Church/Mission
Tensions Today

Church/Mission Tensions Today

Edited by
C. PETER WAGNER

MOODY PRESS • CHICAGO

Library of Congress Catalog Card Number: 72-77940

ISBN: 0-8024-1549-0

Printed in the United States of America

CONTENTS

5

PREFACE

Most evangelical missionary leaders I know are activists. They have committed themselves to the cause of foreign missions and spare no energy and effort in burning out their lives for the kingdom of God. Forty-hour weeks are unknown to them, and they think as little of spending two days in New York, two more in Los Angeles, and the next two in Singapore as most people think of going to the barber and the supermarket.

Most of them are loaded with information and creative ideas, but generally speaking, organizing and writing down these ideas takes a rather low position on the list of priorities. Therefore, pulling thirteen of them together to contribute to a symposium on mission/church relationships has been no small undertaking. In most cases, meeting the deadlines has meant changes in plans, time taken from their families, and long hours over the typewriter. But now the book is born, and the labor pains are forgotten. As the reader will agree, it was worth the effort; and we have here a major contribution to contemporary evangelical missionary thinking.

Working with this select roster of men has been a privilege and a pleasant task on the one hand, and relationships with the editorial staff of Moody Press have been most satisfying on the other. My hearty thanks to all of them, to the Executive Committee of GL '71 for the unmerited assignment, and to my wife, Doris, who labored through this with me, as a good helpmeet, and who typed the manuscript.

C. PETER WAGNER

INTRODUCTION

by VERGIL GERBER

The Green Lake '71 Conference (GL '71) on church/ mission tensions which gave birth to this volume was certainly not the first of its kind.[1] Conferences on church/mission relations can be traced back to the very beginning of the church.

By nature, church and mission are incendiary. "The church exists by mission," says one theologian, "as fire exists by burning." Sparks of tension are inevitable. Church and mission have always been in tension. The missionary mandate which spawned the church also spawned agencies for assisting the church in her mandate. In the course of history, churches produced missions. Missions produced churches. Their success produced tensions.

VERGIL GERBER serves simultaneously as Executive Director of Evangelical Missions Information Service and Executive Secretary of the Evangelical Committee on Latin America, both joint committees of the Interdenominational Foreign Mission Association and the Evangelical Foreign Missions Association. Combined, the IFMA and EFMA represent some 16,000 North American missionaries. Dr. Gerber is a graduate of Fort Wayne Bible College, and holds the B.Mus. from Taylor University, the B.A. from Northern Baptist Theological Seminary, and the D.D. from Conservative Baptist Theological Seminary. He served as a missionary to Argentina, Costa Rica and Mexico under the Conservative Baptist Foreign Missionary Society, and is presently on loan by that organization to IFMA/EFMA. He is the editor of the recently published book, *Missions in Creative Tension,* and his articles on missions have appeared regularly in evangelical periodicals.

THE FIRST SENDING CHURCH AT JERUSALEM

Strained relations between older and younger churches began with the very first church at Jerusalem. Fanned into life from the coals of the Great Commission, the Jerusalem congregation ignited tiny sparks on the day of Pentecost which rapidly spread across racial, cultural and geographical boundaries. Christian congregations were soon kindled on pioneer mission fields in Asia, Africa, Europe and the Middle East.

THE RECEIVING CHURCH AT ANTIOCH

Among them was the flourishing Gentile church at Antioch (Ac 11:19-21). No sooner were the flames of a successful indigenous congregation kindled there than the white heat of missionary fervor began to glow. The receiving church was turned into a sending body (Ac 13). Paul and Barnabas were appointed as the first missionaries of the new agency (13:2-3). Their early missionary efforts ignited congregations in Lystra, Derbe, Iconium, Antioch of Pisidia, Perga, Pamphylia and Attalia.

As the missionaries returned on furlough to report to the Antioch church from which they had been sent out (Ac 14:26-28), it was clearly evident that tensions were smoldering as a result of their successful missionary endeavors. They had to do chiefly with matters of relationships. Some of them were innerpersonal and negative, ending in division (15:34-41). Others were interpersonal and positive, producing creative guidelines for spelling out future relationships (15:1-31).

THE CHURCH/MISSION CONFERENCE AT JERUSALEM
(A.D. 49)

The strained relations which had developed eventually reached the point where they were a threat both to the older and younger churches. Certain pressures needed to be alleviated. Misunderstandings needed to be clarified. They called for an honest reexamination of these issues:

• Should the Gentile converts of the younger church be required to follow all the Jewish customs and ceremonies practiced by the Jerusalem church (Ac 15:5)?

• Which of these are mere cultural accretions, and which are essential to the Christian faith?

• When and on what basis should the younger church be given authority to act on its own?

• What relationship should be sustained between sending and receiving congregations?

These are some of the hard questions which led to the calling of the first church/mission conference at Jerusalem in A.D. 49 and to which representatives of both the older and younger churches addressed themselves. Caught in the middle of these tensions were missionaries Paul and Barnabas.

POSITIVE TENSIONS

Tensions can be positive as well as negative. The tensions which result from stretching the cables of a great bridge serve to give it strength and stability. Properly related, they fulfill an exceedingly important function. So the cables which held together and sustained the early church had to be properly related. And much depended on the existing structures.

In the Jerusalem/Antioch controversy, the tensions created by the success of both church and mission had a stabilizing influence on the future spread of the gospel. The decisions reached had a twofold effect: (1) They served to relieve undue stress and strain, and (2) they gave new strength and stability to the missionary program of the future.

PHENOMENA UNIQUE TO TODAY

Although church/mission tensions, therefore, are not new to our time, they have literally exploded to such extent and magnitude today that they represent a major turning point in the history of the church. Several phenomena unique to this generation have contributed to the crisis:

THE PHENOMENON OF THE CHURCH WORLDWIDE

Today, as in no previous generation, the church can be found in every part of the world in eschatological fulfillment of the Great Commission. Ralph Winter calls the phenomenon "unbelievable" as "churches displayed vigor and put down national roots in a way that could hardly have been believed in 1944."[2]

Actually the unprecedented growth of the last several decades exceeds everything that has gone before in the twenty centuries of the church's existence since Pentecost. Even more astounding is the virile, dynamic and permanent character of these churches. Though maturing in uneven patterns and at varying stages, they are beyond doubt there to stay. Their existence, as Winter points out, is "no longer based on any significant foreign financial or organizational support, much less control."

THE PHENOMENON OF THE THIRD WORLD

The emergence of independent nations worldwide has given rise to the term "Third World." The Third World is characterized by a growing resentment to the pressures and influences of the so-called "Great Powers." This has its effect on the church worldwide, as both nations and churches struggle for independence and identity. Both assume new forms compatible with their indigenous cultures. Both face the dilemma of demanding independence on the one hand while recognizing the absolute necessity of interdependence on the other.

THE PHENOMENON OF THIRD WORLD MISSIONS

Just as historically churches produced missions, and missions in turn produced churches, so the phenomenon of indigenous missions created by the younger churches of the Third World have added a new dimension to church/mission/church relations, in other words, church/mission/church/mission. Today, United States-based mission societies send missionaries from New York to Santiago, Chile. Third World mission boards in Santiago, in turn, have Chilean missionaries ministering in

New York City. At GL '71 the Korean general director of a national mission society with roots in the Korean church sat on the platform beside a United States-based mission director whose missionaries are working in Korea as they discussed the implications of the changing role of missions and missionaries in the '70s. The "home base" now is everywhere, and the terms "receiving" and "sending" churches are almost obsolete.

CRISES IN CHURCH/MISSION RELATIONS

The phenomena unique to this generation point up a series of contemporary crises facing the missions related to the IFMA and EFMA with some hard questions for which answers are needed now:

The crisis of identity. Should IFMA/EFMA missions merge completely with their churches overseas (fusion)? Or should they remain separate identities (dichotomy)?

The crisis of eschatology. How does the eschatological fulfillment of the Great Commission in the existence of the church on a worldwide scale affect IFMA/EFMA missions and their future, should the Lord tarry His coming? What role should they have?

The crisis of relations. What is the relationship of IFMA/EFMA missions and missionaries to churches overseas? To the churches at home? How will they function?

The crisis of structures. Are present mission structures effective? Feasible? Adequate? What part should the church overseas have in future organizational patterns?

The crisis of theology. What are the nature and mission of the church in the '70s? Are the concepts "The church *is* mission" versus "The church *and* mission" biblically defensible? Are there scriptural bases for the existence of mission societies as paraecclesiastical agencies?

GREEN LAKE '71

Although in a sense the Green Lake '71 Study Conference might be considered an extension of the "great missiological debate" which began at Jerusalem, the complexity of today's "global village" leaves little doubt that there are no easy answers to the problems that face us in this last quarter of the twentieth century.

The objectives of the consultation were clear:

1. To identify the points of tension which exist today between mission and church.

2. To share experience, input and cross-fertilization of ideas that will help us constructively to cope with these tensions.

3. To develop guidelines which will help each mission to chart its own individual course of action in terms of changes which need to be made.

No one was under the illusion that a general consensus would emerge. The wide divergence of IFMA/EFMA missions in their church/mission relationships precluded any such consensus. "Unity in diversity" characterized the week-long gathering.

The main benefit of GL '71 was to give each delegate a fresh exposure to the problems and possible solutions of church/ missions tensions today. Unlike most conferences, the number of speakers and papers was few. The program was geared to delegate participation and small-group and full plenary discussion sessions, rather than positional presentations from the platform. It was a work conference with advance study and reading assignments for all who attended. Participants got out of it exactly what they put into it. Said one mission administrator, "The advanced reading prepared us to *think widely.* Discussion groups helped us to *look broadly* at each other. Feedback sessions demanded that we *act wisely* in the days just ahead."

Unanimously the "Green Lake 400" confessed their—

- failure to work consistently toward the development of fully responsible churches at home and abroad,
- tendency toward paternalism, authoritarianism and lack of trust in our relation with our Christian brethren,

- slowness in building scriptural bridges of unity and fellowship between North American and overseas churches.

Their concerns as they left Green Lake centered in the need for—

- discovering forms of church-mission-church relationships that allow for the fullest scriptural expression of the missionary nature and purpose of the church;
- sharing with their missionaries and their constituencies what is being done around the world to develop new patterns of church-mission-church relations;
- evaluating their relations with home and overseas churches through fellowship and consultation in biblical and related studies;
- fostering reciprocal ministry between churches at home and overseas on the basis of mutual love, acceptance and oneness in Jesus Christ.

It was evident that, although as one prominent educator expressed it, "GL '71 marked a milestone in the progress of church/mission relations," the conference itself was only a springboard for a great deal more creative thinking and study which needed to be done, and on a much broader basis. For one thing, the basic bibliography prepared specifically as a part of each delegate's preliminary study materials revealed that conservative evangelical mission leaders have written very little on this subject to date. Stimulated by the exposure papers given at Green Lake, the assembly charged the executive committee with the responsibility of initiating and developing further writing and thought among Evangelicals. Before the sessions ended at Green Lake, the editor of this book had been chosen, writers for the chapters had been confirmed, and arrangements had been worked out for its publication.

The book will be key reading material for every pastor, missionary, and theological student concerned with the missionary task of the church in this last quarter of the twentieth century. It constitutes the most valuable, up-to-date textbook available on the subject today. Designed among other things for classroom use on either the graduate or undergraduate level, it undoubtedly will have a wide circulation as a textbook in evangelical colleges and seminaries.

Missions will also find it a basic guide for field conference discussions and study, as well as for the preparation and orientation of new missionaries.

As you read these pages prayerfully, God grant that they make you sensitive to that which the Lord Himself wants to do through His church in the accomplishing of His missionary purposes before He Himself returns.

NOTES

1. GL '71 stands for Green Lake (Wisconsin) where 400 carefully selected mission and church leaders related to the Evangelical Foreign Missions Association (EFMA) and the Interdenominational Foreign Mission Association (IFMA) spent an entire week in September, 1971, grappling with the most serious issue facing world missions in the '70s: mission/church relationships.

   GL '71 took the place of the triennial Missions Executives' Retreat sponsored jointly by the EFMA and the IFMA, which represent a combined total of 102 evangelical mission boards and approximately 16,000 missionaries around the world. Much more than a retreat, GL '71 was a study conference designed to come to grips with a gnawing topic: MISSIONS IN CREATIVE TENSION. A 457-page compendium bearing this same title has been published by the William Carey Library, South Pasadena, California.

2. Ralph D. Winter, *The Twenty-Five Unbelievable Years 1945-1969* (South Pasadena, Calif.: William Carey Library, 1970), p. 27.

*Most Evangelicals agree that the first step toward
an understanding of church/mission/church relationships must be theological. With unusual
perceptiveness, Jack Shepherd extracts from the
Green Lake conference the main threads of discussion concerning the theology of the church
and weaves them into a new and fascinating
pattern, colored, and rightly so, by his own biblical
insights. In a sense, the chapters that follow
gain full meaning only when seen against the back-
drop of this initial theological presentation.*

1

IS THE CHURCH REALLY
NECESSARY?

by J. F. SHEPHERD

GL '71 was a conference on missions planned by mission
organizations for missionaries, and yet the most prominent
single theme was *church*. It was not that pastors and leaders
from overseas churches who were present insisted on calling
attention to the church. *Church* and *churches* were directly
emphasized in all the papers, speeches, debates and prayers.

J. F. SHEPHERD is the Education Secretary of the Christian and Missionary Alliance in the United States and Canada. A graduate of Nyack
Missionary College, he also holds the B.S. from the Hartford Seminary
Foundation, the M.A. from the Kennedy School of Missions, the B.D.
from Bethel Theological Seminary, and the S.T.M. from Union Theological Seminary, New York. Mr. Shepherd was serving as a missionary in China when forced to leave because of Communist pressure; he
then spent several years in the Philippines. His varied career includes
key posts as a professor of missions, mission personnel secretary and
pastorates.

This fact in itself demonstrates a notable and solid contribution that GL '71 can make if the issues it raised continue to be taken seriously. We who were there had our disagreements about the past, present and particularly the future of missions. In fact, plans for dissolution, "euthanasia" or phasing out of mission had some supporters. But whatever happens to *missions,* the really important thing for all was that *churches* continue to mature and multiply.

It is appropriate that the first essay in this collection should have the church as its subject because it certainly had the place of priority and precedence at the conference itself. For example, Edmund Clowney's great series of messages which carried the subtitle, "Biblical Ecclesiology and the Crisis in Missions," was the first item on the agenda each day.[1] He laid a sturdy scriptural foundation for thought and discussion about church and mission. Reflection on the whole experience and review of the published materials produce the conviction that the way toward a proper concept of mission begins with clear thinking about the church.

While there are things that need clarification and probing, it is worth noting that in contrast to the denigrating opinions of many today, GL '71 not only thought highly of the church but held great hope for it.[2] In fact, the amazing growth and multiplication of churches throughout the world have created the most urgent issues confronting the conference. It is striking that the one-page affirmation which was adopted in the closing session had no direct reference to *missions* as such, but spoke emphatically of "church/mission/church" relationships. This was a way of emphasizing that missions cannot really be independent of churches. Missions only have being, and reason for being, in a context where they relate to churches on both sides.

This church-mission-church equation underscores a fact that needs to be understood. While GL '71 was deeply concerned to consider church and mission with complete theological integrity, the issues it sought to grapple with had to do primarily with the structural aspects of churches and missions. The problem was to determine what institutional relationships were most suitable for productive spiritual and personal fellowship in service as Christ's church.

The purpose of this article is to point out some of the theological implications of the GL '71 perspective on the church. These observations are more nearly an interpretation or commentary than a reformulation of any of the proceedings. Before coming to the theological points, however, it might be helpful to engage in a kind of methodological procedure which should bring into sharper focus some elements of the GL '71 perspective of the church.

WRESTLING WITH DEFINITIONS

There has probably never been an occasion in which *church* was introduced as a subject for discussion when it would not have been appropriate to ask the question, "What do you mean by *church?*" GL '71 was no exception. In fact, in addition to the series of general ways in which the word can be used, some specifically missionary nomenclature introduced complications and ambiguities. These two categories of definition can be reviewed in a summary way and then checked out in terms of the biblical use of *church*.

WHAT DOES "CHURCH" MEAN?

There are at least nine different ways in which the word *church* is commonly used. Nearly all of these could be identified in the Green Lake discussions. It might have eliminated some ambiguity if varying usages could have been classified and standardized in the course of the debate. It would be possible to pick out a set of examples from the written materials, but perhaps it is enough to suggest the variations with a kind of illustrative observation in each case.

1. Church—the body of Christ consisting of all Christian believers. (Many at Green Lake, in disagreement with Clowney, would limit this use of the term to true believers since Pentecost.[3])

2. Church or churches—congregations of professing Christians. (This for several reasons would have been the most frequent kind of reference at GL '71.)

3. Church—all true believers in a given area, though they may be related to differing congregations. (Ideally, this would be what Clowney referred to as the metropolitan *church,* for example, in Antioch.[4])

4. Church—an international denominational organization. (Some were present from the Presbyterian *church;* some from the Mennonite or Nazarene *church.*)

5. Church—a national denominational association. (CAMACOP is the C & M A *church* of the Philippines.)

6. Church—a collective term for all who call themselves Christians. (We were given statistics on the world *church.*)

7. Church—all professing Christians in a given country. (We heard what kind of missionaries the *church* in Africa or the *church* in Mexico wants.)

8. Church—a building. ("Should mission funds be used to build a *church?*")

9. Church—a specific service or meeting. ("In our country we have *church* at 7:00 A.M.")

SPECIAL MISSIONARY VOCABULARY

When the church is discussed in terms of missionary expansion and mission relationships, things get even more complicated. Translation into other languages that are more precise than English is sometimes helpful, but in the Green Lake discussions the traditional polarizing combinations were hinted at, even though efforts were made to be sensitive and inoffensive. Direct organizational contact has nearly always been mission to church. However, when relationships begin to be discussed and described, there is usually a tendency to imply contrast between churches rather than between mission and church. Here the good word *church* gets combined with adjectives that are almost inevitably irritating.

1. Some relational terms:
   a. sending churches and receiving churches
   b. home (North American) churches and overseas churches
   c. home-base churches and field churches
   d. older churches and younger churches
   e. mother churches and daughter churches
   f. Western Christendom churches and indigenous churches
   g. white Anglo-Saxon churches and native churches
   h. our (?) churches and the nationals' churches

Some terms were employed at Green Lake to describe the churches which had come into being as a result of mission activities. These terms had a certain positive quality; but when used in this sense, no attempt was made to suggest a relationship to the churches responsible for their having been "planted," "established" or "organized."

2. Some descriptive terms:
   a. growing churches
   b. developing churches
   c. emerging churches
   d. maturing churches

There may not have been explicit reference to all of the terms listed above, but there was evidence in the discussions that the basic meaning they convey was there. Even in the case of those terms that are now regarded as outmoded and offensive, their pejorative sense came through at times. Everyone must have been aware that "white churches" and "colored churches" might have been a neat and obvious distinction for the two worlds of mission and church. If the North American mission establishment were not suffering such a tragic lack of black participation, it might not have appeared in such sharp "color" contrast to Third World churches.

What words can we use if communication is really to take

place when we talk of church/mission/church? That certainly is part of the problem. All of that missionary vocabulary under "relational terms" seems to have a flavor of inferiority and patronage. Even attempts under "descriptive terms" to be more complimentary might be seen as emphasizing an underprivileged background or a kind of adolescent improvement. Looked at another way, the terms could be regarded as implying that the sending church was smug in present attainments and had ceased to advance.

How can we talk of church and churches so as not to allow historical and environmental factors, which seem to disclose a kind of unequal partnership, to be a source of tension? What is needed is a strong biblical accent on the essential character of the church as church. Its inherent vitality, authenticity and dignity must have priority over such considerations as culture, ethnic identity, geography, affluence, age or size. What makes a church a church is not its derivation from the efforts of an eccleciastical enterprise, but its origin and identity in relation to God's presence and power. The true church, as Clowney put it, is "formed in God's presence."[5] The Bible is the primary guide in defining the church as to its essential nature and function, as well as form. Before looking at the theological implications of the sort of biblical teaching and exchange we had about the church at Green Lake, it might be well to put the terms noted above to a kind of biblical test.

BIBLICAL NORMS FOR THE WORD "CHURCH"

LOOKING AT THE SPECIAL MISSIONARY VOCABULARY

A generalization can be made with regard to both the relational and descriptive terms. The whole Bible has a dimension in which the purpose of God is that His people reach out to peoples that are "foreign" to them. There is even an emphasis on the deficiencies of the background of such peoples. A strong theme is that before people come into life in fellowship of the church of God they have been lost and corrupt. However, the

unfolding doctrine of the church distinctly asserts and cele-
brates the unity and oneness of those who are now in the body
of Christ. This emphasis transcends every other factor which
might make for inequality or differentiation. Moreover, it is
evident that "new-born believers" and newly planted churches
frequently manifested more vitality and productivity than those
that were older in the faith and in more highly structured organizations. Too often in mission history, factors that are human, historical and even sinful have influenced the shape and
character of organizational relationships. Such factors must be
judged and eliminated by thinking about the church in a manner that is consistently biblical.

LOOKING AT THE GENERAL USAGES OF THE WORD "CHURCH"

It is too late to try to revise ecclesiastical nomenclature. We
are going to continue attending *church* in a *church* on Sundays
at 11:00 A.M. We will persist in speaking of the influence of
"the church" in the political and social world quite without
reference to doctrine, experience or ecclesiastical character and
tradition. We will generously lump together all kinds of religious groups in compiling statistics on "church and churches"
and their growth. We will identify people and organizations
as "church members" and "churches," who from another standpoint we would classify as unbelievers in heretical and even
apostate organizations. The historical accumulation of diverse
meanings that the word *church* is made to convey make it
frustrating, if not nearly hopeless, to make sense when using it.

In looking at the nine suggested usages, some at Green Lake
would have insisted that only the first two are strictly biblical.
It might have been possible, by correlating 1 and 3, to win
agreement on definition 3 as being the local counterpart of the
"invisible" universal church. Many of us would have balked,
at least in debate, at the loyal attempt of those who would try
to make a biblical case for *church* as denomination. This
would apply to definitions 4 and 5. This is not to say that
denominations, as such, are wrong or evil or even in tension

with Scripture. The question is whether it is proper to call such organized institutional structures *church*.

It is not my intention to say that a word is not to be used or that it is inaccurate or suspect because it is not explicitly scriptural. Inevitably words can tend to diversify and extend to broader usages. Nonetheless, if we take seriously the biblical norm for all things Christian, we should distinguish between those things essentially biblical and those that are derivative. Clowney, commenting on the use of Scripture in such matters, said that we are in danger of going to two extremes in handling the Bible. That comment certainly applies to Scripture texts and church teaching. Some will claim *too much* for its teaching. They will say the Bible gives us everything we can know or need to know or do about the church. Others claim *too little*. They will say it gives us the basic primary truth; but beyond that, we improvise and have no fixed directives or principles from the Word to which to appeal. There needs to be a balance between these two views. What is given in Scripture must be accepted as authority and guidance in all matters of faith and practice. While we can call things *church* which Scripture doesn't, we must distinguish primary and secondary, biblical and historical or even theological types of usage. Moreover, we must bring all that has to do with *church* under scrutiny of what is explicitly taught about the church in Scripture.

Church defined against the broad background of Scripture should always hold these three elements together: (1) its essential nature—relationship to God, (2) its specified function—service to the glory of God, (3) its basic but adaptable form—an effective and consistent institutional expression of its nature in fulfillment of its function.

When this norm for definition is applied to the usages listed under "relational terms," it is evident that there is an incompleteness that shows some of the terms to be inadequate. It is a contradiction to claim a churchly form for that which does not have the vitality of the divine nature, that is the source of true membership in the church. Ministry, mission and service are *manifestations* of what the church is if it is "formed in the presence of God," but these are not the source from which it has its being.

There has long been controversy over the question of visibility and invisibility in relation to the church. In spite of the apprehension such a view elicits, it must be insisted that that which is most important about the church is invisible. That is its essential divine nature imparted through the Holy Spirit. One hastens to insist that this nature will invariably be visibly expressed and take on discernible form in the community of those who share in the life of God. However, it is important to realize that none of the visible signs of the church's form or function are indisputable evidences of the presence of divine life. Unfortunately, it is quite possible to have a form that may be called *church* without possessing the life or fulfilling the biblically defined function of the church.

Another fact relevant to this discussion is that though the people of God all share in the one divine life, and although the character and service the church is to manifest are carefully set out in Scripture, the form it is to have is defined so as to allow for adaptation in every generation and in a variety of cultural situations. The implications of such a definition of the church have very practical significance for the church/mission/church relationship which was the concern of GL '71.

THEOLOGICAL IMPLICATIONS

Such theological implications of a biblical view of the church for missions are framed and outlined with four objectives in mind: (1) to report on GL '71 so as to highlight some of the crucial issues with which it grappled; (2) to try to point out in this chapter on the church which, in my view at least, represents the most important aspect of the acknowledged tension in church/mission relations; (3) to offer a kind of personal, but hopefully representative, commentary on the GL '71 affirmation; (4) to set out at least this chapter of this volume as another modest but insistent challenge to the ecumenical compromise and distortion of a biblical theology of church and mission.

THE NATURE OF THE CHURCH

Clowney's lectures at Green Lake were a good sample and summary of sound teaching on the nature of the church as the people of God who have life in the Spirit through an individual experience of regeneration. I am assuming that the theological persuasion of IFMA-EFMA on this doctrine need not be spelled out and supported with Scripture in this short paper. I simply want to suggest three aspects of truth concerning the essential nature of the church that have special implications for church-mission relationships.

UNITY

The unity of the church is in the Holy Spirit by whom we are baptized into the *one body*. It is clear that this unity is to be expressed in the life and service of the church. The search for unity in the early stages of the ecumenical movement has impeccable missionary credentials.[6] The church needs the kind of unity that the world can *see* and in consequence believe in the one God who sent His Son as Redeemer.[7] Unfortunately, the movement for ecumenical organizational uniting, without proper concern for doctrinal truth, has come to focus more on the form of the church than its nature. This would have been the opinion of most of us at Green Lake. Our convictions or prejudices may have prevented our thinking clearly enough about this unity in terms of our own relationships. It is to our shame that little was said, and nothing affirmed, about *unity* at GL '71. We must, however, remember:

1. That our unity in Christ at the congregational and every other organizational level must transcend every kind of structural separation and hold us together as fellow believers in bonds of peace and love.

2. That unity in Christ is more important than any differentiation of nationality, race, politics, economics, social standing,

age, or even loyalty to ecclesiastical tradition. We should be willing to set these things aside in order to attain and maintain deep unity in Christ.

3. That true unity is never at the expense of truth. However this does not mean that conformity on every point of orthodox belief is necessary to share oneness in Christ. In the view of this writer, we are called to unity with all who have personal, experiential belief in saving truth. "Saving truth" is what a man has to believe in order to be saved.

4. That we very much need to do what Clowney urged: "Renew our consideration of the New Testament teaching respecting the unity of the church."[8] That teaching obliges us to have an open concern for unity with those whom we acknowledge to be in Christ with us. This is a much-needed note in terms of our relationship, or lack of it, with those within the ecumenical movement.

In his timely little book, *Missions: Which Way?* Beyerhaus is discerning and correct when he calls for continuing dialogue with the World Council. He says, "By abandoning diaglogue, the evangelical movement might purchase the rescue of its evangelical missionary concern with the price of a proper view of the church."[9] The immediate lesson for Green Lake is that the unity of the church is more important than separation of churches and missions. A larger and more disconcerting lesson may well be that the unity of the church is more important than the safe, isolationist separatism we have with our own conservative evangelical brethren.

IDENTITY

It may seem equivocal to utilize a nonbiblical term like *identity* after all this emphasis on direct reference to Scripture. However, identity seems to me to be the word that most nearly corresponds to the fine expression used by Beyerhaus and LeFever, "the responsible self-hood" of the church.[10] As is acknowledged in their book, the New Testament use of the word *self* does not really commend it for endorsement even in the classic "three-self" missions formula. *Self* in Scripture has more to do with carnality than with identity, so it seems awkward to try to add another *self* category to describe the church. Better to use the contemporary word and try to give it biblical content.

Is there not a proper biblical concept that can be used of believers and churches that fits very well into the term *identity* as it is frequently used today?[11] Can this not simply mean a church which knows who and what it is? There are texts from Old Testament and New in which God's people were exhorted in one way or another to recognize who they were and whom they served. This kind of clear, informed sense of spiritual identity is an important factor in mission/church relationships.

The fact of the true identity given to the people of God by grace should make it clear:

1. That the church should know itself over against the world out of which it has been called in salvation. While the church in every situation should recognize itself as in one sense part of the world, it should also be aware that there is that other part of the rebellious world which is not under obedience to the gospel. For that reason, it is outside the church, without hope and without God.[12]

2. That sense of identity through which those who are born of God know they need to be holy, as the Father is holy, comes from the indwelling Spirit, not legalistic pressures especially from foreigners.

3. That any company of true believers, even the two or three who are gathered to the Lord, constitute a church of His. They have the right to every privilege in worship and ministry, as well as the responsibility for full obligation in witness and service.

AUTHORITY

Now we are back to an explicitly biblical word, *authority*. There are those texts which pointedly emphasize the authority of the sons of God. We can single out the implications of the missionary commissions in Matthew 28 and John 20 to make this point directly. Several aspects of the authority of the church, because of its nature as formed in God, are especially relevant:

1. A church has authority through the Son and in the Spirit to carry out that great word of the Lord Jesus: "Receive the Holy Spirit. If you forgive the sins of any, their sins have been forgiven them; if you retain the sins of any, they have been retained" (Jn 20:22b-23, NASB). This is the mandate for participation in evangelism and mission for every true church.

2. The church's authority is derived from Christ as its Lord and Head, not from some authorization bestowed through the agency of a "sending church" when it decides that things can be "turned over" to the church which it has nurtured.

3. If this authority of the church is taken seriously, those who share in its ministries locally or regionally should come in some measure under its jurisdiction.

4. This kind of jurisdiction should be exercised by the sending church over its delegated representatives in mission. While both function and form enter in here, this pattern of authority may be seen as deriving from the missionary nature of the church.[13]

THE FUNCTION OF THE CHURCH

The comments on the nature of the church should make it clear what would certainly have been a presupposition to the GL '71 affirmation, namely, that "there is no salvation outside the church." Such a claim, which is offensive to some, can only be made with the essential nature of the church in view, not considerations of relationship to some prescribed organization. Related to that doctrinal position are two correlated views that are in distinct tension with popular ecumenical notions.

The first is that in God's redemptive mission in the world the church is the unique instrument of *His* saving work. The order of relationships, then, is God-church-world and not the inversion of these to God-world-church as is proposed in the

World Council studies on "the missionary structure of the congregation."[14] One of the most perceptive critics of these ecumenical concepts states the case in a way that would have found acceptance at GL '71, even though he represents the Lutheran World Federation:

> Not all acts of God which are related to the world are *missio*—only the sending of the Son and the Holy Spirit (the structures of which were preformed in God's election of Israel) and the consequent sending of the Church into the world for its salvation. If the concept of *missio Dei* is strictly conceived as the sending of the Son (and the Spirit) and as the sending through the Son (and the Spirit) into the world, then the order God-Church-world is justified, as long as it is kept in mind that God acts in the world in a *saving* way exclusively through the Gospel proclaimed by the Church.[15]

The corollary of the God-church-world formula is another dissent from ecumenical phrase-making. Instead of saying that "the church is mission" which relates to *being,* it seems more to the point to say, "The church has a mission." This is to emphasize the functional aspect of mission as that which the church is to *do.* My intention is not to insist that the whole function of the church is mission. On the contrary, I want to quarrel with that idea. However, since the primary concern here is with the church in mission and in the kinds of relationships resultant from missionary action, the three points to be suggested regarding the function of the church highlight the *missionary* function.

THE PRIMACY OF THE MISSIONARY FUNCTION

An attempt was certainly made at Green Lake to set mission in the context of the many-faceted comprehensive ministry of the church. This is set out most strikingly in Ephesians 4. It does seem that much of the ecumenical/evangelical tension over the tendency to polarize social action over against mission comes from the notion that these two are the same thing and can be substituted the one for the other. Peter Beyerhaus adds a new and respected voice to this whole controversy. His recent statement underscores the fact that social action is not only a secondary aspect of mission, as he describes it, but actually resultant from the effect of the primary saving mission. When there is proper perspective, he insists that the two points of view can be balanced and brought together. His statement is a beautiful example of the intimate relation of the nature and function of the church:

> Mission occurs when—and only when—it is directed toward putting man's existence, through a conscious decision of faith, under Christ's Lordship and His effective spiritual power. In this way, man experiences lasting salvation, a salvation in which his non-Christian environment may temporarily participate. But salvation in the full sense of the word is not found primarily in these indirect effects. Rather, salvation is the new communion of the Holy Spirit through the bond of peace. For this reason, the center of the missionary commission always remains its call into communion with Christ. This communion finds its visible representation and sacramental realization through responsible incorporation into the Church. The planting and growth of the Church as the Body of Christ in the world remains the primary goal of mission within history. The transformation of the structures of this world is the result of a membership which is prepared to serve. This theological association of the primary Christocentric *being* and the world-oriented *function* arising from it could in principle make possible a synthesis between the evangelical and the "ecumenical" understanding of mission.[16]

To apply the truth of this statement to the GL '71 issue is to insist that mission should have a place, even a *first* place, in the life of every church. It was clear at Green Lake that there had not been sufficient persevering faithfulness to guide the so-called "younger churches" into participation in mission.

THE DISTINCTIVENESS OF THE MISSIONARY FUNCTION

Chapter 2 of this volume discusses mission, as such, but an allusion needs to be made, in passing, to the fact that mission, as a particular function of the church, needs to be distinguished from other essential but different functions. The serious warning of Stephen Neill cannot be repeated too many times: "If everything is mission, pretty soon nothing is mission."[17] There is need to coordinate our mission terminology, but I want to urge that mission be defined specifically as "multiplication of churches." Such a definition could helpfully distinguish mission from evangelism or prophetic, pastoral, or didactic ministry. It would distinguish it as well from worship, fellowship and whatever other things properly belong to the doxological activity and service of the church.

THE CONTINUITY OF THE MISSIONARY FUNCTION

One more observation can be added to the insistence that every church has, as a primary function distinguishable from all else it does, a responsible, organized missionary involvement; that is, there is to be an unending, dynamic continuity in the outreach in mission of every church "old or young." In other words, mission obligation is not fulfilled and exhausted when a new church is planted. Instead, mission is then to be reshaped and extended. Is this not the clear meaning of the Pauline concept of the apostolate as he described it to the young church at Corinth: "Our hope is that as your faith increases, our field among you may be greatly enlarged, so that we may preach the gospel in lands beyond you" (2 Co 10:15b-16a, RSV)? Green Lake revealed that we had not taken seriously enough the need to keep mission going right on into the regions beyond the churches that were brought into being in the first phases of outreach. Too often we have lapsed into what Peter Wagner calls "the church development syndrome."[18] We have gotten a fixation on the churches with whom we are in "modified dichotomy" or "fused parallelism" and have failed to keep going after that which is lost, as the parable has it.

THE FORM OF THE CHURCH

As has been noted, the purpose of GL '71 was to study and discuss issues relating primarily to the form of the mission organization or society in its relationship to sending and receiving churches. The consideration of missions in this sense quite logically raised the question of the organizational form of the church. In fact, one of the main contentions of the first conference paper was that just as the church must have visible form, so mission also must have visible form. To sacrifice this in the interest of integration of the church and mission was perilous for both, in the opinion of the writer. That position, incidentally, was reinforced by later conference proceedings.

It must be acknowledged that there is much less biblical teaching about organization for mission than there is for church organization. It might appear that at GL '71 there was too much emphasis on the lack of biblical teaching on organizational structures. This elicited corrective protests from Clowney on a couple of occasions.

There was cordial agreement on all sides that even though the New Testament did not explicate details on the form of the church, it did emphasize that it *always* had some visible organized form. A vast literature has been produced to defend and support episcopal, presbyterial and congregational forms of church government. In most cases such work falls into the position against which Clowney cautioned—that of trying to claim *too much*. It seems to me that some of the recent literature on "the believers' church" has brought new and important dimensions into the whole discussion of the church. One quotation from the most eminent of the Free Church scholars, Franklin Littell, is relevant to this point:

> In the history of Christianity there have been some who said that the Bible was ambiguous as to doctrine and organization. The traditional orthodox view has been that it gives clear indications on doctrine but is ambiguous as to organizational pattern. The Anabaptists maintain that the New Testament

was clear, both as to the content of the Christian faith and the organizational procedures in the true Christian community.[19]

The sort of Free Church congregationalist view held by Anabaptists not only fits the New Testament picture very well, but it seems remarkably well suited to contemporary ideas about congregational life-style. As I see it, the claim that the Scripture is as clear in its teaching on church organization as it is on the doctrinal content of the faith can hardly be substantiated. However, there are same basic teachings about the form of the church that can be summarized in the following observations:

THE BROAD DEFINITION

It has been helpful to me to try to decide what you have to have to have a New Testament church. This is a means of suggesting the basic elements of any church organization. With this in view, the shape of the organization may vary, but the basic constituent elements must be there if they are essential for the church.

Of course, you have to begin with a people who hold a common belief and "congregate" with reference to it. The question, which is not absolutely ridiculous, about whether one believer constitutes a church is a bit technical for this discussion. You might say "yes" on the nature-and-function aspect. The question would, of course, be on the matter of form. Putting that aside, I would suggest that there are five basic things that you must have to be a church as a visible, social institution: (1) Scripture (in oral form perhaps for a nonliterate culture); (2) leadership; (3) the "sacraments"— baptism and communion (or their equivalents, as in Quakerism); (4) giving; and (5) consensus of belief.

Roland Allen limits the necessities to four.[20] He omits "giving," but I add it, possibly because I am of the Christian and Missionary Alliance, at the same time recognizing that some Christians who live outside of money economies give in their own way. Number 5, which I have called "consensus," Allen refers to as "tradition." He has in mind both a New Testament and an Anglican emphasis. It is not just having Scripture that is a constituent factor for a church, but having a consent or commitment to what it is understood to teach. In my judgment you cannot really have a proper church without all of these things, and actually nothing additional is really needed to constitute a church. You could, of course, have all of these things without the people "taking shape" as a church, but that would be from failure to be gathered together around the Christian teaching or, more properly, the person of Christ. Perhaps it does need to be emphasized that having church form does not in itself insure either truth or life in Christ.

ADAPTABILITY

It is not difficult to see that the basic elements mentioned above could all be present in an organizational framework in a multiplicity of different ways. This is the genius of the indigenous church idea. *Indigenous* has to do with the adaptation of the form of the church's life to varying cultural situations. *Support, government* and *propagation* are three things that correspond to the five elements suggested above. They are concerned with the form and function of the church, *theologically* understood. The *indigenous* aspect has to do with that prefix *self* that is properly added here. This relates to the way in which the church governs itself, supports itself, and expresses itself in witness. This is the cultural or *anthropological* side of missions theory.

This is the area of mission/church relationships in which there has been the danger of a weakening paternalism or a repressive dominance that has not allowed churches to develop their own shape and style so as to be at home in their own culture and to relate relevantly to their own people. Much more could be said on this, but the fact that such adaptability is a proper biblical characteristic of the church is a crucial one for missions. In terms of mission *strategy,* the most important single element of ecclesiology is the doctrine of the local church.

It is only as a visible congregation that the church can be indigenous.

EFFICIENCY

It is the potential for adaptation and the possibility of diversification in the development of the basic elements that form the church that the Holy Spirit can use to make the church effective in ministry. As the GL '71 affirmation declares, we must rely on the Holy Spirit to gift the church for ministry. We can quench the Spirit by efforts to confine people to a structure which may seem proper to us, but could conceivably be unsuitable for them.

In New Testament passages there is a kind of indistinguishability of meaning between *local* and *universal* in references to the church. This may be because the universal church is only manifest locally. In the same sense, the local church is only a real church as it participates in the universal. For the same reason the form of the church is only proper if it is effective in its function and expressive of the essential nature it has as the body of Christ.

The assumption that the basic source of tension between missions and churches is structural did not go unchallenged at Green Lake. Some insisted that spiritual and personal problems were much more fundamental and serious. That point of view is not easy to argue with, and yet it does appear that structures in themselves become sources of tension in two special ways. On the one hand, they can become a medium in which wrongly motivated or mistaken ideas and concepts get fixed and then perpetuated. In such a case, good and well-intentioned people and efforts can be limited or impeded by the improper structures themselves. In another sense, structural limitations and defects resulting from failure to change and update can produce the kind of frustration and irritation that becomes corrosive and corrupting to those who are trying to work together within organizational relationships.

The GL '71 affirmation included some sincere expressions of repentant confession. It reads as follows:

and we confess . . .

. . . our failure to work more consistently toward the development of a fully responsible church at home and abroad;

. . . our tendency toward paternalism, authoritarianism and lack of trust in our relations with our Christian brethren;

. . . our slowness in building scriptural bridges of unity and fellowship between North American and overseas churches.

It does seem safe to assume that, even if we all make the spiritual and personal adjustments appropriate to such confession, unless we work with industry and imagination to carry out the central stated objective of the affirmation, we will have failed. We must work to do what the affirmation declares:

. . . to discover forms of church-mission-church relationships that will allow for the fullest scriptural expression of the missionary nature and purpose of the church.

NOTES

1. Edmund P. Clowney, "The Biblical Doctrine of the Ministry of the Church (Biblical Ecclesiology and the Crisis in Missions)," in *Missions in Creative Tension,* ed. Vergil Gerber (South Pasadena, Calif.: William Carey Library, 1971), pp. 231 ff.
2. See, for example, Pierre Berton, *The Comfortable Pew* (Philadelphia: Lippincott, 1965); Stephen C. Rose, ed., *Who's Killing the Church?* (New York: Association Press, 1966); J. C. Hoekendijk, *The Church Inside Out* (Philadelphia: Westminster, 1966).
3. Clowney, pp. 238-40.
4. Ibid., p. 294.
5. Ibid., p. 238.
6. Kenneth Scott Latourette, *A History of the Expansion of Christianity* (Grand Rapids: Zondervan, 1970), 7: 26, 34.
7. Harry R. Boer, *Pentecost and Mission* (Grand Rapids: Eerdmans, 1961), pp. 186-204.
8. Clowney, p. 298.
9. Peter Beyerhaus, *Missions: Which Way?* (Grand Rapids: Zondervan, 1971), p. 92.
10. Peter Beyerhaus and Henry Lefever, *The Responsible Church and the Foreign Mission* (Grand Rapids: Eerdmans, 1964), p. 134.
11. Eric Erikson, *Identity: Youth and Crisis* (New York: Norton, 1968).
12. For a protest against this view, see T. Wieser, ed., *Planning for Mission* (New York: World Council of Churches, 1966), p. 47.

13. See "A Green Lake '71 Affirmation," in *Missions in Creative Tension,* ed. Vergil Gerber (South Pasadena, Calif.: William Carey Library, 1971), p. 383.
14. World Council of Churches, *The Church for Others* (Geneva: World Council of Churches, 1967), pp. 16 ff.
15. Herbert T. Neve, ed., *Sources for Change* (Geneva: World Council of Churches, 1968), p. 84.
16. Beyerhaus, p. 68.
17. Stephen Neill, *Creative Tensions* (London: Edinburgh House, 1959), p. 80.
18. C. Peter Wagner, "The Church Development Syndrome," *World Vision Magazine,* Oct. 1971. See also Donald F. Durnbaugh, *The Believers' Church* (New York: Macmillan, 1968); James L. Garrett, Jr., *The Concept of the Believers' Church* (Scottdale, Pa.: Herald, 1969); Francis A. Schaffer, *The Church Before the Watching World* (Downers Grove, Ill.: Inter-Varsity, 1971).
19. Quoted in Ross T. Bender, *The People of God* (Scottdale, Pa.: Herald, 1971), p. 71.
20. Roland Allen, *Missionary Methods, St. Paul's or Ours?* (London: World Dominion, 1960), p. 107.

*This chapter is a strong, biblical oriented argument
for the perennial need of foreign missionaries.
But the kind of missionary and the auspices under which he works are carefully defined. Robertson McQuilkin warns against uncritical acceptance of either the old comity system or the new
"organizational fundamentalism" of amalgamation.
Here is some fresh, pragmatic input for the current dialogue.*

2

THE FOREIGN MISSIONARY–
A VANISHING BREED?

by J. ROBERTSON MCQUILKIN

Is there still a valid role for foreign missionaries? Raised by
honest people, this question has been accused of deflecting
many young people from the mission field, of sending tremors
through the ranks of missionaries, and of causing many to
leave the foreign field.

Whether or not this question alone can bear such heavy responsibility, it obviously is the type of question that, just by
being raised, has enormous practical impact. Therefore, it must
be answered. At root it is a theological question, not merely a
pragmatic problem. Consequently, it must be answered theologically: Is there still a valid role for foreign missionaries?

J. ROBERTSON MCQUILKIN has been President of Columbia Bible
College since 1968. Previously he served for twelve years as a pioneer
missionary to Japan under The Evangelical Alliance Mission. Dr. Mc-
Quilkin is a graduate of Columbia Bible College and Fuller Theological
Seminary. His articles on mission theory and practice have appeared
in leading evangelical periodicals.

To answer this, four other previous questions must be handled. They are:

1. What is the primary mission of the church?
2. What is the evangelistic mission of the church?
3. When may the mission be judged complete?
4. Who is responsible to accomplish this mission?

I will simply outline a brief answer to the first three questions, laying the groundwork upon which I build an answer to the last question, really the central issue.

WHAT IS THE PRIMARY MISSION OF THE CHURCH?

According to the Bible, the church has many functions or purposes. The congregation of God's people is a *temple* for worship and observing the ordinances, a *family* for the fellowship and discipline of its members, a *school* to teach and learn the Word of God, and a *fold* for pastoral care, counseling and healing. All of these are functions of the ministry of the church for its own members. Incidentally, all of these functions will be fulfilled far more effectively when God's people are with Him in His presence, the "church triumphant." But is there no ministry of the church toward the world, a function that only the "church militant" here on earth can fulfill? What is its obligation toward those outside the family of God?

The apostle tells us that we are to do good unto all men, speaking of financial assistance (Gal 6:10). Though he qualifies it by saying, "especially to those of the household of faith," a reader of the New Testament would be dull indeed not to sense that God's people should be concerned for the welfare of those outside the family—their physical and social welfare as well as spiritual. The church is concerned for the whole man.

But the underlying assumption of this paper is that such a mission is not the *primary* mission of the church. The primary mission of the church we call *the* mission, the *Great* Commission, repeated with a different emphasis by our Lord on at least four different occasions following His resurrection.

This is the same mission that brought Christ to earth. "Jesus Christ came into the world to save sinners" (1 Ti 1:15). "The Son of man is come to seek and to save that which was lost" (Lk 19:10). This great mission of our Saviour in providing eternal redemption for lost and aliented men is the same mission which He gave His disciples to complete. The "Wheaton Declaration" puts it this way:

> We regard as crucial the "evangelistic mandate." The gospel must be preached in our generation to the peoples of every tribe, tongue and nation. This is the supreme task of the Church.[1]

The church thus has many functions and even more than one responsibility to those outside the church. However, the primary mission of the church to those outside is to bring them inside the evangelistic mandate of our Lord. What is that mandate?

WHAT IS THE EVANGELISTIC MISSION OF THE CHURCH?

The evangelistic mission of the church includes three elements: proclamation, persuasion, and establishing congregations of God's people.

Our mission is to go into all the world and proclaim the good news to every person (Mk 16:15), to be a witness to the very ends of the earth (Ac 1:8), to proclaim repentance and remission of sins to all nations (Lk 24:47). Of course, a proclamation of the gospel, even when "proclamation" is taken to mean effective communication, does not exhaust the responsibility of the church in its evangelistic mission.

The church is responsible not only to inform people but to win them. Only when men are won will God be satisfied. The great Commissioner defined the mission as discipling the peoples (Mt 28:19).

Finally, not only are the people of God responsible to win men to faith in Christ, but they are responsible to bring them into the visible congregation or family of God's children. If there is no such congregation it must be established. "I will build my church" (Mt 16:18) states in advance what Christ intended to do, and the book of Acts shows how the Great Commission was understood by those who heard it. They set about establishing churches. Birth is an individual matter, but in God's plan it is birth into the family.

Once a congregation has been formed, there is the immediate need for all the functions of the church. If the evangelist has the capability or gift of providing for these other functions, his role may begin to change. Normally, however, the congregation itself as it begins to mature, should provide for these various ministries. Certainly if the evangelist continues to "evangelize" the Christians, there will be little maturing. And if he alone provides for all the pastoral and teaching ministry, the church may be stunted in its growth. The ideal would be for the church to mature rapidly, assume its responsibility for ministry to its own, and join the evangelist in winning those yet outside.

These three, then, are the components of the church's evangelistic responsibility: proclamation, persuasion, and establishing congregations of believers.

The official stand of the United Presbyterian Church emphasizes these three elements:

> The supreme and controlling aim of the Christian mission to the world is to make the Lord Jesus Christ known to all men as their divine and only Savior and to persuade them to become his disciples and responsible members of his church in which Christians of all lands share in evangelizing the world and permeating all of life with the Spirit and Truth of Christ.[2]

The International Missionary Council meeting in Madras in 1938 put it this way:

> Evangelism . . . must so present Christ Jesus in the power of the Holy Spirit, that men shall come to put their trust in God through Him as their Savior and serve Him as their Lord in the fellowship of His church.[3]

This is the evangelistic responsibility of the church. When it has been fully discharged, what will the world look like?

WHEN MAY THE EVANGELISTIC MISSION OF THE CHURCH BE JUDGED COMPLETE?

Since this question is eschatological, it may not be possible to answer it with dogmatic precision. But we can judge to some extent. The church's responsibility can hardly be assumed discharged until every person has had opportunity to hear with understanding the good news of the way to life in Christ.

Of course, saturation proclamation alone does not fully discharge the church's responsibility. That will not be until all whom God is calling have responded to the call, accepting Christ as Lord and Saviour, and have been brought into the fellowship of His people. God alone may judge when this has been accomplished. And yet, so long as the Lord Himself does not proclaim a consummation by His own appearance, the church must assume that it is her responsibility to do what He said to do.

Without trying to probe the part of God's purpose He has not seen fit to reveal, what does the present state of obedience to His command seem to be? Has the evangelistic mission been accomplished? Actually the need is greater today than it ever has been. There are more people outside of Christ in the one land of Indonesia than there were in the entire Roman Empire when the Great Commission was given. According to the conclusions of some demographers, if our Lord should return today there would be more people in hell from this generation than from all preceding generations combined.

The evangelistic task is great and growing greater. But who, specifically, among all Christians, is responsible for seeing that it is done? Are local Christians alone responsible? What of lost people who are out of reach of any "local Christians"? What of people who live within reach but are not being reached? Are such people the responsibility of Christians from afar, that is, of foreigners? If so, of which foreigners? American foreigners? Only foreigners invited by local Christians to do the job? Or also foreigners sent by their own people to do the job?

WHO IS RESPONSIBLE TO ACCOMPLISH THIS MISSION?

The apostolic church did not take this great evangelistic mission as the responsibility of a select group of full-time professionals. The early church accepted the mandate as the responsibility of every disciple of Christ. Not all would be equally effective in bringing unbelievers to a commitment of faith. Not all would be equally effective in landing "fish," but all were equally responsible to be good bait in (1) demonstrating a supernatural quality of life, and (2) giving testimony (witness) to genuine, personal experience. The evangelistic responsibility is for all Christians, particularly all Christians in concert. Together they win men, each contributing his share. The body as a whole reproduces. We might call this "evangelism through the total church-in-witness."

But God also gave evangelists to the church, those who were particularly gifted in "landing fish," bringing men to commitment. Thus some Christians were given ability to be more *persuasive* than others, though all were to be faithful *proclaimers*. These evangelists were never intended to function independently of the church, but were designed as representatives of the church. Patricularly for people at a distance, whom the "total church-in-witness" could not reach, God provided the means whereby the church could delegate this evangelistic responsibility to certain of its members, gifted and sent to accomplish that mission.

Paul was such a representative of the church at Antioch, reporting back to the church what had been accomplished. This same function continued on after the apostolic era.

Eusebius, writing of the time from A.D. 100-150, speaks of "numberless apostles" or "preaching evangelists" who were living then. He describes them:

They performed the office of Evangelists to those who had not yet heard the faith, whilst, with a noble ambition to proclaim Christ, they also delivered to them the books of the Holy Gospels. After laying the foundation of the faith in foreign parts as the particular object of their mission, and after appointing others as shepherds of the flocks, and committing to these the care of those that had been recently introduced, they went again to other regions and nations, with the grace and cooperation of God.[4]

The contemporary word *missionary* does not precisely describe this function, however. As we now use it, the term has to do with location rather than vocation. No matter what the vocation, one seems to be a missionary if he is employed by a church in one place to serve in some way elsewhere. Especially, we use the term when a person serves in a culture other than his own, while being supported or paid by a church or mission in his own culture. Normally this means an overseas ministry and thus the term *missionary* normally means an overseas servant of the church.

This definition contributes to some of the confusion concerning the "missionary call." Actually the "call" may have little or nothing in common with what has traditonally been considered a "call to the ministry." What it really boils down to is geographical guidance—the conviction that God wants one to work in some place other than his native land. Each person who has such a conviction may be considered to have a "missionary call." He may be an airplane mechanic or a farmer; but if he is convinced that he should do this in a foreign land and is to be paid by the church of his own land, he has a "missionary call."

This particular definition of *missionary* means that we only confuse the issue by asking a general question such as that proposed as the theme of this chapter, "Is there still a valid role for foreign missionaries?" Of what role do we speak? We must discern the exact role or it will be impossible to judge whether or not the need for that role still exists.

For example, does the role of the outsider or foreigner include supplying funds for the relief of human need or to provide financial aid to a weaker sister church? Then foreign *funds* are what is necessary and the foreign *person* may actually prove an embarrassment. This administrative role of distributing money sent by more affluent Christians of other lands, if necessary at all, could hardly call for a large foreign staff. Is the foreigner a technical expert with skills needed more in another land than his own? Then, so long as some area of the world needs him, and wants him, the doctor, educator and agriculturalist will have such a role.

Is the foreigner's role that of ministering to Christians as teacher, pastor or administrator? If so, his role is normally a diminishing one in a maturing church. Furthermore, once the church has come into being, such ministers should be invited or called by those who desire the service or ministry, not sent by others who feel the ministry is needed. Of course, in the life of an emerging church there may be a legitimate period of weaning when maternalism or paternalistic oversight may be needed or at least tolerated. But in the nature of the case the need for roles of ministry to Christians imposed by "sending churches" from outside will decrease in direct proportion to the success or spiritual growth of the church.

THE EVANGELISTIC ROLE

But what if the role is evangelistic, particularly pioneer evangelism? This original missionary role will never cease to exist until the evangelistic mandate of the church is finished.

It may be argued that the responsibility for a given area passes from the foreign sending church to the local church once it has been established. This may be a legitimate delegation of responsibility, just as the original sending congregation may have delegated its evangelistic responsibility for those at a distance to the specially called evangelistic missionary at an earlier stage of evangelistic outreach.

But if there is a church that either cannot or will not reach the lost nearby, those churches outside that range of direct responsibility cannot delegate their evangelistic responsibility to it any more than they could to a nonfunctioning evangelist. The church universal has an obligation to all people outside of Christ, and it may not attempt to discharge this responsibility by delegating it to representatives who are not fulfilling it. God alone may judge whether they cannot or simply will not, but the church at large must judge whether a local congregation or group of congregations is in fact fulfilling the responsibility.

Adaptation to local circumstances can make the evangelistic task more successful: sometimes in cooperation with others, sometimes independently of others, sometimes under the direction of others. Perhaps certain people should be sent to one area and not to another. But the evangelistic representative is sent to a lost world by a sending, responsible church, not called or invited to a receiving church. He may be invited by one church to join it in evangelism so that his home or original sending church may be joined by a second forwarding church, nearer the evangelistic objective. Paul asked the church in Rome to share in sending him to Spain, for example.

Recognizing these things, evangelical missions generally bypass the old denominational comity system which allocated evangelistic responsibility for an area to one mission. The system served some good purposes, no doubt, but when it became a hindrance to completing the task, God raised up dynamic groups that bypassed the system. So with emerging nationalistic comity. If it aids in completing the evangelistic mandate, good. But if it blocks it, God will raise up fresh, dynamic movements and will bypass the new system just as he did the old.

We tend to accept the new way as inevitable. For example, in commenting on the "nationalization" of the Africa Inland Mission in Kenya, the news writer for *Christianity Today* assumed this. He said, ". . . mission societies similar to the AIM were watching and looking for guidelines . . . many of them doubtless will follow the AIM's lead . . . the 1970's will be the decade for 'passing the baton.' "[5]

Often the sole criterion in judging whether or not organizational changes should be made seems to be the question of unity and harmony, what will make for smoother running of the organizational machinery and more pleasant interpersonal relations. This undoubtedly has entered our missiological bloodstream through massive transfusions of ecumenical thinking. To be sure, the unity of the body of Christ is of great importance indeed. But it is not the only criterion.

Donald McGavran puts the primary criterion into clear focus:

> Is the over-riding goal cordial church-mission relationships? . . . If principles governing cordial relationships are stated regardless as to whether they guarantee an ever more effective evangelization, the two billion will be betrayed. . . . *Church-Mission relationships have little importance in themselves. They are important chiefly if they enable effective discipling of men and ethne to take place.*[6]

If evangelical missions dissolve staff, facilities and organization into a national church because they have no choice (the government demands it, for example) or because the evangelistic mandate in that area is being fully cared for by the national church, or because, through amalgamation, both foreigner and national can become more effective in the evangelistic responsibility, the amalgamation may indeed be the step of wisdom. However, if action is taken because of an uneasy feeling that this type of union is the only truly right way and as a consequence the evangelistic initiative is lost, the error is fatal.

The danger inherent in this indiscriminate move to amalgamation of church and mission was seen more than ten years ago by the director of the Missionary Research Library. Herbert C. Jackson says:

> A second "old pattern" I would propose is the restoration of an aggressive independence of foreign mission activity, breaking the current pattern which holds that missions must

be completely subservient to the younger churches and to the cooperative relationship in the rather narrow and technical sense in which we in the ecumenical groups have come to use that expression. This is not to be understood in any sense as a rejection of ecumenicity, which I believe profoundly to be the work of the Holy Spirit in our age; but it is to recognize that quite unintentionally a tyranny has arisen which stifles apostolate and militates very greatly against any real fulfillment of the great commission and against the freedom of the Holy Spirit to move where he will. . . .

The current view of both younger churchmen and older churchmen is that "mission" and missionary agencies must be subject to the younger churches, and work only where and when and how the younger churches should dictate. This has produced a retraction in the missionary witness that is worse than tragic and at the same time when there are still vast areas that have not heard the gospel. . . . We must have a breakdown of the contemporary view that if a church is established in a given country, or even in a region of a country, it has "homestead rights" (if not squatter's rights) and no one may enter except with the approval of the existing church, to work under the direction of that church. . . .

We must replace the present pattern in the cooperative groups, to once again swing wide open the doors so that the largest possible number of missionaries may enter to proclaim the gospel to as many people as possible.[7]

Jackson has given us fair warning of what we may expect if we blindly follow the evolutionary interpretation of missions, accepting as inevitable and good whatever the "new pattern" may be. In area after area, the evangelistic mandate is going unfulfilled because a miniscule group of Christians has assumed or has been delegated full evangelistic responsibility for a population it cannot reach alone.

Of course there are areas in which the local church is discharging effectively the responsibility for evangelization and little, if any, outside help is needed. A mission that has served

in such an area will need to refocus its aims and perhaps reallo-
cate its resources, keeping in mind the primary mission.

But instead of concentrating on our primary reason for existence as missions and missionaries, namely, to develop new
relationships and innovative programs to forward this evangelistic task, we tend to resist change—or seek change—for ex-
traneous reasons.

On the one hand we tend to conform to the old structures,
sending unneeded or uninvited servants to churches that feel
increasingly responsible for their own ministry. We may do so
because "the old is good"; God has seen fit to bless the ways of
godly men who laid the foundations. Change is difficult and
dangerous. Besides, jobs and income may be threatened by the
new way.

On the other hand, we become fascinated by the new organizational orthodoxy: amalgamated mission and church. And
we rush to the altar of union as the only really valid option.
Then we sit and wait for an invitation from the "receiving
church," while neither they nor we evangelize the unreached
world.

Does the answer lie in such either/or solutions? Why do we
lump all "missionary" activity into a single rigid structural relationship? Why do we not distinguish the roles of those we
send overseas? Certainly when *ministry* to the *church* is the
task, a move toward the servant role is long overdue in many
places. But when our *mission* to the *world* is the task, we must
maintain enough structural flexibility to assure its completion.

If the historic missions can cut free from inhibiting traditions
concerning the role of the "missionary," refuse indiscriminate
adoption of emerging organizational fundamentalism, and act
creatively, the role of world evangelization through them may
well be accomplished. However, if they become bound by
either the old or the new, God may well pass them by and accomplish His purpose of world redemption through new, free,
dynamic movements.

CONCLUSION

"Is there still a valid role for the foreign missionary?" We may answer categorically: so long as the evangelistic mandate has not been completed, the church of Jesus Christ has need for representatives with evangelistic ability to which it may delegate this responsibility. The role of the missionary evangelist is more needed today than ever before.

Therefore, we can face young men who are seeking the will of God for life investment and say: If God has given you a gift and calling of service to the church—teaching, pastoring, healing, literature—you may serve in needy America or needy Africa, long-term or short-term, full-time or part-time. But you must go as a servant of the church to which you minister. If you do go to a foreign land, you would be wise to ride light in the saddle—you may be phased out instead of fused in.

But if God has called and gifted you to bring sinners to repentance and plant the church of Christ, here is a band of pioneer evangelists we call a "mission." It works in partnership with other groups—other missions, churches at home, churches overseas—in some cases by fusion in a single organization, in some cases by consultation with other autonomous organizations. But, my young friend, they're in business till Jesus comes. They are obeying His great command. They have His promises. They will succeed, for the gates of hell shall not prevail against them.

NOTES

1. Harold Lindsell, ed., *The Church's Worldwide Mission* (Waco, Tex.: Word, 1966), p. 221.
2. *Missionary Research Bulletin,* 11, no. 8.
3. *Christianity Today* 11, no. 3 (Nov. 11, 1966): 4-5.
4. Philip Schaff, *The Oldest Church Manual Called the "Teaching of the Twelve Apostles"* (New York: Funk & Wagnalls, 1886), p. 68.
5. *Christianity Today* 16, no. 5 (Dec. 3, 1971): 41.
6. Donald McGavran, ed., *Church Growth Bulletin* 7, no. 6 (July 1971): 151-52.
7. Herbert C. Jackson, ed., *Occasional Bulletin* 12, no. 10 (Dec. 1961).

Are home churches the unwitting victims of missions searching nervously for support bases? While churches in the homeland have long recognized their responsibility to missions, it is possible that missions have not adequately fulfilled their responsibilities to supporting churches. Rarely have pastors spoken out on the subject as clearly as Gordon MacDonald does in this chapter. Here is a constructive and authoritative word from an experienced pastor who has attained a higher-than-average involvement in missions.

3

CLOSING GAPS BETWEEN MISSIONS AND HOME CHURCHES

by GORDON MACDONALD

Late evening television viewers in my hometown have been treated recently to a daily scanning of a weather-radar screen. For a radius of 150 miles, we are able to see the formations of weather fronts which are due to move through our area. As we watch this electronic gadget, an expert analyzes the data and informs us as to what kind of weather we can expect for the next forty-eight hours.

GORDON MACDONALD has been pastor of the First Baptist Church of Collinsville, Illinois, since 1966. He has traveled extensively in Africa, Latin America, and Europe, speaking to missionary groups and ministering to missionaries' personal spiritual needs. In 1971 he delivered the Fall Lectures in Missions at Gordon-Conwell Seminary, South Hamilton, Massachusetts. Pastor MacDonald received the B.A. degree from the Univeristy of Colorado in 1961 and the B.D. from Conservative Baptist Theological Seminary, Denver, Colorado, in 1966. His articles are familiar to readers of *World Vision Magazine, Eternity, Evangelical Missions Quarterly,* and other evangelical publications.

What an asset it would be if a mission executive could turn on some sort of radar which would perform a similar function in his line of work. How helpful it would be if we could electronically "quantify" the storm clouds of tension which arise on the missionary scene of each generation of church life. But no such radar exists. We can only probe the moods and feelings of people involved, praying that the Spirit of God might make us properly sensitive to what is really happening.

One area of the missionary effort that must be probed is that of the relationship between the mission agencies and the sending church. In this article we use the term "sending church" to define those groups of churches which are located in North America and support the worldwide mission effort with dollars and personnel.

Many of us within the context of the sending church sense an ever widening gap between churches and the agencies of mission. The ultimate result could be a drying up of home-base support just when there seems to be many breakthroughs in other parts of the missionary enterprise.

THE BIBLICAL PATTERN

We cannot talk with any accuracy about sending church-mission relationships without placing them in their biblical perspective. The pattern of the sending church can be studied with clarity in Acts 11—14. The new believers at Antioch had been molded together under the leadership of Barnabas and Saul. The result was a well-balanced sending church which understood how to witness in the streets, teach new converts, and enter into a caring ministry for believers who were not as economically fortunate as they were. Under these conditions, churches will necessarily mature. And the greatest evidence of Antioch's maturity was the Spirit-led decision in Acts 13 to send out Barnabas and Saul as an overseas extension of their evangelistic ministry.

Luke records no opposition to the Spirit's leading; the men were enthusiastically sent forth. The Greek text aptly employs a verb which literally interpreted reads, "They released them." Until a booster rocket reaches the zenith of its power output on the launching pad, giant clamps hold it firmly to the earth. But when the thrust has been built up to the critical point, the clamps release the rocket; it is sent forth by the releasing action of the hold-down devices. The same picture is seen in that dramatic scene when the Antioch congregation became a sending church by releasing Saul and Barnabas.

Our particular note of interest rests in the fact of Paul's continuing relationship with the church once he had left Antioch. While he seems to recognize that the seat of authority of the church fathers was at Jerusalem, and while he was engaged in a daily involvement with many of the churches he had founded, Paul never forgot that *his* sending church was at Antioch. We have no record that Antioch had a financial interest in Paul's work, although it is quite possible. Nevertheless, Paul maintained a unique relationship to that church that was never forgotten. Why?

Paul is saying something to us here. He is revealing his comprehension of the dynamic relationship which ought to be present between a sending church and missionary personnel. Apparently the believers in Antioch had to be part of Paul's missionary effort, not only because Paul needed them but because they needed to be part of an international ministry. Through Paul and Barnabas, Antioch was fulfilling part of its own purpose for existence.

There is no change in that need today. Every sign in the biblical doctrine and historical practice of the church points to the fact that a contemporary congregation cannot experience the fullness of God's plan for its existence unless it has an intimate involvement in missions as a sending church. The sending church is international in character. Whenever that international dimension has been curtailed or dulled, or whenever that international involvement has become stifled by ecclesiastical bureaucracy or artificial relationships, the life of the church is retarded.

The great genius of the church is the fact that Christians thrive on the melting together of men of different races, ages, mentalities, cultures and economic classes through the blood of Christ. Such an experience cannot be had on a community level only. The Great Commission was not a simple command to "Go." Within it was the key to the success of the future church. The more expansive the church became in its international evangelistic efforts, the greater would be its inner strength and vitality.

Having set forth this principle—that the church reaches maturity only when it has become a sending church (international or cross-cultural in scope)—we can turn our attention to where mission/church relationships seem to be souring today. Anything we can find which jeopardizes the chances for the local congregation to have firsthand outreach experiences into the world ought to be identified, studied, and promptly corrected. Let me suggest some places where we might search for such storm clouds of tension.

TRAINING THE LAITY

One ought to begin this analysis by looking to the laity: the human lifeblood of the church. We should concentrate our interest on men and women who are not members of the missionary committee or the top level of church leadership. It would be reasonable to suggest that, beyond these brief boundaries, the viewpoint of missions which confronts us would be sheer confusion. Put very simply, the average layman in the church just doesn't understand at all the reason missions exist or what they are supposed to do.

As long as he has been a member of the church, he has been aware that mission had something to do with the church's life. He may even have been convinced at one point or another that the success of the church depends upon some sort of continued and growing missionary involvement. The sad result of this, however, is that while being involved in missions, he is not necessarily receiving the type of experience which God intended for him to have as a product of international involvement.

Mr. Churchman is not normally hostile to missions—unless he has been shortchanged at one point or another by some ill-conceived missionary scheme. But he doesn't really know what is going on "out there." He hears only what key people—the mission board and the mission's public relations department want him to hear. The sum total of his understanding of mission often amounts to a series of missionary slogans ("Why should anyone hear the gospel twice until everyone has heard it once?"), the 172 slides of "the mission field," and the encyclopedic lists of statistics about world population growth and the projected sweep of the pagan cults.

Confusion over mission, its meaning and its conduct is not only the result of lack of information; it also comes from some of the *mis*information which is coming to him. James Michener's novel *Hawaii* is a case in point. Sacrificing some historical accuracy to the shrine of literary entertainment, Michener proceeded to portray nineteenth-century missionaries to the Pacific in such a poor light that many American Christians have become uneasy about the role of missions abroad. Humor on television, the criticisms of some national leaders in emerging nations, and the influence of such organizations as the World Council of Churches, which proposes the withdrawal of missionaries on a wide front, all serve to distort the perspective of Mr. Churchgoer. It is in vogue for people coming home from world travels to repeat half-truths about missionary exploitation. More and more pastors hear responsible people suggesting that missionaries be brought back home.

In addition to lack of information and to misinformation, the layman sometimes suffers from too idealistic a view of the missionary effort. The backlash to Elizabeth Elliot's brilliant novel, *No Graven Image,* should have warned us that most Christians were not equipped to see the missionary venture in anything but romantic terms. Mrs. Elliot's attempt to inject some realism into the thought patterns of her characters bruised

the sensibilities of many Christians (some of them missionaries) who never have wanted to face the fact that there may
be times of depression, even defeat, for missionaries and missions. It confronts us with the fact that many laymen are simply not prepared to face and react to the real truths about missionary life around the world.

Where does the fault lie for such confusion? Is it the missionary's for not telling us the inside story of his life situation
on the field? Does the blame rest upon the mission agency for
casting all missionary information in such a light that it is
sure to look good "for the constituency"? Or has the sending
church simply not been trained to listen perceptively to what
missions is all about?

CAUSES OF THE COMMUNICATIONS GAP

But we must go far beyond the mere problem of confusion
in terms of the distorted image that some laymen have of missions. I am convinced that many missions are equally confused
when it comes to *their* image of the sending church. Preoccupied by the turmoil of the emerging national church and the
pains of its development, they have tended to invest all their
creative thinking overseas. While heads have been turned in
the overseas direction, massive changes have occurred here at
home.

For one thing, church specialization has set in. Church staffs
are now studded with directors of Christian education, youth
pastors, business managers, and a host of other hired personnel.
They have tended to fragment the church's interest so that
people now see missions as only one of the many categories
of church life. In other words, mission no longer enjoys a top-
line priority in the church program. Mission agencies seem
to be waking up to this fact just a little too late.

In addition to the complexities of contemporary church pro-
gramming, there has come a change in the mood and outlook
of church members. The new quest for honesty has brought

a new element into Christian thinking. The modern mind inquires far more deeply into the "why" of things. There is a new cynicism which regards almost everything as guilty and worthy of suspicion until proven innocent. In a whole new way the motivations, the methods, and the results of any aspect of church life are being questioned.

Returning missionaries are often shocked at the questions which they are being asked by churchmen, especially by the younger generation. Having the title *missionary* no longer entitles one to immunity from frank questioning. Those who are ready to give straight answers are gaining new friends, fresh support, and a more involved home-base commitment to their work. Conversely, those who tend to veil their answers in clichés, or who wish to countercharge the new church *mind* as being unspiritual and apathetic, are losing out.

The fact that many Christians have now had travel experiences makes them much more curious about missions. Their questions are far more intelligent once they have been in the area where missions is in operation. They look for missionary personnel who are doing hard thinking about contemporary realities. They search for missionaries who are employing the tools of the new age to spread the old, old story. When they find them, they are delighted. But when they cannot, they are disillusioned.

Add to the sophistication of the church's life and mind the reality that mission life and theology have also become complex, and you have a serious gap of communication. Missions and missionaries have adopted new philosophies and theologies. New vocabularies of terms and concepts make for a feeling of bewilderment as the layman attempts to find out what in the world is going on. Hence, a knowledge gap which neither layman or missionary seems to be able to cross.

It might be wise to pause in this assessment of things as they seem to be, to add that I am not saying that what is happening in the sending church or the mission agencies is wrong. In a complex world, sophistication of operation arises. The knowledge explosion has not been limited only to secular areas. But the result is that the layman is going through a kind of "future shock" as he attempts to cope with the vast amount of motivation and information now available to him. It is becoming increasingly difficult for him to react and get excited about the cause of worldwide missions under the present circumstances. One of our prime questions, then, must be how can we overcome this vast gap of confusion, misinformation and multiple inputs and help laymen settle into a healthy experience of mission involvement on a practical and spiritual level.

We may want to begin by pointing up the inadequacies of mission today to provide the sending church with a uniform understanding of biblical foundations for mission practices. The history of missions reveals that they were born out of Bible study and teaching. It was a full comprehension of the Word of God that compelled the first men in modern mission to take corrective action within the church and call for men to face their missionary responsibilities.

But what is the sending church hearing today? All too often it is the devotional message, geared to inspiration, guilt or emotional persuasion. Few are the men who are sounding out the biblical imperatives for mission. We are in need of champion speakers who can plumb the depths of Scripture and call the church to attention in order to face its supreme responsibility to the worldwide evangelistic cause. We need expositors who can inspire laymen with the Word of God, challenge them to face the biblical commands, and implement them in this age. Reformations are always the result of rediscovered doctrines, not the kind of insipid missionary preaching that so many pulpits are filled with today.

Beyond clarifying what the Bible teaches about mission, I would like to call upon missions to provide an intensive campaign of indoctrination of pastors and laymen, a campaign geared at opening up the strategy of mission to the church. With some frankness, I confess that most pastors I know have little, if any, knowledge of the difference between "good" missions and "bad" missions. We are forced to rely upon person-alities like brand names (If Billy Graham endorses it, it has got to be good!).

How many laymen (and pastors), for example, know the difference between service missions and church-planting missions? What does the average church know about the problems of mission administration? How can laymen make an intelligent decision about the proper place to invest the Lord's money? Why is it, in short, that a church is called "missions-minded" on the basis of how much money it gives?

I recently saw a copy of a letter written to an evangelical mission canceling support of a missionary who was being transferred to a North American office where he was going to be a director of the mission. Even though the missionary needed continued support, it was the policy of this "missions-minded" church never to support any missionary who wasn't located outside of the country. It seems to me that it would have been "missions-minded" to have realized that this new director was probably in a better position now to further the church's missionary interest than ever before. The church was misinformed and misguided. No one had taught it effectively. The joy of intelligent missionary investment and participation was denied them through ignorance.

Therefore, the storm clouds of tension between sending church and mission arise largely because of the lack of teaching that we in the churches are getting. Mission agencies *owe* the sending church an intensive program of education on these matters. Such knowledge will make the sending church more discriminating in its choices of fields of missionary involvement.

THE FINANCIAL CREDIBILITY GAP

One cannot talk about tensions in these relationships without finally getting to the problem of mission-sending church finances and the friction often created by money. When asked about the first word which comes to mind when *missions* are mentioned, many laymen will respond with an answer that is financial in implication. In that reaction, they reflect a growing suspicion and hostility that whenever missions are on the program, the "bite" will be put on. "Leave your billfold and checkbook home tonight—your pen too, in case they just happen to have blank checks; there's a missionary speaker in the pulpit." So might go the thought pattern of Mr. Churchgoer. An unspiritual idea, true, but quite real. Real enough that it ought to be reckoned with.

Missionary leaders have lamented the fact that money once easily raised is now becoming harder to find. Where, they ask, are the fervor and enthusiasm which were rampant in the '40s and '50s? Why are people reluctant to give to projects, administrators and agencies? The answer is not difficult to find, but it is a good deal more significant than the tightness of money!

One might wish to face, first, the growing American mentality of isolationism. As a whole, the American people feel that investments overseas have not achieved the success we once thought possible in terms of gaining political and diplomatic success. Some of that mentality splashes upon the church. Money once earmarked for projects abroad is much more easily invested at home. The feeling is that we have some missionary work to get done here first.

Then, suspicion is a large part of the answer. Ignorance is another. Too long, missions have allowed the local church member to feel that they only wish his dollar. The missionary who journeys two hundred miles, preaches his heart out, and then says that the most important thing he needs is prayer is simply not believed. The follow-up letters and the private comments all prove that what he really wanted most of all was money—*support* is a more diplomatic word. Now that is not bad. But where has the atmosphere of frankness and understanding of these things gone? A half-dozen experiences of this sort make the layman wary; he begins to ask, "Is this all the mission ever wants from me?"

Now here is a serious point of tension. A missionary should not have to come to a church like a beggar with his hand out. The church should not have to feel that the "bite" is always being put on. And yet the current practices of many faith missions promote this unavoidable atmosphere. A solution will have to be found, or laymen will withdraw more and more from an active interest in the missionary program.

It has been demonstrated over and over again that the money is there for the organization or the man who can show a plan for the investment of gifts. Organizations which have approached the church with a plan that gets results within the context of their work, which have shown the church that there is substantial justification for the kind of work that they are doing, are getting the support they are looking for.

It will be helpful for both the sending church and missions to remember always that the man in the pew today handles significant amounts of money. He is accountable to his company and to the Internal Revenue Service for the handling of his money. He understands principles of investment. He learns that money poured down a rathole is not a good investment. He is burned once but seldom a second time. Finally, he has learned not to mix his investments with his emotional feelings. He makes solid, objective strategic decisions.

He will do likewise when he is led to give to the missionary effort. Show him a plan, a strategy which is going to work, and he will invest. Prove to the laymen that the missionaries and projects you want him to support are well managed, that they are set in strategic situations, and that their activities are evaluated. Show him that his money is going to get some kind of specific result which is in alignment with the biblical mandate.

Financial tension can easily arise in the heart of a pastor against missionaries. The pastor, already committed to a church budget of Christian education expenses, mortgage payments, not to speak of salaries, is usually pushing hard to maintain the support level of other missionaries previously pledged to. Thus he cannot help but be on the defensive when a missionary comes, stays in the home of his church members, and walks away with chunks of personal support which may come out of the layman's tithe. The appeal to give to a specific project or person rather than an impersonal, dull church budget is almost too great to pass up.

This all places the pastor in a weird tangle of mental feelings. He wants to sell the missionary to his congregation, but not so strongly that he will overburden other aspects of the current church budget. A real tightrope! While some missionary leaders may bristle over these thoughts, they will nevertheless have to wrestle with the fact that—rightly or wrongly —the feeling exists. It has frequently crippled the confidence that a pastor has had in a mission board.

We cannot ignore the fact that the varying financial policies of missions have often put the missionary in the guise of a beggar. A missionary comes to a church and gains pledged support. The church is happy with the established relationship. It has a missionary; the missionary has a supporting church. But then a chain of letters begins to come which follows a monotonous pattern. First it is a car fund that has to be raised. Would the church give an extra offering to purchase a car for this term? Then it is "outgoing" expense, a miscellaneous item which can number several thousand dollars to "outfit" the missionary. Finally, the letters come for special projects: taping equipment, a ham radio, a portable public address system. Pastor and people are confused. Is the missionary supported or not? Can he really go to the field? Or is there more money to be raised? How many new projects must there be?

Now it should be repeated that the intention of these paragraphs is not to label such practices as "wrong." But it would certainly be accurate and reasonable to call them "misunderstood." Either the missions and their missionaries are going to have to be more candid in telling us the full sum of money needed to put a missionary unit on the field fully equipped, or the image of a missionary is going to be further jeopardized. For when it comes to money, what *is* the truth?

The fiscal problems of sending church/mission relationships may stand at the top of priority lists for solving. I do not think that we solve these problems by entering into what is called the "pool" support system, where churches simply give their missionary money to a central fund which then administrates salary and equipment expense to each missionary it chooses to support.

Fellowship with the Receiving Church

Another dimension of potential tension in sending church/ mission relationships is seen in the absence of fellowship between the sending church and the more recently established receiving church. Inadvertently, mission agencies tend to stand as a buffer between the two groups, denying both sides a vital link of relationship which they badly need. Often the mission agency is guilty of telling the sending church and the receiving church only what it wants each to hear about the other. A full-orbed fellowship is difficult to establish on this basis.

Having been biased against contemporary forms of ecumenism, we Evangelicals have tended to shy away from church unity in general. But the fact is indisputable; there *is* a worldwide church of Jesus Christ. In every land there are congregations of believers serving the same God. How little we know of each other! How insipid our attempts to help one another! I am suggesting that we have forfeited one of the great rights of the church: the chance to have international fellowship, the strengthening of one another.

The American church does not really understand that there are church groups all over the world which are highly mature, which are able to sustain themselves, to reach out as sending churches in their own right. The American church is not fully aware that there are Bible preachers and teachers around the world whose insight and wisdom in the Word of God are the match of our finest men. Furthermore, the American church has not become aware that there are churches and churchmen in the world who may have a ministry to us.

Where is the mature church today? Is it in America? Are we the mature dimension in the world today simply because we have a stranglehold on most of the world's wealth? What of the dynamic movements of revival and renewal in other parts of the world? While not marked with material wealth, they show depths of power and strength that the American church has rarely known. For example, consider the lay revival of East Africa, the Pentecostal surge in Brazil, the vitality of the church in Nigeria, the amazing durability of the believers in Soviet Russia and South Vietnam. Who is the mature church today? Is it possible that these are church groups which ought to be coming to America to tell us something about the plans and promises of God?

. If these churches have something to say to the church of North America, there are few of us who know about it. Hardly ever has a national churchman come from Asia or Africa to "care" for us by teaching the Word of God. Of the few who have been sent to the States, most were on fund-raising tours. We have to believe that one of the strongest links the international church has at its disposal has never been truly forged: the fellowship of mutual caring and teaching. Too long it has been a one-way street of men and material. It is time for mission to see that, as a bridge across the waters, it can provide a mutual ministry which moves in two directions.

To be fair, we must recognize that if communication lines were opened up between local churches of every continent that undisciplined believers from poor countries might attempt to take advantage of wealthier Christian brothers. Mission leaders have often stated that this is a serious problem. It is time, however, to take that risk. We simply cannot be convinced that mission has completed its job to any extent until it has forged a strong tie between sending and receiving church. This tie may begin by helping the sending church to listen to what the receiving church has to say.

THE TURNOVER PROCESS

Another of the potential misunderstandings which easily moves to the surface of sending church/mission relationships is the whole question of the disposition of mission properties and equipment on many fields. With some frequence we are seeing the wholesale turnover of buildings, organizations and equipment to national personnel. This may be a landmark experience to the missionary on the scene, but it is confusing to the man at home who financed the property through his giving.

As the national church has matured on many fields, the whole agonizing question of the ownership of mission property has become a priority question. We begin to read statements such as the one which suggests that the American missionary now enjoys simply the status of a "guest" of the national church. We often read of situations where the missionary now becomes part of the national church organization, is assigned by nationals to a particular type of work, and is made generally accountable to the national for his productivity. Beyond that we are bombarded with the reports of the national churches being given the title deeds to hundreds of thousands of dollars worth of buildings, printing presses, vehicles, etc.

These things are not wrong. They do produce tensions, however, because they generally rub against the grain of the American mentality. It is difficult for Americans to understand the seeming rebellion of the national church in wanting to assume leadership and ownership. The churchman in America has not been sufficiently prepared for such turnovers. He is unable to understand the new concept that money given to American-based missions can suddenly become the property of groups whose name he is unfamiliar with, or that the missionary he supports in answerable to an unknown national.

Again, the need here is a massive information program. Something is needed which would acquaint the sending church with the ultimate aspects of mission strategy: that of planting the church and setting it free on its own.

As much as our national brethren would like to protest our "colonialist" mentality, they must accept our cultural heritage every bit as much as we have been asked to accept theirs. The transfer of authority and ownership may be Christian, biblical and strategic, but it must be accompanied by slow and painstaking educational methods here at home, lest there arise a lack of confidence in mission projects and needs on the part of the giving church.

THE PROBLEM OF PROLIFERATION

Perhaps nothing is more bewildering to the sending church than the proliferation of new missionary organizations. Rarely does a month go by that there does not seem to be the announcement of another new organization with a unique sales pitch based on a new twist of scriptural interpretation or some strategic idea which the church in the world has completely overlooked.

One wonders if the extrachurch organizations have any idea what a confusing picture they present to the church and its bevy of giving laymen. It might be charged at the outset that the church itself has much the same problem with its denominational stratification. This is a reasonable charge. However, perhaps it can be said with some accuracy that the church is often divided on doctrinal lines while extrachurch organizations tend to divide on personality lines.

The independent spirit among Evangelicals seems to reveal its vital flaw at this point. We view with alarm the tendency for men to split and split again, starting new movements each time, building buildings, purchasing computer time, mailing lists and expensive publicity material. The redundancy becomes scandalous as personnel, equipment and time are often needlessly duplicated. On the home front the churchman finds his head swiveling from side to side as he worries over the correct place to send his funds. Every organization has a need which is just a bit more urgent than the next!

Because there is so little discipline among Evangelicals, due largely to their lack of organization, what can be done about this problem of proliferation? Perhaps very little. Every man who joins the rush to be a new "founder and director" will find some rationale to justify the existence of his movement. Little will have been accomplished.

But this is such a serious problem that to do nothing would be more than injurious. Why cannot some of our evangelical leaders, honest men of God, give us some forthright principles on organizationalism? Would it be possible to help us to discriminate between the good and permanent as opposed to the fly-by-night? Could organizations such as the Evangelical Foreign Missions Association and the Interdenominational Foreign Mission Association strengthen themselves as accrediting agencies? This, of course, runs the risk of having a superagency calling all the shots. But would that be any worse than the situation which is so seriously fragmenting our honest efforts at worldwide evangelization right now?

PASTOR TO THE MISSIONARY

The role of the church in the pastoral care of the missionary is a glaring point of need as we enter the '70s. I question whether a missionary organization can capably discharge the duties both of administrator-strategist and pastor to the missionary. One is strictly a business relationship, while the other has to do with all the aches and personal conflicts which arise out of living in that system.

For years a church's specific responsibility for a missionary ended with the giving of money and a few scattered gifts on various holidays. Add to this a tiny involvement during the stage of appointment, and you have generally outlined the extent to which most churches are involved in the personal life of the missionary. It would be easy to say that most churches are not interested in becoming more involved than this; but, on the other hand, little attempt has been made to initiate creative attempts to bring the church into the pastoral orbit of the missionary's life.

The local church, if adequately trained and informed, could offer much to mission and missionary in addition to money. The local church is quite capable of leading a person through the complete series of missionary phases: recruitment, training, appointment, sending, maintenance and evaluation.

A pastor, for example, is often able to challenge people in his congregation to fill certain spots on the mission field as he is made aware of specific needs. Recently I returned from a Latin American country where I had been doing some missionary research. While on location, I saw a need for a couple to work in a particular situation. At the same time I was aware of a young couple in our congregation wrestling with the call of God in their lives. Upon my return home, I visited and shared with them the observations I had made on the field. Within weeks they had made application and been accepted by the mission. Shortly they will be fitting into a slot which God prepared and revealed through a local church pastor and congregation.

But the church must also have some sort of pastoral ministry while a missionary recruit is in formal training and when he reaches the field. Some thought should be given to the possibility of assigning every missionary a pastor (assigned on the basis of the missionary's choice). The mission agency could take time to train that pastor to do an intensive job of "caring" throughout the years of the missionary's career. If a crucial need of personal or spiritual dimensions arose, it might be necessary for the mission to call the pastor in to help arbitrate the situation. A wise pastor could bring perspective to a problem. Many churches are ready to loan their pastors for short periods of time to missions. Such men could make great contributions in counseling, Bible teaching and exhortation.

AMERICAN INTROSPECTION

Any student of the American scene realizes that the people of the United States are beginning to look inward. Who knows where it really began. But national introspection is upon us.

and it has not been without its effect upon the church. Church-men are calling for a new look at things around home. We can easily be criticized for the millions we have spent on our own lavishly appointed buildings and equipment, a tragic imbalance in proportion to the amount sent out into the rest of the world. On the other hand, an uneasiness pervades the soul of many Evangelicals. We have neglected the minority groups, the poor, the urban dweller. Suddenly the cry is rising to appro-priate more funds for home projects.

This introspection is going to make it even more difficult for funds to become available for overseas development. A new understanding of the balance of investments will have to be gained.

A helpful solution to this growing dilemma will be a redefi-nition of mission and its area of involvement. But in the final analysis, the need both at home and abroad will be equally acute. More men, more support, and greater creative thinking will be the answer. Instead of becoming defensive against "home mission" activities, the foreign branch of the church will simply have to show us how both can be incorporated into the international program of evangelism. In the long run, ill-defined, unproductive missionary efforts are going to be weeded out.

There are serious tensions on the horizon between missions and the sending church. Often these tensions are the product of ignorance, immaturity, or changing circumstances no one could predict. Missions are going to be confronted with a new cynicism in the churches. Some of it will be the outcome of poorly led churches, congregations whose leadership has been lax in challenging them with the worldwide mission of the church. For other churches, the cynicism will be the result of feeling that they have been "used," and that too often the great appeals were badly misrepresented.

For others, the cynicism will be a healthy sign. It will mean that a new day could be arising, a day in which pastors and laymen are taking a long, hard look at their involvement in the strategy of the church. Men will be looking for the right investments of time and money. The support will go to those organizations which are demonstrating their usefulness to God. Their strategy, their results and their manpower will all point to that fact.

Much of the sending church in North America languishes today in a general state of despair. Here and there are bright lights shining: churches where God is obviously at work, churches with pastors and laymen who are happy with their joint vision of sharing and living the gospel. But that is not the trend of things in most places. Let us be frank and admit that general church morale is low. It is reflected in the growing difficulty of getting people excited over evangelism, Bible study and fellowship.

Such a mood means that the sending church is in need of some kind of reformation. This is not a reformation of programs, but a renewal of the inner spirit of things. From some source must come a new call to vitality and energy. From some place must come new leadership, a new direction which will spark a commitment to Jesus Christ and His commission. I believe that call could come from the mission dimension of the church. Here are men and women who are veterans of the "wars." They understand suffering, they comprehend involvement, they know well the painful experience of reaching out and of caring for the hearts of men. These men and women have something to bring to the sending church. We need to hear it. Reformation simply awaits its leadership.

Thus, we have a choice in this time of tension between the home church and mission. We can choose to become more rigid, to kick obstinately against the onrushing forces of change. Or we can welcome such winds of change as breaths of fresh air, a new day in which a greater, in-depth experience of mission-sending church relations can be improved. The next few years will determine the alternative we choose.

Would your church be likely to consider forming a "Committee to Investigate Our Missionary in Ethiopia?" With their tongues only slightly in their cheeks, Charles Mellis and Bob Lehnhart suggest that something like this be done by churches in order to evaluate the effectiveness of the missionaries and mission boards they support. This chapter is full of new, and at times, controversial ideas, which, if implemented by home churches, could go a long way toward revitalizing the entire North American evangelical missionary movement.

4

CHURCHES: YOUR MISSIONS NEED YOU

by CHARLES MELLIS and ROBERT LEHNHART

We mean it. We need *you;* not just your money—you!

Oh, we know that's not the image we missionaries usually project. The pastor delegates who met with us at GL '71 were gracious men. But as they held up the mirror, the message was clear: too often we've come through as looking to the churches principally as supply houses. We've placed our orders for recruits and money. Our requests may be ever so low-keyed. But the result is the same.

CHARLES MELLIS has been President of Missionary Aviation Fellowship since 1970. After serving as a pilot with the Air Force during World War II, he joined MAF toward the end of its founding year. As Secretary-Treasurer, he spent most of the next two decades in administrative responsibilities. This was punctuated during the 1950s by four years of overseas service, most of it in the Southwest Pacific, establishing new services and surveying future possibilities. Mr. Mellis also

We have to acknowledge that there is a significant degree of validity in this image. Our purpose in this chapter is to make some suggestions which may modify this—not just the image, but the relationship itself.

First of all, we'd like to see this change because we sense we may be missing God's best for us. We feel a new sense of needing you pastors at this point in time. For more than half of this century we as missionaries have enjoyed some notable successes. Sometimes we forget how much we need each other when things are going smoothly. But now that history is changing our job description (as missions), we've got to grapple with some hard questions. When we're faced with a struggle, we need each other more—and at a deeper level.

OF TREES—AND FORESTS

Probably the need which we feel is the greatest from our viewpoint as mission administrators is a more complete understanding within the churches of "the big picture" in overseas missions. Most churches get their mission information from two sources: individual missionaries they are related to, and periodicals (including house organs of the agencies). Both these sources have developed problems as adequate barometers, for different reasons.

There was a day when the *best* source of mission information was the individual missionary. The evangelistic and church-planting task *centered* on his efforts. What was happening under his tree was at least approximately representative of

serves as a member of the official board of the Interdenominational Foreign Mission Association.

ROBERT LEHNHART is Director of Planning and New Developments for Missionary Aviation Fellowship. After graduation from Bryan College and the Moody Bible Institute aviation program, he joined MAF in the late 1950s. Mr. Lehnhart gained his field experience as a pilot-mechanic in Brazil and Ecuador. In 1967 he became MAF Director of Recruitment and Orientation, and in this office developed a new concept of orientation for overseas service which he continues to co-ordinate for MAF and other missionary personnel in the annual Orientation Institute. He is also Director of Operations for MAF.

what was happening under many other trees. Today those trees make up a forest, which is something more than the sum of the trees. An understanding of this forest is crucial.

Most periodicals dealing with missions major on success stories. As already mentioned, we've experienced enough success that we've come to expect it as a norm—possibly even as a test of spirituality. As the church has absorbed this success orientation, our mission agencies, consciously or unconsciously, have catered to it. This has continued in circular fashion to the point where it now takes real courage to place integrity ahead of emotional impact in our written communications.

Both these media (personal reports from missionaries and success-oriented periodicals) have produced the often-discussed hero image, not only of the missionary, but of the movement as a whole. Neither the movement nor its participants are allowed by its friends to "fail." This places an unbearable burden on both administrators and overseas missionaries.

The first step toward a solution is, of course, theological. God won't allow *His* work to fail. But that's true despite *our* batting average, not because of it! If we can firmly transfer this burden from our shoulders back to God's, this will free us to be real people, relating realistically to the sticky problems we'd rather ignore.

But let's go back to this primary need: the "understanding" of churches, and particularly the leadership, as to what we face in "the big picture" today. As indicated above, there isn't very much in popular periodicals on this subject. There are exceptions. *Eternity, Christianity Today, Church Growth Bulletin, His, Evangelical Missions Quarterly* and some others have tried to grapple with the mission picture as it really is.

Ex Libris

More often this needs book-length treatment. Pastors should be seeking out good, concise, analytical books like Dennis Clark's *The Third World and Mission*[1] to recommend to their elders, deacons and mission committee members. This won't happen easily. Some of these books will be viewed as "negative" by some mission-hearted people. The pastor may have to help them see that missions, as such, are not being "attacked." The author may at times overstate his point (don't we all?) but what he's really trying to do is separate temporary, outgrown practices from the basic continuing principles. Unfortunately, we usually are more comfortable with methods (from order of worship to one-year furloughs) than with principles. Our comfortable thought patterns become presuppositions. When these are scrutinized we too easily see this as an attack on "basics." It takes conscious effort to avoid this confusion.

While we are talking about books as an important part of mission awareness, we ought to say a word about biography. For many years we as mission leaders have urged the churches, and particularly candidates, to read mission biography. This can still be valuable, *providing* one remembers what he is reading. In the first place, biography represents history. If it's faithfully written, it gives a good personalized picture of the mission scene in that day, which, of course, might be quite different from the mission scene today. Also, a biography usually represents the particular locale where the personality lived and worked. And this may even be a very nontypical situation, since the exotic makes more interesting reading.

CONFERENCE AND COMMUNICATION

These two classes of books, biography and analysis, illustrate the distinction between challenge or inspiration on the one hand, and information or education on the other. We feel this distinction also needs careful consideration in planning the oral presentation of mission in the local church. Most churches center almost exclusively on the former. Today we need a much stronger emphasis on the latter. And it need not be dull!

We're not recommending the *elimination* of challenge/inspiration mission presentations. They still are valid in some situations. For example, the missionary representative on furlough should not only be asked to report, but he should be encouraged to speak from his heart.

The challenge presentation is probably *least* valid today (and here we are going to have to speak to a sacred cow) in our missionary conferences where we're speaking to people already committed to missions. Here we should shift emphasis from inspiration to education. And while we are making the shift, let's go with the best current thinking on education; let's not think only in terms of teaching, but rather of *learning.* The goal is to lead the congregation through a process of discovering what God is doing in the world, particularly through His church *today,* then to lead them to involvement in that larger world in some personal way, beginning in the local community (not just inside the walls of the church) and moving out from there.

PROCESS AS COMMUNICATION

We feel that the best way to achieve this goal is through a preplanned learning experience which emphasizes *process* rather than merely challenge, on the one hand, or plain facts on the other.

What do we mean by process? Facts don't change people; the learner must experience the *reality* of the facts and be faced with the struggle to integrate them. For example, rather than a missionary *telling* about how difficult it is to communicate across a cultural barrier, why not bring into the conference several articulate non-Christians from another culture or subculture (international students, minority groups, etc.)? Then in a small-group context, if possible, seek openly to interact regarding values, beliefs and commitment. If a larger group is the only option, then choose several from the congregation, along with the missionary, to carry on the interaction. Afterward the missionary should help the congregation draw the parallels and interpret what actually happened. This way the people not only will understand the problems but will be able to pray intelligently for their missionaries, since they will have felt to a point what missionaries feel. Some may also gain confidence enough to allow them to move out themselves into the community arena of minority groups and/or international students. Even more elementary, it might enable them to take the first step in communicating their life and faith to those most like them.

Learning "processes" can be designed to fit the local situation. Consider some of the "involvement" films designed to touch an audience at the level where the people encounter a conflict of values, experience and belief. These should be followed by a discussion to draw out the reactions and feelings of the audience.

What are we driving at here? Simply this: We can no longer afford to allow the man in the pew to stay comfortably uninvolved, either in the communication of the missionary task or in the task itself. Most people remain uninvolved because they are afraid. They may need to experience "encounter" in the comparative safety of their friends before they are willing to risk themselves out in the world.

ENTER THE TEAM

We'd like to suggest a small-team approach to the selection of speakers and resource people. This differs from the usual practice in that they would (1) be few in number, (2) be chosen for particular gifts and insights, and (3) plan *together* the learning experience.

The value of a small team is that each man is involved significantly in the missionary conference. This is good stewardship. It might be frightening to know how much it really costs to have thirty, twenty or even ten missionaries at a week-long conference. Figuring a realistic salary, travel, and living costs, isn't it a high price to pay for what we're getting? Of course, with the team approach it is highly important that we involve the right people if we're going to accomplish our goals. Who should make up these teams?

Most of them will probably be experienced missionaries, though not necessarily "fresh from the field" (a former expectation). They may now be studying, teaching or doing research, taking a good solid look at the big picture. Mission administrators also bring a needed dimension.

By our emphasis on the big picture we do not mean to avoid specifics. In fact, they are the meat on the bones that gives meaning and comprehension. What we are pleading for is that specifics be integrated constantly into the whole by someone with experience and insight.

A second qualification is the ability to communicate. Let's define that too. If you think of a communicator as one who can tell the best story in an interesting way, you may already be asking for and getting him. But that's not what we are suggesting. The good communicator does not have to rely on dramatic interest. He can hit head on the issues of the day and make them live, for he involves the participants in the learning process, as we have already discussed.

We have placed a heavy emphasis on two-way communication, or interaction, to use the current idiom. And the kind of interaction we're talking about should not be confused with a forum, panel or question-and-answer period in the main sanctuary! The group has to be small enough so that all but the most timid will get a chance to talk if they want to. And it should not be limited to asking questions of the "expert." People can learn by sharing their ideas, even weak ones.

This need for interaction adds another qualification in selecting men to lead these seminars. They're going to have to be pretty secure people who are not too easily threatened or too defensive. This is particularly crucial when it comes to communicating with the group we most want to reach: the youth and young adults who must take the torch from us. The over-thirties may prefer to be spectators for a while longer. But our new generation learns primarily through interaction, and they want to talk about the "gut" issues.

We as mission agencies probably need to take some of the

initiative in developing such teams. But even this would
happen faster if we knew you pastors would welcome this approach. We hope you'll do more than welcome it. How about
insisting on it? Push us a bit! It's going to put demands on us
that we would often rather not have to face, but the results
will be good for both of us.

SHORTER SEMINARS

Once we've put together an effective team, how are we going
to use it? Good stewardship is probably going to require that
we concentrate the team's efforts in shorter periods. Let's look
at one format. It's more a seminar than a conference. Some
churches have found a quarterly emphasis (Saturday night and
all day Sunday) keeps the momentum rolling better than an
annual production. Saturday night can be used for small-
group discussions in several homes. The small number on the
team can be most effectively used if some groups meet early in
the evening and others later, with the resource person moving
from one to the other halfway through the evening. Content
should be facts and issues illustrated from real life, both successes and failures, to keep it alive and believable. Some of the
recent concepts that are having such a significant impact on
missions should be discussed: church-growth studies and philosophy, or the fast-spreading theological training-by-extension
movement, to name two of the key ones.

Sunday can be used in a variety of ways, again taking advantage of the natural groupings within the church and Sunday
school and zeroing in on two-way communication. If the
church is large and the Saturday evening groups were not
adequate, Sunday afternoon can be utilized in the same way.
Perhaps some of the ideas we shared earlier for involving
people in the *process* would fit either the Saturday or Sunday
evening.

To summarize: the goal is understanding and participation,
not the extraction of the most money possible in pledges and
cash. Not that money isn't important (we'll say more about

this later), but some things need to be said that may hurt us missionaries in the pocketbook. We need to ask ourselves: Is it right selectively to feed our supporters only the information which we know will give them the right vibrations? This can undermine our integrity and destroy our credibility with thinking people, especially the young.

Even those who try the hardest to be honest communicators seem to have difficulties sharing unless the churches encourage and push a little. It's difficult to share defeats or weaknesses when others share only victories. Oh, they may tell of the obstacles and difficulties which hinder the work, but these just highlight their successes. This is not the same as sharing failure. None of us likes to fail or to admit it, especially missionaries. Could this explain why we are so often put on a pedestal and why we sometimes appear phony to our youth?

COMMUNICATING ACROSS THE GAP

And, of course, communicating with the young is particularly vital. The future of the church's mission depends on them. So our chosen form of communication has to be one they'll at least tune in to. And interaction, or "rapping," is very much their style.

Consider asking your youth groups to tell you in advance what their *real* questions are about missions. Let them tell you what kind of approach would communicate to them. Then plan that kind of a communication even though you find it threatening. You'll also have to make sure that we as mission agencies deliver what you've asked for, even if it's threatening to us.

If your youth group isn't sure what they prefer, here's something you might suggest which is oriented to their style. During Billy Graham's Oakland Crusade, some creative Christians organized the "Committee to Investigate Billy Graham" and provided nightly bus service from Bay area campuses to the stadium. It was highly successful. Hundreds went, and many committed their lives to Jesus Christ.

Why not a "Committee to Investigate Our Church's Mission Overseas?" Or, "Committee to Investigate Our Missionary to Ethiopia?" In the latter case you'll have to be sure, of course, that your missionary to Ethiopia has backed off from his trees far enough to get some real understanding of the forest, and that he is not threatened by blunt questions! For in *both* cases you'll need to create a climate in which the interrogators can fire away without being put down for their questions.

FINDING GOD'S MEN

Now let's turn to the areas where we missionaries need the help of the churches in some of our most crucial decision-making: selection and periodic evaluation of our people.

At GL '71, and related study sessions, a good deal was said about more church participation in the calling of special messengers. Reference was made to Acts 13:2, where the Holy Spirit's call to two specific men was issued not to them alone, but to the acknowledged leaders of that congregation. The call was highly personalized but it was delivered through a group. This is not to suggest that Paul and Barnabas did not sense the call personally. In fact, they had to, for they also were a part of the group. Yes, they were already a part of the acknowledged leadership.

This is hardly the common picture today. The call has become highly individualized. An individual's sense of call has become so sacrosanct that his brethren may feel guilty for even evaluating it. We need to take a closer look at this in the light of Scripture. It would appear that our present trends are less a product of scriptural understanding than of our frontier heritage of rugged individualism. This, of course, has affected our American churches in other important ways also.

It's one thing to say that we need the help of churches in evaluating candidates. Even if we are all (including the candidate) agreed that this is scripturally proper, there are still massive practical problems. Probably the greatest one is our tremendous mobility. The candidate's father may have been an engineer whose company shifted him to different branches every two or three years. In any case, he went away to college just about the time he was emerging as an adult, just when the first really valid opportunity to assess his future potential was surfacing. Unless his home church makes a special effort to maintain communication with him, there may not be any group of church leaders who could adequately speak to his call when his training is completed. Those of us who read candidate reference papers can attest to the fact that this is a common picture today.

How do we overcome this problem and get back to the scriptural pattern? Maybe we're going to have to take a fresh look at whether we should be assigning people fresh out of school to longer-term service. As indicated, Paul and Barnabas were already involved in active ministry when called; their gifts had already been demonstrated and confirmed. Maybe this should be our most important qualification, more important even than academic degrees, specialized professional training, or formalized Bible study. Some missions do require a year or two of Stateside internship. This may or may not constitute real involvement in the life and ministry of the church. It can become the checking off of just another requirement from the list of qualifications.

Ideally, we need to see a revision of the educational process so that emergent leadership—whether pastors, laymen or special messengers—will remain deeply involved in the life of the church throughout the training process rather than being isolated for a substantial period. In any event, there is a need for reemphasizing the role of church leadership in the selection process.

It is the mission's responsibility to describe the job to be done and the qualifications. The church leadership, in a church in which the candidate has been deeply involved, should be able to provide objective readings on the gifts, the strengths, the weaknesses and the areas of growth of the candidate. This kind of interchange would go far toward correcting a serious weakness in missions today.

Ideally, the church should also work with the mission agency in periodically evaluating the effectiveness of their representatives. This is a lot harder to accomplish, both emotionally and practically, than involvement in the original selection.

There's an interesting factor in supporting church/mission relationships. Dedication, good motivation, and doctrine are significant; hard facts about accomplishment of goals are not.

A missionary executive in a large, well-known agency recently said that he had been personally supported in his ministry for over twenty-five years and had never, up to that time, been asked any direct questions about goals or accomplishments by those who have invested thousands of dollars in him and his work. Competence seems to be taken for granted, or perhaps the church is depending entirely on the mission board to guarantee it. However, the mission probably hasn't been asked tough-minded questions on effectiveness by its supporting churches either.

Missions do get quizzed, but usually this is limited to questions of doctrine, or relationships with some group that is not on the "approved list." Sometimes it concerns the method of raising money. Curiously, they are seldom asked about goals and performance, in spite of the fact that this is one of the best ways to determine if a mission or missionary deserves to be supported. Maybe a "Committee to Investigate Our Missionary to Ethiopia" or one to investigate his mission agency isn't just an attention-getting gimmick after all!

An example can illustrate how this works. The Trinity United Presbyterian Church of Santa Ana, California, has a mission budget of well over $100,000 a year spread widely across both denominational and nondenominational ministries. Several of their leaders recently became concerned that they were simply continuing to approve the existing budget each year. They were careful to update to cover inflation and to extend their outreach by adding several new ministries or missionaries. However, the latter were usually chosen because someone rallied the interest of the committee on their behalf.

These leaders wanted to know if there was a way they could determine that all of these ministries and people were really doing a job, a relevant job, and doing it well. Did the church really have a strategy to their giving? Are there priorities or are all things of equal importance? Did they have a balanced program of assisting various types of ministries, or were most of their dollars going in just one or two directions?

They decided to find out. They called in the entire faculty of a nearby school of missions for consultation over a period of several weeks. Goals and priorities were dealt with realistically. They identified the responsibility of their local church and its mission in the world. Criteria were set up as the basis for an evaluation of existing and new ministries. Three questionnaires were designed. They were not the vague and general questions often seen, such as, "What kind of work does your mission do? Where does it work? How many missionaries do you have?" etc. Rather, they asked the hard questions, such as, "What are your goals? Are you accomplishing your goals? What are your strengths? Your weaknesses? What are you doing about your weaknesses? If you were a member of our church, could you explain why we should support you?"

Yes, the questions no doubt bugged the missionaries and administrators who had to answer them. Yet, some indicated it was a worthwhile exercise. They were forced to stop long enough to look at themselves and those working with them. It pinpointed areas where they were slipping. Surprisingly, the church received almost 100 percent response to the questionnaires. The process of evaluating the response tested the dedication and sincerity of the committee, forcing them to struggle with their own understanding of missions in the light of the response to the questions. A heavy time-commitment was demanded, and budget deadlines put them under pressure. Part of the process was facilitated by the committee's spending a weekend in a mountain cabin away from outside distractions.

They gained amazing new insights about missions, especially those which they support. They were able to see that some were drifting and uncertain while others were dogmatic and defensive. They also found, to their great encouragement, that some were quite honest and open about their struggles and efforts to meet the challenges of the '70s.

Overall it was quite an educational experience. Decisions, for a change, were made from a basis of knowledge. A few ministries which they felt had lost their significance were dropped. However, the committee realized its inexperience and was cautious not to move too drastically on this initial effort. They also knew that yet ahead was the important task of educating the congregation so it could understand and participate in the process more fully.

This is just an example of what one church did. If others would repeat it, the results might be some revitalized mission committees, as well as missions, and ultimately churches.

You may be wondering how this desire to support those who are *accomplishing* goals relates to our earlier plea for more honest communication regarding both success and failure. Wouldn't the admittance of failure indicate a lack of performance? Possibly so. And if severe enough it could mean the person should change his place or role of ministry. However, some failure is a normal part of life and experience. The crucial question is: Has he learned from it, and is he now working on his weaker areas? In fact, people often accept us more for our humanness, if we are open, than for our strengths. Experiencing some frustrating failures while pursuing goals is much more tolerable than to be "successful" in a ministry where no one knows what the real goals are.

What are the risks for the churches in utilizing this evaluation approach? Several. Mission committees can get in over their heads pretty quickly. They can misinterpret the data. But Spirit-led common sense can help keep that in balance.

Committed men who have management experience in the business world know many of the right kinds of questions to ask. They may need the help of others who know the mission task better theologically as well as practically. But a *team* of the right people should be able to do the job effectively. Education of the committee through good books such as we have suggested earlier may be the first step. Good resource people are available to hold educational seminars for a committee or the church, especially near the major population centers.

At this point we can predict the reaction of some of our mission administrator colleagues to the implications of our suggestions. Should an avalanche of questionnaires hit their desks, our names will be anathema. We'll probably be burned in effigy at the next meeting of the mission association!

Seriously, though, there are some potential problems for us here. Care should be taken in the design of such questionnaires. Busy mission executives and missionaries can be diverted from their primary task by spending too much time answering questions. If this idea catches on, both a standard format and well-planned timing would be very important in implementing it. The Missions Advanced Research and Communications Center (MARC) is already developing a model questionnaire.

MONEY, MONEY, MONEY

We could hardly deal with the subject of this chapter without talking about money. Most evangelical Christians believe that the church in North America has some responsibility for sharing the gospel with less-evangelized parts of the world. Relatively few of us can become personally involved in this mission abroad. Most will have to settle for involvement through a medium of exchange that represents a piece of one's life and labor. This is the good side of money that too often gets buried in our materialistic, overcommercialized society.

As we look at the existing relationship between our agencies and the supporting churches, we'd like to discuss two principal concerns, and then a third which grows out of the first two.

Our first concern, shared by many throughout the churches, is the amount of time and money we spend to raise money. For most of our mission agencies, this amounts to a great deal more than ever shows up on our financial statements. Even if our public relations departments are very small, we have 20 to 25 percent of our staff regularly on furlough, and our accepted candidates represent another 5 to 10 percent. Granted, these people are involved in more than fund-raising; they have a genuinely important ministry of sharing. But this could be planned into much shorter and more effective periods if fund-raising were not involved.

Our second concern is closely related: what we normally tell people in order to raise money. We spoke earlier in this chapter about the success-orientation we have all acquired. Consciously or unconsciously, we end up emphasizing what people *want* to hear, what they have become used to hearing and have translated into values.

It is because of these two concerns, rather than any pious downgrading of money, that we have chosen to discuss financial relationships late in this chapter. We have pleaded earlier for learning experiences where our church people can come to grips with the mission picture as it actually is today. If this really happens, we may be able to break the current cycle of wasted human resources, frustrating furloughs, and a progressive following (even if from afar) of Madison Avenue.

While we are frankly facing these two concerns, we will also have to take a look at a venerable institution: personalized support. To suggest that there may be some ills in personalized support is a bit like attacking motherhood and apple pie! But we all know that mother love *can* get off the track and become "smother love." And not all apple pies are of equal quality.

Few students of missions in this century would deny the crucially important role personalized support has played—important not only in terms of enabling (getting the job done *there*) but also of involving (the supporting churches *here*).

At the same time, it produces by-products which can cause problems in *today's* mission picture.

For example, individualists tend to be confirmed in their preference for independency. This was no great handicap in the days when it took a rugged individualist to plant the gospel flag in new ground. But today the crying need is for sensitivity and interdependence. This more difficult role calls for more loving, prayerful hand-holding-up partnership than ever before. It *also* calls for the objective shared counsel of colaborers, mission leaders and national churchmen. These leaders need to be freed, as much as possible, to render their honest counsel in terms of the task, rather than in terms of possible constituency reaction. The latter is more apt to come from individual close friends and relatives than from responsible church leaders.

Despite such by-products, we are not about to recommend the dismantling of the personalized support system! But there are some things we can do to bring it up-to-date. As has been true throughout this chapter, we're thinking in terms of churches rather than of individuals.

Probably the greatest need is to take a hard look at the *number* of families supported by a church, and the amount of support contributed to each. For the past two decades, some mission agencies have strongly encouraged a widely distributed support. And many churches have set a maximum amount per family—$50, $100, $200, often depending on the size of the church. These policies have usually been advocated on three grounds: more prayer for the missionary, more security for the mission agency, and more of a worldwide interest for the church.

We have some questions about each of these. Is quantitative approach to prayer an adequate view of God's purpose in prayer? From an administrative viewpoint, distributed support is a good pragmatic "hedge" against loss of support, yet what we rationalize as "practical" often has its roots in fear.

In any case, we feel the time has come to *reverse* these policies. Perhaps we are paying too heavy a price for these minimal, possibly questionable, advantages of distributed support. Far and away the largest disadvantage is that the missionary family's loyalties are torn between many churches and geographical areas, whereas, as we have said earlier, a deep involvement with one or two sending churches would fall more within the biblical example pattern and help correct some of the problems we are facing.

As a hugely important by-product, the furloughing missionary family could experience a rich, refreshing relationship instead of (1) an exhausting rat race for young families with preschool children, or (2) a deserted mother coping with her children's adjustment to a new school while the absentee father faces the tiring circuit alone.

Making the changeover to fewer missionaries who are more adequately supported won't be easy. But it is possible. In fact, it's made easier by today's trends. Career changes are as much a fact of life in the mission picture as they are elsewhere in our world, maybe more so. We're not speaking of "failures." We're speaking of those who (1) have finished their task and have recognized that the church they planted is better off without them, or with a different type of ministry; or (2) recognize that the Lord has called them to their family responsibilities also, which may require reassignment in their homeland. This has created a "turnover," much of which is necessary and some very healthy.

We would encourage churches that have mission funds released due to such career changes to think not just in terms of finding a *new* missionary representative, but of utilizing those funds to strengthen the support of the missionaries they are already responsible for.

A major exception, of course, would occur if that church had a family newly called of the Lord to overseas service. In that case, we would hope this call were felt by the church as well as the family and that the church would undertake to become *fully* involved with them! And if the mission board had also made a point of fully involving that church in its decision-making, we would have a new kind of relationship that could restore the blessings of the personalized support system to some of its original luster. Terms and furloughs could be planned with a view to what was best rather than to what was expedient. Fund-raising per se could decrease and allow truly spiritual sharing to become predominant.

Finally, we believe that a truly "involved" church, involved in an understanding of the big picture today, involved with the agency in original selection and periodic review of its representatives, involved heavily in a supporting partnership, would also *want* to be involved in the financial needs of the mission agency that cannot validly be personalized. This includes more than the cost of administration. (Never very popular even though necessary—it seems too much like taxes!) The big picture today simply demands less paternalistic handling of the nonsalary expenditures than "work support" under the direction of an *individual* missionary.

PRAYER TARGETS

We have purposely left the subject of prayer until this late point, and our comments will be few. This is hardly because we feel it is of lesser importance, nor because we are satisfied with what we observe in ourselves or in our brethren! We can't even accept, without reservation, the panacea that people generally pray more consistently for that which they're involved in financially. This may or may not be true.

On the one hand, we must face realistically that we live in a day of rush and pressures—internal pressures we *should* control (but who's qualified to cast the first stone?), and external pressures we cannot control. Probably few people in our churches or in our mission agencies are satisfied with the quality of their communion with God. Yet, planning additional church prayer meetings hardly seems to be the answer.

It is our observation that programs to encourage prayer usually breed more program than prayer! Should this surprise us?

We can program activities. But relationships cannot be programmed. And prayer is, at the core, a relationship.

So is renewal. And if there is any one dynamic we desperately need today, this is it. We as mission agencies are products of the churches we represent. If you are doctrinally sound, but comfortable with, and even defensive of, yesterday's applications and methods, we may be too. If you are open to new applications of eternal truth, new forms, new methods—so will we learn this openness. Doctrinal purity alone will not insulate us from an Ichabod rating.

Isaiah enjoined his contemporaries, "Let the people renew their strength." We believe our evangelical churches need this message today. In fact, we're praying more for renewal than revival. North America has many churches that are dead, or as good as dead. A careful use of language tells us *those* churches need to be revived, brought back to life. We're praying for that too.

But our deepest concern here is for the churches that *have* life—middle-aged life—settled-down life—conserve-what-we-have-and-don't-rock-the-boat life. *We* need *renewal*—a real work of the Spirit at the deepest levels of attitude, commitment and values.

What can the sending church do for their agencies? Pray for —trust God to give us *all*—real renewal. Nothing else is as crucial as that to the future of our worldwide mission.

NOTES

1. Dennis Clark, *The Third World and Mission* (Waco, Tex.: Word, 1971).

*No easy formula for mission/church relationships
can be developed which may be applied anywhere
and at any time. Even among missions and
churches of the same denomination, historical
and geographical factors often determine varying
patterns of relationships. In an incisive way,
Warren Webster pinpoints these time-space factors, as he calls them, and shows how flexibility is
required to face contemporary mission/church
problems. Some of Webster's observations on
the traditional "indigenous church" theories of mission will be of special interest to readers.*

5

MISSION IN TIME AND SPACE

by WARREN WEBSTER

"The Mighty One, God the Lord, speaks and summons the
earth from the rising of the sun to its setting" (Ps 50:1, RSV).

"The God of the *whole earth shall he be called*" (Is 54:5).

The Bible is a missionary book from cover to cover. In Genesis we read of a time past when God made all things. In Revelation we read of a future time when all things shall be made

---

WARREN WEBSTER is General Director of the Conservative Baptist
Foreign Mission Society, under which he served in literature and linguistic ministries among Muslim and Hindu peoples for fifteen years
in West Pakistan. Extensive travels throughout the Muslim world and
Orient have given him a broad perspective on mission activities in that
part of the globe. A graduate of the University of Oregon and Fuller
Theological Seminary, he also holds the D.D. degree from Conservative
Baptist Theological Seminary. Dr. Webster's writings have made him
much appreciated as an evangelical missiologist, and he has lectured
on missions at Fuller Theological Seminary and Gordon-Conwell Theological Seminary.

new. And in between we follow the outworking of God's purposes in time and space.

The universal range of divine concern for the whole created world permeates the Old Testament as well as the New and is seen in two dimensions:

The temporal or historical dimension—"to the end of the age."

The spatial or geographical dimension—"to the end of the earth."

In a context bounded by these dimensions, contemporary mission/church relations find their meaning and substance.

Historical and geographical factors have influenced the Christian world mission from its inception. At the midpoint of redemptive history, when the Word became flesh midway between East and West, the Mediterranean world had been prepared religiously, politically and linguistically for the coming of Christ. Forces were at work that contributed greatly to the early growth and spread of the Christian message. It was neither the first time nor the last that God used the interplay of historical and geographical realities to effect His purposes.

CHRISTIAN AND SECULAR HISTORY

The rise of Islam in the seventh century A.D. offers an example of external factors affecting the spread of Christianity. Sitting astride both land and sea routes to the Orient, Islam formed an immense barrier between Western Christendom and the Far East. For more than a thousand years repeated attempts to penetrate this barrier largely failed. As a result Christian influence moved northward and westward in the Christianization of Europe. The expansion of Christianity in Asia and the launching of the modern missionary movement had to await finding a way to circumvent the barrier of Islam through the discovery of an all-sea route to India and China. In the process, North and South America and sub-Saharan Africa were also discovered, thus opening vast new mission fields in addition to Asia. The very historical forces which impeded Christian missions at one point actually contributed to a new and greater outburst of missionary expansion.

Dr. Kenneth Scott Latourette in his book *The Unquenchable Light* traces the ebb and flow resulting from such interaction of Christian and secular history. From the time of Christ to the twentieth century he sees four major waves of Christian advance, alternating with periods of stagnation or recession. However, he notes that each successive recession has been progressively briefer in duration and each ebb period has produced forces leading to a fresh advance of the Christian faith which has carried the influence of Jesus Christ to a new high point in the total life of mankind.[1]

While we cannot predict that this ebb and flow must inevitably be the course of the future, we know that "The Great Century of Christian Advance" (A.D. 1800-1914) established the body of Christ as a worldwide reality for the first time in history. The presence of the church throughout the world is one of the great facts of the twentieth century. As Bishop Stephen Neill has observed, "In the twentieth century one phenomenon has come into view which is incontestably new—for the first time there is in the world a universal religion, and that the Christian religion."[1a] At the beginning of the 1900s the promise of the risen Christ that "repentance and forgiveness of sins should be preached in his name to *all* nations" (Lk 24:47, RSV) was nearer fulfillment than ever before.

The era of the two great world wars which followed was a time of mixed spiritual advance and decline. If, overall, the forces of spiritual regression appeared to dominate, it may have been the briefest and most short-lived ebbing of the Christian tide to date. The very events which seemed so foreboding on the political scene actually prepared the way for a new outburst of Christian vitality in quite unexpected places.

COLONIALISM AND MISSION

Ralph Winter in his book, *The Twenty-Five Unbelievable*

Years, chronicles the postwar era from 1945 to 1970 as a generation that witnessed four hundred years of Western colonial expansion rolled back like a rug.[2] Prior to the end of World War II most of the non-Western world was under Western domination of one type or another. Twenty-five years later, 99.5 percent of non-Western countries were independent.

This political "retreat of the West" led many observers to conclude that the fate of Christianity would ultimately parallel that of European colonialism. This viewpoint as set forth by Professor K. M. Panikkar, a prominent Hindu philosopher and historian, maintains that Christianity is nothing more than an epiphenomenon of Western political expansion and as the West retreats politically, so also will the Christian faith. While this may have been Panikkar's hope as a cultured Asian who rejected Christianity, it has not been borne out in the intervening period. In the past "twenty-five unbelievable years" the church of Jesus Christ has grown significantly in nearly every area from which Western colonial powers retreated. It is now more evident than ever that the growth of biblical Christianity is not dependent upon Western political presence and power.

While it cannot be denied that the modern expansion of Christianity and the spread of Western civilization have gone on at the same time, they have not always gone hand in hand, and their relationship is not a simple one of cause and effect. Some critics allege that Christianity is, and always was, the handmaiden of imperialism. This is a widely current falsehood which deserves to be labeled for what it is. In many places the mission of the Christian church has spread in spite of, rather than because of, Western diplomatic and commercial interests whose representatives have often impeded the spread of the gospel, both through direct opposition and through personal lives that sometimes reflect the worst rather than the best of Christian culture. The East India Company, for example, initially did not want missionaries in the East at all and exerted strenuous efforts to keep them out of its territories in India and elsewhere. In Java, the Dutch colonial rulers decided not to permit the Christianization of the Muslim inhabitants of the island and for over two hundred years almost nothing was done to take the gospel to the Javanese. Now in free Indonesia the church is growing dramatically in areas from which it was largely excluded by Western colonial rulers. Similarly, British colonialists prohibited missionary work in Malaya. And in recent years in at least one Asian country American government representatives proved a bigger hindrance to the importation of Bibles than the local Muslim officials.

In place after place the gospel has spread in spite of this opposition of vested interests in the West. Today in independent nations of Asia, Africa and Latin America, evangelical churches are growing faster, with deeper roots, than they did during the era of Western dominance, which is evidence that the church is not the servant of colonialism and that its mission is not a form of religious imperialism.

NATIONALISM AND MISSION

In reflecting on an era when the Christian world mission was too often identified with colonialism and Western culture, it seems necessary to separate the life-giving kernel of Christian truth from the culturally colored shells which embody and carry the seed. In proclaiming Christ as the Saviour of the world, both mission and church need to distinguish clearly between the gospel and Christianity.

The gospel is God's gracious provision of salvation through Jesus Christ to all men in every age and clime who submit themselves to Him in faith and trust. Christianity, on the other hand, is the human response to the gospel. The gospel is the power of God unto salvation—divine, pure, universal in its application. Christianity is the local expression of the gospel as it takes root in the soul and in the soil of a given place. The gospel message is universal. Christianity is often compounded with provincial customs, local tradition and human fallibility. While we can say with Paul that we are not ashamed of the gospel of Jesus Christ, we may sometimes be embarrassed by things that go on under the banner of Christendom. Apparently this is what one Asian student meant when he said, "We want your Christ, but we do not want your Christianity."

Nationalistic pressures have encouraged the "rediscovery" of indigenous church patterns in this century. While the principles of "self-government, self-support and self-propagation" are necessary disciplines for a church learning to develop its own character in the face of political and cultural nationalism, some leaders, both missionary and national, have made the mistake of looking upon the establishment of indigenous churches as the end and goal of missions and the final answer to nationalistic pressures. The fallacy of this, however, became apparent when some churches became so indigenous, so nationalistic, that they no longer had room for anything foreign, including missionaries and Christians of different racial and national origins.

While it is right for a people to want to stand on their own feet religiously as well as politically, there is a point where nationalism and the church must part company, for the church cannot be itself when imprisoned in the framework of a narrow nationalism. While churches must take root in the soil as well as in the soul of a people, they must also learn to see their relationship to other believers in Christ who is the Head of the church.

Mission and church both need "a new grasp of the biblical truth that the church is the 'people of God' an elect race, composed of people out of all nations, transcending all nations and races."[3] The body of Christ which ultimately includes men of "every tribe and tongue and people and nations" is by definition supranational, supraracial and supracultural though locally it may be largely national, racial and cultural.

From the biblical standpoint, a truly Christian church is not one without a foreigner in it, but one in which a believer is treated like a brother; or more precisely, one in which all believers—without distinction of nationality, race or cultural background—fellowship as members one of another in the household of God. This understanding of the essential oneness of all the people of God was what enabled an African churchman to say with deep spiritual insight in the face of rampant nationalism, "We do not want an African church, we want a Christian church in Africa, a church which is truly missionary and in which there is neither black nor white."[4]

The Christian answer to divisive nationalism and the false brotherhood of Communism lies neither in patterns of dependence nor of independence, but in the recovery of that interdependence in the one Spirit which marked the New Testament churches. In the biblical interdependence of both younger and older churches lies the future of the church's mission to the world.

GEOGRAPHY AND CHURCH GROWTH

Not only *historical* considerations influenced church growth and mission/church relations, but *geographical* factors have played a bigger role than is often realized.

The factor of accessibility to the Christian message has often determined the timing and sequence of Christianization. But the religious distribution of mankind has even more profoundly affected the growth and success of Christian missions. While in the last century and a half men have come to Christ from every culture and climate, from every religious background as well as from every major language family, the movement to Christian discipleship has by no means been of equal dimensions from all religions.

The great ingatherings into the church from pagan backgrounds—virtually all the major people movements—have been from among basically animistic peoples. This was true in times past of the "conversion" of northern Europe and the Christianization of Latin America. It remains true today of the rapid spread of Christianity in Africa and most significant Christward movements in Asia. All are among peoples whose basic religious patterns have been animistic, however much influenced by contact with the major ethnic religions of Buddhism, Hinduism and Islam.

In Indonesia, which has the world's largest Muslim population, there is a growing Christian community of approximately ten million people, but more than 90 percent of these have come into the church from Indonesia's sizable animistic minority. On the island of Sumatra where Batak tribesmen ate the first two missionaries who visited there a century ago, there are now indigenous Batak churches with their own ministry and institutions and over a million members—all former animists or their descendants.

The notable church growth reported from Korea and Taiwan in this century have taken place primarily among people with animistic beliefs, however much influenced by traditional national religions.

The progress of the church has been much less marked where the majority of people are adherents of one of the major ethnic religions. "In fact," Nida and Smalley report, "in no major pagan region in the so-called 'missionary world,' apart from the aboriginal areas, has Protestant missionary work gained more than one per cent of the population."[5] This is true of the Muslim world, long known for its resistance to the Christian gospel. In West Pakistan three-quarters of a million Protestants and Catholics comprise slightly more than 1 percent of the total population, but fewer than one-tenth of 1 percent of Pakistan's Christians have come out of Islam.

In Japan where Buddhism and Shintoism are strong, Protestant Christians after a century represent less than one-half of 1 percent of the population. In Thailand less than one-tenth of 1 percent of Thai Buddhists have become Christians, and the picture among Burmese Buddhists is similar, although there are more than 200,000 Christians among the hill tribes of Burma—all formerly animists.

In India fifteen million Protestants and Catholics comprise 2 to 3 percent of the population and might appear to be the exception to Nida and Smalley's statement about accessions to

Christianity from the lands where ethnic religions predominate. But on closer study, it is evident that most of India's Christians have come as a result of people movements from the scheduled castes or outcasts whose religious beliefs and practices have more in common with animism than with philosophical Hinduism. In India's state of Nagaland, between Assam and Burma, Christianity has spread to the point that all of its 850 town and village communities are reported to have both a church and a school, and 60 to 70 percent of its 500,000 people claim to be at least nominally Christian. It is doubtful that any other state or province in Asia (with the possible exception of Roman Catholic areas in the Philippines) has a higher percentage of Christian population. But the Naga believers formerly were animists—some of them headhunters— just a couple of generations ago.

By way of contrast, the accessions to the Christian faith in India from Hinduism's upper castes, while not entirely lacking, have been almost microscopic in comparison.

The significance for world missions of geography as it relates to the distribution of established ethnic religions and of responsive animistic peoples is quite evident. The success of different churches and missions in various parts of the world frequently owes less to their theological and methodological distinctives than to the responsiveness of the people to whom they have gone, and their readiness for change at a given point in history. Baptists, Methodists, Anglicans, Lutherans, Pentecostals and Roman Catholics have all shepherded large group movements into their churches—and all from basically, or formerly, animistic peoples.

In the long debates over missionary principles and "the indigenous policy" many protagonists have failed to see that the policies of Roland Allen, Alexander Hay or Donald Mc-Gavran, which apply well to growing Christian movements from among responsive peoples, do not necessarily work in the same way when applied to static or resistant situations. When people are coming to Christ in great numbers as part of a homogeneous movement, the so-called "indigenous principles" give helpful direction in guiding and broadening the movement. But where there is no movement or where conditions are not right for responsiveness, a doctrinaire application of so-called "indigenous principles" has seldom, if ever, been adequate to elicit such a response.

Because large group movements into the church come from responsive (largely animistic or previously Christianized) peoples, they call for a different structuring of mission and of mission/church relations than the much slower growth of the church among more resistant peoples (often found in the major ethnic religions).

DENOMINATION BY GEOGRAPHY

There is another direction in which mission-church relations have been influenced by geographical considerations. In the history of modern missions when societies for the proclamation of the gospel multiply to the point of competition and rivalry, Protestant missions generally attempted some type of cooperation known as *comity* in terms of which participating missions agreed to work in well-defined geographical areas which did not overlap or duplicate the outreach of others.

This meant, however, that in many places congregations grew up which had no choice in the matter of denominational affiliation. Where Methodists began work, people became Methodists. When one of those families migrated to an area assigned to another mission they might become Baptists or Presbyterians overnight, but for the most part comity agreements tended to perpetuate sectarianism on a regional basis—"denomination by geography."

In time, national Christians became increasingly sensitive to the fact that the particular distinctives of their group often owed less to personal conviction than to the accidents of geographic location and comity agreement. Not infrequently younger churches began to express impatience and dissatisfaction over being "united" to fellow denominationalists thousands of miles away while being discouraged from close fellowship with believers of another communion across the river, or even across the street. Comity, the younger churches say, may relate to missions as missions, but it has little meaning for the church as the body of Christ which cannot be contained or divided by lines on a map. It is not surprising that where national churches have outgrown dependence on missions they have sought to expand their circle of fellowship with other Christians on national, but interdenominational, lines, rather than through extending international, but purely denominational, ties. It has been observed that "whatever the historic justification of denominationalism in European Christendom, it represents an irrelevant pattern for the younger churches which cannot be made indigenous, because it is not rooted in the gospel nor related to the soil in which these churches exist."[6] This undoubtedly has been one of the factors behind church-union movements among Third World churches. It may also help explain why some of the fastest-growing and most virile Christian groups in Asia, Africa and Latin America today are spreading along indigenous lines largely outside the historic denominational churches.

In any event, one of the present tensions in mission/church relations revolves around attempts to undo or to transcend artificial patterns of "denomination by geography" through the discovery of a biblical unity in which all who are "sons of God through faith in Christ Jesus" (Gal 3:26, NASB) come to experience their relationship one to another in the household of God.

The "Home Base" Is Everywhere

Both church and mission now find themselves in an age when the body of Christ is more broadly planted and more deeply rooted among more peoples than ever before in history.

One corollary of the church's presence in virtually every land is that the home base for mission is everywhere—wherever the church is found. Now that the church has become a worldwide fellowship, the "home base" of missions can no longer be thought of as one or two countries in the West. Even if it were possible (and it manifestly is not) for the Christians of one country to evangelize the world, from a biblical perspective it would work an irreparable loss upon the churches in other lands who are also commanded to "go and make disciples."

There may have been a time when people thought of the mission field as something "out there," equated with "dark continents" and "regions beyond." Now we see more clearly that the work of mission is not simply a matter of crossing geographical frontiers, but rather of discipling men and women on the frontier between faith in Christ and unbelief, wherever we find it. As such, the true missionary frontier—the conflict with paganism—runs through every land.

This points up the importance of church and mission cooperating in every nation to bring the whole gospel to the whole world. The establishing of indigenous churches is no longer seen as an adequate end and goal of biblical missions *unless* such churches become "sending" churches in, and from, their own milieu. The New Testament knows nothing of "receiving" churches which are not also in turn to be "sending" churches. To this end the founding of national mission societies and the entrance into mission of national churches on every continent are cause for profound gratitude and continued encouragement. If Western nations and institutions are on the decline, Eastern nations, and the churches rooted in them, are bridging the gap. We are beginning to see churches in Japan, as well as in Taiwan, Korea, the Philippines, Indonesia, India and elsewhere accepting the missionary responsibility which of necessity lies upon the church in every place, not just in Western lands.

Partnership, Not Paternalism

While Christianity did not spread simply as an accompaniment of Western political expansion, the spirit of the colonial era not infrequently influenced Christian missions in directions that were frankly paternalistic. Today, among nations that are free and independent, the key word for mission/church relationships is *partnership,* and new patterns are emerging along biblical lines which offer hope for spreading the gospel of Jesus Christ more widely than ever before in history.

In an effort to lead Evangelicals in the West from a pre-colonial to a postcolonial understanding of mission, Dennis Clark in his book *The Third World and Mission* proposes a number of major policy changes for a new and creative partnership between "sending" churches, missionary societies and the growing churches of the Third World. He envisions the transfer of all major policy-making for Third World ministries from Western bases to the nation and region concerned. He also advocates the multiplication of leadership training centers, communications consortiums and evangelistc teams—in all of which nationals would lead and direct the program with a minority of Western colleagues.

Further proposals recommend the dismantling of all foreign mission compounds and the breaking up of concentrations of foreign mission personnel (with the possible exception of pioneer base camps in primitive areas). For "sending" churches who still think "West is best" the author pleads for an embargo on exporting Western ecclesiastical disputes and cultural taboos to the new churches of the Third World. Having talked with Christian leaders in some fifty nations, he notes the heavy-handed influence of home boards and churches which often try to control field policies from a distance without firsthand knowledge of the situation.

Partnership for mission in the '70s requires that Third World believers be free "under God and led by His Spirit" to determine what is best for the evangelism of their people, even if it means dumping tracts, tapes and techniques from the West. They must also be free under the Holy Spirit to choose and follow their own accredited leaders and not simply those hand-picked by missionaries.

A Philippine representative at GL '71 observed that too often in the past, mission/church relationships have resembled the proverbial "horse and rabbit stew" supposedly mixed in "equal" proportion, that is, one horse to one rabbit! The present decade requires almost everywhere a greater "partnership of equality and mutuality."

Another delegate at GL '71, Arsenio Dominguez of the Christian Nationals' Evangelistic Commission, outlined four principles for church and mission leaders in the '70s:

1. Work with national colleagues in such a way that they do not appear as tools of the West.

2. Avoid those things that could suggest new believers have taken up a white man's religion.

3. Seek to minimize disfavor on the part of Third World governments.

4. Structure ministries in such a way that the gifts of national believers are brought into prominence.

Worldwide "partnership in obedience" among believers will accomplish what we cannot do separately. The key is not simply better ecclesiastical structures, but transformed attitudes and relationships based upon partnership, not paternalism.

THE END OF THE CHRISTIAN MISSION

It seems fairly certain, as far as we can interpret history, that the Western orientation of the world is rapidly coming to an end. However, this need not in itself pose a threat to the Christian world mission.

One of the striking characteristics of the Christian faith has been its repeated ability to survive the passing of an era and an order of which it once seemed to be an inseparable part. This has been in evidence ever since the decline and fall of the Roman Empire which was survived by the very faith it once sought to destroy. In a similar way the Christian church outlived the darkness of the Middle Ages and outlasted the Renaissance and the Age of Reason. The Christian message spread during an era of exploration and discovery. It adapted to the changing demands of the industrial revolution and gained strength. In this century, the Christian hope continues to spread despite the rise of Communism, the advent of the atomic age, and the inauguration of space travel.

In an era of "wars and rumors of wars" marked by the two greatest conflicts in world history, the church of Jesus Christ has demonstrated the vitality not only to survive but to expand. While the church may have lost ground during this time in some areas where it was once strong—most notably in Europe —this is no new phenomenon. Elsewhere the postwar years have seen a fresh extension of the church into half a dozen countries that had previously been "closed lands" with neither believers nor Christian churches. The modern record of rapidly growing churches has often—as in Indonesia and the former Congo—been one of triumph through tragedy, and transformation through testing.

In the twentieth century, for the first time in history, it can be truly said that the sun never sets on the church of Jesus Christ. With the possible exception of the Mongolian People's Republic, there does not appear to be another independent nation on earth in which the church of Jesus Christ is not represented. Samuel Moffett of Korea reminds us:

> Even where there are no organized churches, even where missionaries are turned away with guns and Christianity is a forbidden faith, you will find Christians. Perhaps only one, two, a handful, perhaps only foreigners, but they are there, and they belong to the oldest and strongest world-wide fellowship the world has ever known, the people of God, the Church of Jesus Christ.[7]

The great missionary fact of the present day is that *"the Church is there. . . . ,* the Body of Christ in every land, the great miracle of history, in which the living God himself through his Holy Spirit is pleased to dwell."[8]

It is estimated that in the last 180 years more people have become Christians and more churches have been planted than in the previous 1,800 years of church history. In the last 60 years Protestants are said to have multiplied 18 times in the non-Western World.[9] Due in part to the population explosion, the number of professing Christians is greater than it ever has been before.

UNTWISTING STATISTICS

We frequently hear, however, that church growth is not keeping up with biological growth, so that while the *number of Christians* in the world continues to increase, the *Christian percentage* of world population has been steadily declining from about one-third in 1940 to less than 30 percent today, with an expectation that it may not be more than 16 percent by the year 2000. Since many began to question these pessimistic prognostications, a group of former engineers and systems analysts in the missionary enterprise went to work to check out the figures and concluded they are based largely on false premises and poor arithmetic. In this connection Stephen Neill recently observed that

> for the first time an attempt has been made to arrive at a scientific estimate, based on population figures supplied by the United Nations and on the best available statistics from Christian sources. . . . It appears that in the past the Christian percentage has been overestimated, since the population of China, almost entirely non-Christian, is now held to be larger than was earlier supposed. When the necessary corrections have been made, the conclusion is reached that the *percentage has been slowly increasing* since the beginning of the century, *is slowly increasing* and *will continue to increase;* so that, if present trends continue, it will in the year 2000 stand higher than ever before in the history of the world. What is a little startling is that at that date less than half the Christians will belong to the white races.[10]

While the Lord of history is sovereign, and no man can say what must happen tomorrow, we know from Scripture that the

God of the whole earth is at work in this age calling out a people for His name which ultimately will embrace some "from every tribe and tongue and people and nation" (Rev 5:9, NASB).

It has been said repeatedly that the day of missions is coming to an end. This is nothing new. The Bible says the same thing. But rightly understood, the end of the mission will be the end of history as we know it.

Many students of the Word and world events believe that in the closing interplay of Christian and secular history there will be one final ebbing of the faith—perhaps the briefest, yet most intense, recession to date—marking the advent of Antichrist and preliminary to the triumphal appearance of the coming King. This is to be followed by the greatest wave of spiritual advance ever seen, when "the kingdom of the world has become the kingdom of our Lord" (Rev 11:15, NASB) and "the earth shall be filled with the knowledge of the glory of the LORD, as the waters cover the sea" (Hab 2:14).

Whatever the precise sequence of eschatological events, it is clear that in God's program the geographical and historical are integrally related. When our Lord commissioned His disciples to go "to the ends of the earth" (the spacial dimension), He promised to be with them "to the end of the age" (the temporal dimension). He also declared that the gospel of "repentance and forgiveness of sins should be preached in his name *throughout the whole world,* as a testimony to all nations; and *then the end will come"* (Lk 24:47; Mt 24:14, RSV).

This is the divine program for church and mission in time and space. The historical culmination awaits the geographical fulfillment. The end of the age awaits the completed proclamation to the ends of the earth. The indications are that the "Omega point" of history is nearer than it has ever been before.

In this day of opportunity it devolves upon church and mission everywhere to move forward together in discipling men and nations—to make history, not just read about it!

NOTES

1. Kenneth Scott Latourette, *The Unquenchable Light* (New York: Harper, 1941), chap. 9.
1a. Stephen Neill, *A History of Christian Missions* (Baltimore: Penguin Books, 1966), p. 559.
2. Ralph D. Winter, *The Twenty-Five Unbelievable Years* (South Pasadena, Calif.: William Carey Library, 1971).
3. Henrik Kraemer, *A Theology of the Laity* (London: Lutterworth, 1958), p. 157.
4. Lesslie Newbigin, *Is Christ Divided?* (Grand Rapids: Eerdmans, 1961), p. 22.
5. Eugene Nida and William Smalley, *Introducing Animism* (New York: Friendship Press, 1959), p. 59.
6. *An Advisory Study* (New York: COEMAR, 1962), p. 37.
7. Samuel H. Moffett, *Where'er the Sun . . .* (New York: Friendship Press, 1953), pp. 4-5.
8. Neill, p. 576.
9. R. Pierce Beaver, *From Missions to Mission* (New York: Friendship Press, 1964), p. 63.
10. Neill, *Call to Mission* (Philadelphia: Fortress, 1970), p. 79.

Missions must determine what they are aiming for before they can establish policies on relationships with the emerging churches. Philip Armstrong here suggests that evangelism should take the top priority in mission objectives. The best relationships come about when the church recognizes this as the supreme objective, and when the mission can therefore be useful to the church in winning the lost to Christ, and bringing them into fellowship. How each of the multifaceted activities of modern missions should be brought under these principles is described in this chapter.

6

SHARPENING OBJECTIVES FOR BETTER RELATIONSHIPS

by PHILIP E. ARMSTRONG

Rolf Syrdahl in his book, *To the End of the Earth,* summarizes the eras of mission history under the hypothesis that every generation has had to preach Christ in a context over which it had no control.[1] Obviously, for Evangelicals the message has not changed. Neither has the goal of missions—total world evangelization. But the context in which any mission

---

PHILIP E. ARMSTRONG is the General Director of the Far Eastern Gospel Crusade, a mission of 260 members in Japan, Philippines, Okinawa, Hong Kong, Taiwan and Alaska. His relationship with the mission dates back to 1945, when Armstrong and other World War II veterans founded the organization. He has lectured on missions at Trinity Evangelical Divinity School, Columbia Bible College and Dallas Theological Seminary. Mr. Armstrong serves as President of the Interdenominational Foreign Mission Association, and is a member of the editorial staffs of *Evangelical Missions Quarterly* and *Moody Monthly.*

sets its objective today is far different from that of any other generation.

AGENTS AND INSTRUMENTS

Where are the pioneer fields today? Hymns speaking of whitened harvests in heathen lands have lost their geographical distinctives. The heathen are lost. That is indisputable. But the darkness may not be "far, far, away." There is virtually no geographical area in the world where some witness does not exist. The church is there.

The tension for both denominational and interdenominational missions in articulating their objective lies in this: Is the task to evangelize or to develop the church? Consciously or unconsciously missions seem to sense two competing priorities: evangelism and the church. But these are not really two. Our *objective* is evangelism. The church, not the mission, is the *agent* of evangelism. The church is not simply a means to the end. It is at one and the same time both the end and the agent. A mission, however, is only an *instrument* of the church. If the church is there, has the mission been accomplished? Not as long as the mission can be instrumental in the church's completing the Great Commission.

A mission's active ministry continues as long as it is an instrument of the divine Agent in accomplishing the divine purpose. When it becomes an end or an institution in itself or when its objectives do not match the biblical call of missions to the church, it goes out of existence. There should be satisfaction, not shame, if an instrument of the church which has served well is no longer needed because that church now has developed effective instruments of its own.

A church-planting mission which does not have a continuing commitment to the task of evangelism will find tensions mounting wherever there is blessing in church growth. This is because a mission's objective must always be the world. George Peters in his second paper at Green Lake '71 states this: "Christian missions must be focused on the world, not on the church."[2] So if a mission is to have a continuing place of use-fulness, it must continue as the instrument of the whole church in evangelism.

Mission objectives are often fuzzy because for the most part they are drawn up as a part of the articles of incorporation of a sending society. These are usually stated broadly enough so the mission can safely enter almost any field of activity without legal compromise. Rather than disciplining the mission into articulating crisply defined objectives, this procedure allows it to diffuse into a wide range of activities. The secondary ministries which frequently develop are the ones that most commonly produce tensions in the receiving church.

MISSION STRUCTURES

An evaluation of the Green Lake '71 conference may well indicate that the matter of structure was a key. Missionaries normally assume that a form they have been brought up on, with certain minor adaptations, has validity overseas. The dominant influence of the sending church has led both denominational and interdenominational missions to try to find one pattern that can be applied throughout the entire mission operation. This will continue to be evasive, for there is need for a variety of forms as long as there is unity within the field. Missions have gravitated toward static structures. Evangelicals have rightly had to take an inflexible stance in biblical theology when surrounded by neouniversalism and syncretism. But frequently that conservatism is transferred unconsciously into nontheological areas. We tend to make infallible our fallibilities, including structure! A structure, when dealing with a growing organism like the church, can best be described as a still photograph, valid for only a moment of time. But the form must change to keep pace with growth.

A mission theoretically should be one of the institutions most capable of change. It works on the growing edge of a changing society, a changing culture, and emerging church. It has the stimulation of developing Christian doctrine in a cross-cultural context. The mission body is geographically remote from its constituency. Its goal is to sell intangible ideas, not a material product. This should all stimulate mission flexibility. The missionary himself is basically an adventurer, seeking new horizons. His furlough provides an automatic job rotation, introduction to new ideas, fresh interpersonal relationships, off-location study and reevaluation. Frequently the missionary himself unwittingly becomes the greatest obstacle to well-defined objectives. Our clichés indicate this. A missionary is sometimes referred to as scaffolding; he is supposed to work himself out of a job. He is temporary; the church is permanent, it is said.

All of this leads the emerging church to question whether the missionary fully understands the objective. Either he does not, or he is unwilling to face the long-term haul toward accomplishing it. Louis King at Green Lake tried to counter this mood when he said, "The mission does not act like an agency retiring from the scene."[3]

The changes taking place in the church today mean that every mission should take a serious look at its present structure. "The struggle for the preservation of organizational identity must not be permitted to disrupt spiritual relationships whatever our rights may be."[4]

In one of the discussions at Green Lake, George Peters referred to the movement of the Holy Spirit in evangelism. He said, "Where there is spiritual life there is function; where there is spiritual function there is form." We cannot eliminate it. In that same discussion, Patrick Arnold of the West Indies Mission said, "Right structures do not provide dynamic, but wrong structures do restrict dynamic."

Strangely enough, most evangelical missions at Green Lake would feel that they have a good working relationship with the national church. Some would say they have good communication. Others, that they always consult with nationals. Others would say their negotiations have been successful. Some might say we treat each other as equals. However, nothing became clearer from the panel of international church leaders at Green Lake than their desire to have barriers removed to clear the way for a massive proclamation of the gospel. Arsenio Dominguez from the Philippines said, for example, "Christ did not say, 'Go into all the world and be equal.' He said, 'Go and preach the Gospel!' "

Actually, never before in the history of the church has the objective of world evangelization been more within reach. Population explosion, mass communications and mass mobility have given access to every corner of the globe. The *agent* of evangelism has not changed; it is still the church. What has changed radically is the location of the church; it is now on the field. If the objectives have not changed and the agent of world evangelization, the church, is present in most countries of the world, there is no reason why that objective cannot be accomplished. The mission, having settled its role, could be the tool to bring it about.

The necessary spiritual resources, technical facilities, financial resources and dedicated leadership are available somewhere in the world. If Evangelicals are ready and will ask and answer the right questions, the church in any given country may, under God, have the resources necessary to see one of the greatest movements of our time. Five crucial areas in which questions need to be asked and answered are as follows:

1. WHAT CONSTITUTES THE CHURCH?

Church leaders overseas seem far more concerned to study the doctrine of the church in Scripture than missionaries. But both the mission and the younger church need to come to a clear understanding of what constitutes a New Testament church. Louis L. King said at Green Lake, "If both are not certain on this so very essential matter, we envision that tragic conesquences for the church, the mission, and world evangelization will ensue."[5]

A large factor producing tensions between mission and church may stem from an unbiblical concept of indigenous principles. Evangelicals, especially in the interdenominational movement, have tended to equate indigenous, autonomous, independent and congregational. These concepts should be seriously studied in the light of Scripture. Overseas church leaders at Green Lake pleaded for unstructured, informal, personal involvement between missionaries and the church, regardless of the structural relationship. The failure of the missionary to recognize the singular goal of church and mission was well put by a missionary who addressed new arrivals overseas: "If you knew you could plant a church in five years by yourself and in ten years with the church, which would you do?" This sums up the tension: The missionary is eager to get the job done, while the church is eager to establish itself as a native and natural witness in its own community.

2. A COMMON OBJECTIVE

Louis King stated, "The pattern of mission/church relationship ought not to have as its final criterion simply a compatible relationship."[6] Rather, "The mission's relationship with the church is primarily at that point in which the church is engaged in witness and mission to the non-Christian world outside its door."[7]

George Peters heartily agreed with him: "Progress in partnership depends in a measure on human insight and adjustment, but its origin is not found in these. Its source is a common obedience to the living Word of God given once for all in Jesus Christ, yet given anew through the Holy Spirit in every generation." Peters then quotes C. W. Ranson, "This command has not yet been fulfilled by the church. It cannot be fulfilled unless all of the forces of all of the churches, older and younger alike are gathered in a common loyalty, inspired by a common task, and mobilized in a common service."[8]

At Green Lake one could detect a growing recognition of the need of mutuality and reciprocity between sending and receiving churches. In fact, North American pastors appealed to overseas churches to select men from abroad to minister in

North America. But this ministry to one another is not the same as fulfilling the Great Commission. One common calling binds church and mission together. Reaching lost men and women is what motivates the sending church, and hopefully this will keep the receiving church constantly looking beyond its own doors.

3. AUTHORITY

Both Dr. Peters and Dr. King refer to the conflict posed when there are an autonomous mission and an autonomous church in a given country. "The autonomy of the church in any given area is not actual until it has complete jurisdiction over and/or freedom in its total life and ministry."[9] Louis King carries it further: "No church can successfully assume another church's obligations to biblical faith, life, and mission."[10] Peters pushes the loss of the mission's right to make unilateral decisions when the church is formed: "As soon as a church has come into being in a geographical area, the administration of the mission extension program should be integrally related to the church."[11] "Partnership and unilateral legislation and administration are mutually exclusive."[12]

Nevertheless, Peters frankly admits that many missions have not faced this dichotomy:

> A principal cause of tension in many fields is the fact of the dual administration which persists long after a church has come into existence. The fact that the national church has no part, or only an advisory part, in the legislation and administration of the work in her land is unnatural and remains a strong point of friction. It is neither the work or the worker, but rather the policy which is resented. . . . Foreign administration in the presence of the national church is a violation of human rights and Christian relationships.[13]

4. PERSONNEL

Authority is represented by personnel. The larger the block of foreign personnel, the stronger the block of authority. While two missionaries might fit into a sizable overseas congregation with little influence, ten missionaries would rob the congregation of all initiative by their dominance. One missionary put it well: "They do not object to me because I am white. I can think, speak, and act as brown as they. They object to me because I represent a source of authority over which they have no control." The missionary himself may be totally unobjectionable: humble, sacrificial, teachable; but as long as he is "sent" he is not invited!

This outside authority may not be resented because its headquarters is in New York, Nairobi or Singapore. It is the decision-making process of the mission itself that often conflicts with the priorities that the national church would like to establish. In the very nature of mission work, the sending church wants a missionary who is a capable leader, adventuresome, aggressive, totally committed in his dedication to Christ. He is probably already an outstanding young leader in his home church. Such traits have an unavoidable effect when he arrives on the field and begins working with an emerging, immature congregation in the process of discovering its own identity.

Furthermore, the mission may unwittingly have changed the course of its own objectives by accepting such a candidate. That missionary may, by his very drive, see needs on the field to which he responds by initiating a hospital, a school, a literature program. A Christian converted through a Bible camp back home, for example, may arrive overseas and find an avenue for service he feels certainly will be fruitful and, in his opinion, is essential. The church knows nothing of a Bible camp. But the missionary having the experience, training, the drive, and probably the financial resources, may seek and get the support of the mission to start a camp. It never occurs to him to consult with the church, since it has nothing to contribute in the area. The camp may even become an effective evangelistic tool. But can the mission afford to move if it is not a priority of the church?

5. RESOURCES

We may talk of the autonomy of the local church, but the presence of trained missionary personnel and designated mission funds may mock our words.

Look first at missionary support. The missionary would not be on the field if it were not for the generous care of the home church for one of its members who decides to go overseas. He arrived equipped the way the sending church wants to send him, not necessarily the way the receiving church wants him to serve.

Normally those resources include more than the missionary's support. He comes equipped with work funds. Essential as they are in pioneer work, if they are *his* they become a great stumbling block as the church emerges. The church faces this dilemma: With a handful of members it cannot afford a pastor, if it could find one. The missionary's outside support makes him available, whether the church wants him or not. While the church may be struggling for survival, the missionary through his resources may be making long-range plans.

Certainly receiving churches do not complain about the generosity of the sending church. But it is tragic for the mission to draw up long-term objectives without reference to those humble believers who are to bear the ultimate responsibility for the evangelization of their nation.

Take a medical work. With available funds and personnel, the mission may initiate a hospital or clinic to break down prejudice to the gospel. It hopes that a church will result. If the mission goes in with a medical program apart from the church, the tail may well wag the dog. The group of believers cannot afford a pastor, but they have a doctor. Rather than spontaneous witness of new converts, the church thinks of its function in terms of maintaining a medical work. Converts often come for physical rather than spiritual aid. Outsiders criticize this as proselyting. The emerging church acquires a stigma that is hard to live down. It would have been better if the mission had waited until the church was established, then assisted the church in a medical ministry as the fruit of its testimony.

To recognize the seriousness with which young churches take their stand, listen to an Asian Christian:

> If we look carefully we can see there is a unity between Asian and Western churches and that is the *calling.* All Christians in a territory are called as one church and by that calling they have responsibility to answer to God for His calling to them. . . . It is the church who calls the missionary from abroad and it is within the right of the church to decide or appoint who is to be called. We do not hinder those who want to come from abroad, but we must resist the pressure which still exists upon the missionaries in some areas from their home churches to carry out the policies they desire and not what is best for the young churches. . . . We have to educate our people not to accept money simply because it is offered. We must teach that we have no right to accept money unless it is relevant to the point of our obedience. On the other hand we must also teach the giving community that their giving cannot carry with it the right to control. . . . It is our task to educate these members not to give on the basis of pity or according to their own standards and values but in obedience to God. All churches new and old must be one in Him. Christ is not divided and it is He who calls us all to obey and follow Him. . . .[14]

Planning for the Future

Partnership, regardless of its form, is not an easy way out of tensions. But the alternatives are devastating. The breakdown of any dichotomy of mission and church overseas is essential for survival. At Green Lake, comments like these were made in the sessions: "Placing the mission over the church is as devasting as placing the church over Scripture." And, "The receiving church? There are none. Biblically every church is a sending church and it relates to the world." Akira Hatori of Pacific Broadcasting in Japan once said, "I have seen churches under the mission. That does not work. I have seen missionaries under the church, neither does it work. Only the church and mission working hand in hand will produce effective evangelism. They were meant for each other."

Simply because tensions arise, missions cannot abandon the church. In spite of the frustration to the receiving church, it must acknowledge the Holy Spirit's right to say that the sending church "*separate* me Barnabas and Saul for the work whereunto I have *called them*" (Ac 13:2). Here is what the future holds.

PROSPECTS FOR CANDIDATES

Standards will change. The church will call for men with proven spiritual gifts, technical skills, and sterling Christian quality. On arrival overseas, the church will be responsible for the new missionary's orientation. Gwenyth Hubble in her article, "In-Service Preparation," points out the necessity of this.[15] Not only will the orientation be more relevant to the country and the candidate more appreciative of the church, but the church, having been responsible for his training, will be far more understanding of the missionary in future relationships. Candidates cannot expect unilateral assignment of duties by the mission, much less clear lines of accountability to the mission or to the church. The church will not only have a voice in the placement of that missionary, but it will also approve his return after furlough.

At Green Lake, overseas pastors looked upon nonformal intercourse between the missionary and the church as the best means of breaking the present credibility gap. "Missions preserve the status quo by avoiding social intercourse." Allusions were made to missionary get-togethers preceding a church-mission advisory committee meeting. The meeting may go well, but the decisions have already been made.

At Green Lake, one overseas Christian worker stated: "Personalized support has a negative effect on the receiving church. It perpetuates a dynasty." Realistic appraisal of budget and personnel on the basis of objectives may eliminate some missionaries who hold their present job simply because they have personal support and therefore are available as an extrabudgetary item. In some countries the equal-pay, equal-job opportunity practices in industry are now being extended to missionary-church relationships.

Most missions feel the local church is responsible for its own leadership. But creative leadership in the church beyond that level is frequently held by a missionary because he is supported from the outside and his responsibilities are less localized and demanding in daily routine. Furthermore, he may add more experience, training and resources to the job. Missionaries in this situation have to create a vacuum if nationals are to move into leadership.

One overseas representative at Green Lake suggested that the mission withdraw all personnel for one year and, at the end of the time, let the church recall those they missed! Drastic? No doubt. If he asked you, would you do it? The Mennonite Brethren in 1970 outlined strategy to withdraw mission personnel as rapidly as possible from institutions. By means of temporary grants, the board would make it possible for national churches to replace such withdrawals with national workers. Simultaneously, in full collaboration with the national churches, they are pouring all of their resources into a ten-year program of thrust evangelism in six countries.

FINANCIAL PLANNING

In the future, indigenous principles will hold little water if the mission's access to funds gives it the right to control their use. At Green Lake, George Peters said,

> The disparity of income and the ability of missions and missionaries to initiate projects, which the national church has no hopes to carry on without financial subsidies, have assured either the permanency of the mission or the paralysis of the program as soon as the mission or missionary leaves.[16]

Louis King's "Five Principles in Mission/Church Finance" provide skilled guidelines for working together.[17]

Foreign investment overseas in mission property cannot help but be labeled imperialistic in the days ahead. In the past we have invested in mission schools, hospitals, institutions. In the future can we invest in skills and tools? Missions must provide instruments of self-help which, when put at the disposal of the church, will help develop the self-respect of the national worker and the self-efficiency of the national church.

In joint projects, the mission may resent turning over funds to the national church. For the mission to withhold contribution to an agreed-upon project because the resources are "ours" has far less biblical example than "interchurch aid." If the initiative in setting the objectives has been truly mutual, there will be mutual responsibility for securing funds as well as their distribution. It is then a case, not of "priming the pump" but of "helping people on the march."

The mission that learns to respond to the felt need of the church may find it is more needed rather than less. The Mennonite Brethren in Mexico demonstrated this. Many missions have experienced tensions when trying to cut off subsidy programs of the local church. The Mennonite Brethren, rather than withdraw, went to the church with an offer: for every church that would become self-supporting, instead of cutting off the subsidy, the mission would double it for evangelism in starting new churches.

Similarly, the Sudan Interior Mission was approached by the national church about providing secondary schools in their educational program. The mission responded by offering to add one year to secondary education for every year of elementary education the church would assume responsibility for.

Today young churches in young republics want to feel that they are not only self-sufficient, but that they have something to contribute to Christians world over. We must not only find creative ways to give without embarrassing the selfhood of believers but also find contributions they can make to fulfill their own sense of worldwide mission.

SERVICE PROJECTS

As far back as 1916, Donald Fleming wrote a book on *Devolution of Mission Administration.* Already mission-church tension existed. Most of it centered around schools and hospitals. While the service itself may be beneficial, the project is often larger than the church can handle. Two or three such projects could totally upset the proper priority of mission objectives. Generally speaking, the larger the physical plant, the more demanding it is on funds; the more curricular the project, the more demanding on personnel. Ownership and management of that project could be a political football in an emerging church.[18] To my knowledge, the Consultation on World Missions sponsored by the Board of World Missions of the Presbyterian Church in the United States in 1962, set forth the best guidelines for resolving this problem. The Glen Eyrie Report on Findings also laid out critical recommendations for missions grappling with institutional problems.

In the future, service missions in particular have two choices before them. They may operate independently, but their wealth and technical know-how could accentuate any inferiority complex the church might have. Or through careful coordination they may provide a vehicle through which the church can mobilize its own witness as never before.

SATURATION EVANGELISM

Beginning with Evangelism-in-Depth, the past decade could be but a prelude to what could be the greatest outreach the church has yet known. Its genius is the spiritual renewal of the church, total mobilization of believers, coordination of all media in public presentation of the gospel, and simultaneous nationwide saturation.

Similar programs have functioned throughout Latin America, Korea, the Philippines and other places. Eighteen nations in Africa either are currently engaged in saturation evangelism or have plans on the drawing board. Japan, with its skill at industrial-product adaptation, has done the same thing to evangelism. The evangelical church there developed Total Mobilization Evangelism, which is really a conglomerate of the memory program of the Navigators, the Andrew System of the Episcopal Church, the Four Spiritual Laws adapted to speak to the Japanese heart, the prayer cells and the year-long program of Evangelism-in-Depth.

The growth of such patterns around the world is an indication that any mission eager to work strategically can find long-range objectives that have been initiated by the church iteslf.

Open Doors

Recent church-growth studies have been almost as revolutionary as the revolution in evangelism. Nationals and missionaries alike are gaining a new understanding and optimism about cross-cultural communication and responsive areas of the world. Working together under the blessing of God, the years ahead should see even greater people movements than previously.

Revolutionary linguistic and literacy techniques and the use of computers are breaking the verbal isolation of primitive tribes. Communication and transportation have made even the remotest tribes a part of Marshall McLuan's World Village.

Theological education has broken out of the seminary. The total spectrum of training from the local church lay institute to theological seminary is now a realistic goal in most countries. Extension training using programmed learning will make education available to the growing church in virtually any area in the days ahead.

Numbers of young men are eager to go into Bible teaching on the mission field. Fred Renich, Director of Missionary Internship, commented on this, saying, "The expression 'to train the national' is the highest form of neocolonialism." How Asians feel about this is expressed by T. Sihombing:

The churches of Asia may fail to communicate the gospel
to their own societies because they have learned the gospel
from borrowed words from the West. Borrowed words can be
understood by minds intelligent enough to understand them,
but they do not speak to the heart of a nation.[19]

A candidate who is qualified should not be limited in future
usefulness if he is willing to study the nature of the non-Chris-
tion world and the needs and nature of the ministry in the
emerging church. But unless he is able to become a part of the
learning community where he teaches and can demonstrate to
his student his own ministry in the power of the Holy Spirit, he
had better stay home.

INSIDE THE CHURCH

Green Lake brought out the frustration of nationals over
the complexity of overseas church structures. They felt that
diversity of form has hindered church growth. This was brought
out by David Cho of Korea International Mission. "Multiplicity of agencies brings shallowness of work," he said. There
has been a push for mission mergers at home for efficiency of
operation. Instead he allowed for multiple sending agencies
but asked for one receiving agency for the sake of the testimony overseas.

Fragmentation of Evangelicals will become intolerable to
Christians in a country where they are a minority. Home constituencies may wish to convey their convictions to a mission,
but they should realize at the same time that the missionary
may have influence but little authority. Strong national leadership will determine its own standards of unity and purity.

The mission that is prepared to live with the church may
find that the missionary's greatest contribution is still to come.
Freed of administrative responsibility by the church assuming
its proper role, the overseas servant of God can dovetail his
gifts into the church's need. The mission will find it greatest
freedom in these three objectives of the overseas church:

   1. cooperation in pioneer evangelism and church-planting

2. training men and women for service in leadership in the church

3. preparing the church for a large influx of new converts in anticipation of the movement of the Spirit of God

Working at this level, the mission's satisfaction comes by completing and not competing with the long-range objectives of the receiving church. It was this satisfaction that Paul expressed to the Corinthians when he said,

> Not that we have dominion over your faith,
> But are helpers of your joy:
> For by faith ye stand (2 Co 1:24).

NOTES

1. Rolf Syrdahl, *To the End of the Earth* (Minneapolis: Augsburg, 1967), p. 152.
2. George Peters, "Mission/Church Relations Overseas," in *Missions in Creative Tension,* ed. Vergil Gerber (South Pasadena, Calif.: William Carey Library, 1971), p. 208.
3. Louis L. King, "Mission/Church Relations Overseas," in *Missions in Creative Tension,* p. 185.
4. Peters, p. 195.
5. King, p. 186.
6. Ibid., p. 172.
7. Ibid., p. 175.
8. Peters, p. 211.
9. Ibid., p. 194.
10. King, p. 155.
11. Peters, p. 214.
12. Ibid., p. 218.
13. Ibid., p. 216.
14. T. Sihombing, "The Church in the World: An Asian View" in *The Missionary Church in East and West,* ed. Charles C. West and David M. Paton (London: SCM, 1959), pp. 41-42.
15. Gwenyth Hubble, "In Service Preparation," *Evangelical Missions Quarterly* 5, no. 4 (Summer, 1969): 219.
16. Peters, p. 220.
17. King, p. 187.
18. Peters, p. 191.
19. Sihombing, p. 37.

*Missionaries and mission strategists commonly talk
about planting younger churches in the mission
fields they are sent to. This is all to the good. But
in this chapter, which may turn out to be a milestone in contemporary missionary thought, Ralph
Winter raises a question that is not commonly
talked about in missionary circles: How about
planting younger* missions? *The matter of moving
beyond the national church is something which
was not stressed at Green Lake, but which is
brought out strongly by Winter and other con-
tributors to this symposium. Here, not only the
goals, but the accompanying structures are ana-
lyzed with unusual perception.*

7

THE PLANTING OF YOUNGER MISSIONS

by Ralph D. Winter

I was in the Philippines recently, staying in the Conservative
Baptist Mission guest home while being involved in a seminar
on theological education by extension. To my delight, different missionaries and nationals were invited to be present at
mealtime from day to day, and through these contacts I re-

Ralph D. Winter is Associate Professor of the Historical Development of the Christian Mission in the School of World Mission at Fuller
Theological Seminary, a position he accepted after ten years of experience as a United Presbyterian missionary in Guatemala. He holds the
B.S. degree from California Institute of Technology, the B.D. from
Princeton Theological Seminary, the M.A. in Education from Columbia University and the Ph.D. in Anthropology from Cornell. Dr. Winter
is widely respected as a missionary opinion-former through his writ-

ceived a good impression of how determinedly the Conservative Baptist missionaries and national church leaders were involved in church-planting.[1]

I observed, however, that the American missionaries, while they participate in local church life, are themselves preeminently members of a nonchurch organization (based in the USA) called the Conservative Baptist Foreign Mission Society. The national leaders in the Philippines neither have joined this United States organization, nor have they formed a parallel mission structure of their own. I do not know that anyone has tried to stop them from doing so. I suppose the idea simply has not come up.

I would like to bring it up here and now. I have selected the people in the CBFMS because they are so up-to-date; if I can make a point in regard to their operation, it will have to apply to practically every other mission!

CLEAR GOALS, CONFUSED MEANS

In Manila there is no question about clarity of purpose in church-planting. The goal is an autonomous, nationally run Conservative Baptist Association in the Philippines, or perhaps an even larger association including other Baptists. "Some day" this Philippine association may sprout its own home mission society or foreign mission society. But when? How will it go about it? Why not now? Why is not a nationally run mission as clearly and definitely a goal as is church-planting? That is, why do the various goals prominent in everyone's mind not include both *church*-planting and *mission*-planting? And why do we talk so little about such things? Or, to take another tack, why is it that only the foreign missionary (no doubt not by

ings such as *The Twenty-Five Unbelievable Year*s (cited by several authors in this symposium), and for his role as one of the architects of the extension seminary movement. The book he edited, *Theological Education by Extension,* has become a cornerstone for that movement, worldwide.

plan, but by default) has the right, the duty or the opportunity to "go here or to go there and plant a church"?

In the present circumstances, for example, if the Conservative Baptist Mission in the Philippines for any reason decides that its particular family of churches ought to be extended to some other country (or even to some other part of the Philippines), everyone would be likely to assume that it will take foreign money, foreign personnel, and even a decision by foreigners. There may be exceptions, but at least this is the usual approach. Without any foreign help, the local churches may be doing an excellent job reaching out evangelistically in their own localities. But if a new church is going to be established at a distance, especially in another dialect area, that will very likely be the work of the foreigner. Why? Because for some strange reason the only *mission* in the situation is a foreigner's mission, and because the vaunted goal of producing a nationally run *church,* as valuable and praiseworthy as such a goal is, has not automatically included the establishment of nationally run *missions* as part of the package.

This is not to say the idea has never been thought of. The American Presbyterian missionaries in Korea, for example, long ago saw fulfillment of their dream of a national church that would send foreign missionaries. The United Church of Christ in the Philippines sends foreign missionaries. The members of the Latin America Mission are in the throes of mutating into an association of autonomous missions in which Latin as well as Anglo Westerners are involved, but they do not include nor at the moment plan to deal with the far more drastic cross-cultural task of reaching the aboriginal, non-Western inhabitants of Latin America. There are many other examples. And as to the future, just wait: the recently established Conservative Baptist Association in the Philippines will before long be sending foreign missionaries.

Nevertheless, what I would like to know is why the sending of missionaries by the younger church is so relatively rare a phenomenon, and, if discussed, is so widely conceived to be a "later on" type of thing. Just as a new convert ought to be able immediately to witness to his new faith (and a great deal is lost if he does not), so a newly founded church ought not only to love Jesus Christ but to be able immediately to show and share its love in obedience to the Great Commission. How long did it take for the congregation at Antioch to be able to commission its first missionaries? Were they premature?

Space does not allow us to describe the outstanding mission work done by Pacific Islanders (over 1,000 in a list recently compiled), by Vietnamese nationals in the seventeenth and eighteenth centuries, or by the famous Celtic Peregrini and their Anglo-Saxon imitators, for example. Perhaps what we must at least point out is that the churches emerging from the Reformation must not be taken as an example. They took more than 250 years to get around to any kind of serious mission effort, but even then it was not more than on a relatively small scale for an entire century.

The most curious thing of all is the fact that precisely those people most interested in church growth often are not effectively concerned about what makes congregations multiply. Those who concede that church-planting is the primary instrument whereby mankind can be redeemed do not always seem to be effectively employing those key structures that specialize in church-planting. We hear cries on every side to the effect that an indigenous national church is our goal, but the unnoticed assumptions are (1) that only a Western mission can start a new work across cultural boundaries, and (2) that once such a church is established, the church itself will somehow just grow and plant itself in every direction. What illogically follows is this: United States churches need explicit mission organizations to reach out effectively for them, but overseas churches can get along without such structures. The goals are clear; the means to reach them are still largely obscured.

What Green Lake Did Not Say

Admittedly this chapter covers a subject the Green Lake

Conference did not plan to take up. As GL '71 unfolded, we all began to realize that what has carelessly been termed "church/mission relations" really refers, it turns out, to mission/church relations: the relations between an American *mission* and an overseas national *church* (which is probably the product of the U.S. mission's work over the years). To these mission/church relations, GL '71 added church/mission relations, namely, the relation of the *churches* back home to the *mission* they support. So now we have what George Peters characterized as the official docket of the conference, namely, church/mission/church relations. This included three focuses: (1) the church at home, (2) the missions which are their overseas arm, and (3) the churches overseas resulting from these missionary efforts. We can call this "second-generation church-planting" and diagram it as in Figure 1.

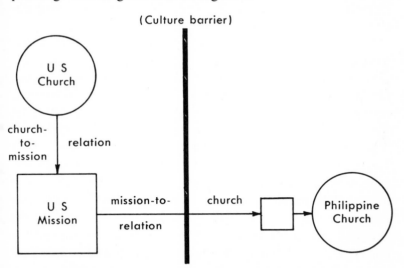

Fig. 1. *Second-Generation Church-Planting.* A new church is "planted" by a United States-based mission across a cultural barrier (mottled line).

It is greatly to be appreciated that this post-GL '71 symposium has allowed for an additional element to enter the picture, namely, the *mission* outreach of the *younger churches*. Thus, while Green Lake tended to confine itself to church/mission/ church relations, this symposium covers greater ground, namely, church/mission/church/mission relations. This may be termed "second-generation *mission*-planting," and diagramed as in Figure 2.

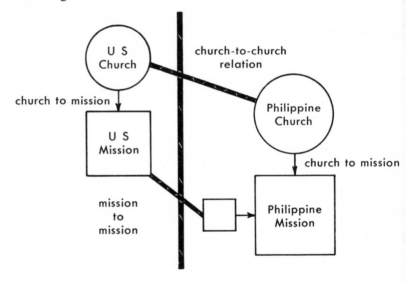

Fig. 2. *Second-Generation Mission-Planting.* A now-autonomous national church develops relations (dotted line) as an equal directly with the United States church body. Next the national church, with the help of the continuing United States mission, founds a nationally run mission.

Note that the appearance of the new fourth element may (in most cases) eliminate the former United States mission-to-Philippine church relation, and will likely create three new ones: (1) United States *church*-to-Philippine *church,* (2) United States *mission*-to-Philippine *mission,* and (3) a new kind of Philippine *church*-to-Philippine *mission* relation that is parallel to the existing United States *church*-to-United States *mission* relation.

In Figure 3 we are anticipating not only the existence of an autonomous Philippine mission, but also its success in establishing a third-generation church across some new cultural barrier. (The existence of such barriers is the primary reason for needing a specialized mission organization, in contrast to ordinary church evangelism, to accomplish such a task.) We call this step "third-generation church-planting." By this time it is possible that the United States mission has reduced its staff sufficiently to be able to move into a new field in a similar way to plant another second-generation church.

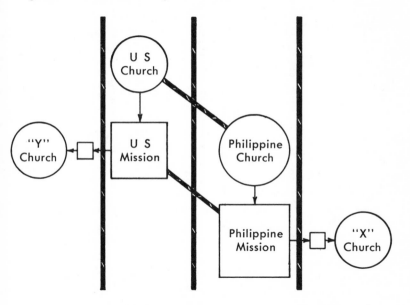

Fig. 3. *Third-Generation Church-Planting.* Both national church and national mission are now autonomous. The national mission establishes relations as an equal with the United States mission, and both it and the United States mission (elsewhere) plant churches across new cultural barriers. This is "third-generation church-planting" for the United States mission and "second-generation church-planting" for the Philippine mission.

Figure 4 assumes that the new third-generation church has now been encouraged to plant its own mission agency before the second-generation mission considers its task finished.

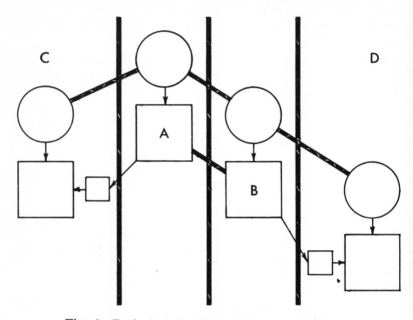

Fig. 4. Both (A) the United States mission and (B) the Philippine mission help establish nationally run *missions* in cultures C and D, respectively, each repeating the stage of Figure 2. In healthy church and mission multiplication this process will continue indefinitely.

FIRST REACTIONS

At this point some may recoil in horror at the thought of all this new machinery to be set up. Some readers may even have compared this to Rube Goldberg. It isn't that we object to the nationals getting in and doing things for themselves. We just somehow can't see the desirability of the nationals, with their limited resources and perhaps in some cases limited knowledge of the rest of the world, having to get involved in all the administrative paper work needed to set up and operate a competent mission agency. It is parallel to our feeling that every nation doesn't have to be a member of the nuclear club. Why should every small nation have to figure out how to make an atomic bomb? Some people may even feel that nationals can't be trusted that far! Can they not be trusted to send missionaries on their own? Western missions made a lot of mistakes in the beginning, and by now they have learned much about government red tape, anthropology, etc. Why should national leaders who have huge problems at home be bothered at this early stage with the problems of other nations?

Furthermore, it is rather mind-boggling to imagine how many new mission organizations will jump into existence around the world if this new kind of mission theory is pursued. The number of new churches (and whole demoninations) springing up in the non-Western world is already astronomical, especially in Africa. You can image the statisticians at the World Council of Churches or the World Evangelical Fellowship going out of their minds trying to keep track of all the new denominations being born (currently at the rate of at least one a day). Isn't that bad enough? So the question naturally arises: Are we serious about every church communion in the world getting into the mission business?

Let's think about it some more. For one thing, we're not necessarily suggesting that the Dani tribespeople of West Irian send a missionary to the Eskimos. Let's reemphasize right here that a specialized mission structure is required not just for work in foreign countries, but also for work in foreign *cultures,* which may or may not be found merely in foreign countries. One of our common weaknesses is that we often take cultural differences more seriously when a political boundary is crossed than when we reflect upon groups of different culture within our own country, especially when those groups are minorities and may appear to be unpatriotic in their adherence to their traditional customs. Certainly, wherever it is feasible, full-fledged work in a foreign country is desirable for several reasons. It not only puts the new national mission on a par with the United States mission which caused its own birth; it also creates a parallelism of circumstances and experience as national workers discover what it feels like to present the gospel while working as aliens in a foreign country. This kind of experience may for the first time introduce key leaders and their families to the psychological dimension of sacrifice involved in being a missionary. Nationals with such experience behind them will be the first to see the foreign missionary in a new light.

However, no matter what the miscellaneous factors pro and con may be, there are two overarching mandates that throw the whole subject of younger missions into the very highest priority.

The Demographic Imperative

In a recent article I found myself presenting a chart which indicated the existence of 2,150,000,000 non-Christian Asians. While Christians constitute a higher percentage of the Asian population than ever before, a far larger number of Asians do not know Christ than when William Carey first headed for India. We must be deeply grateful to God and to earlier pioneers that there are over ten million Christians in India, for example, but the perplexing fact is that there are at least 500 subcultures in India alone, as distinct from each other socially as the blacks and whites in Birmingham, Alabama, and that in at least 480 of these entire subcultures there are no Christians at all. Very bluntly, normal evangelistic outreach from existing Christian churches in India is utterly inadequate to face this challenge.

Note that I am not making a case here for the need of United States missionaries, although in many of these subcultures Western missionaries might be just as acceptable, or more so, than any Indian or Asian. What I am saying is that not even the Indian Christians can do this job unless (1) they understand it to be a task of full-blown *missionary* complexity, and

(2) they set up the proper *mission* machinery to do the job.

What is most needed in India today is the development of liberating fellowships of Christian faith among the hundreds of millions of Indian people who live in the hundreds of unreached subcultures. But the point is that these essential, crucial new fellowships in the unreached subcultures will not be planted by existing *churches* as much as by *mission* structures that can effectively express the true Christian obedience of the existing churches.

We hear that there are already one hundred such mission agencies in India, either for evangelism within the pockets of population where there are already Christians, or for real cross-cultural mission into pockets that are as yet unreached. But who cares? No one even has a list of these organizations. No one thinks it is important enough to make such a list. The new, immeasurably improved, *World Christian Handbook* for 1973 is projected for publications without such a list. There have long been directories of missions originating in the Western world; no one has yet begun a directory of the missions originating in the non-Western world.

This is not a bizarre, offbeat curiosity. It is impressively clear that the two thousand million non-Christian Asians will not be reached unless it can become fashionable for the *younger churches* to establish *younger missions*.

THE THEOLOGICAL IMPERATIVE

One reason why some apathy about missions has been growing in the United States recently has been all the talk (shall we say the "crowing"?) that has gone on during the past twenty-five years about the "great new fact of our time," that is, the emergence of a worldwide family of believers representing every country (but not every subculture) on the face of the globe. As we have seen, this quite distorts the picture demographically. Theologically it is very nearly totally misleading.

When pushed excessively, this "great new fact" ignores the

theological reality of the diverse subcultures of mankind. Let's take a hypothetical example. If the United States were an un-reached country and Christians from Japan planted a church in Seattle, another in San Francisco, and a third in Los Angeles and then headed home feeling satisfied that the United States had now been reached for Christ, this would be the kind of demographic nonsense we pointed out above. But if the three churches that were planted by the Japanese mission were all among the Navajo Indians, it would become a *theological* absurdity as well. And it would be an even greater absurdity if all the rest of the United States were (like Africa and Asia) cut up into hundreds of radically different subcultures rather than being relatively unified in language and culture. This is only a parable of the whole non-Western world today.

The theological imperative, however, does not merely arise from such practical considerations of tough cross-cultural mission. It goes much deeper. Do we dare say that whether or not there is anyone to "win" in foreign countries, that God does not intend for national churches to be isolated from Christians of radically diverse culture? Do we dare say that the Great Commission will not be fulfilled merely by the planting of an indigenous church in every culture so long as those churches remain isolated? Surely the Bible teaches us that the world-wide multitude of Christians constitutes a body, and that the various members and organs of that body need each other. Isn't it possible, therefore, to assume on theological grounds that even if everyone in the world were converted to Christ, Christians in one culture would still need to know Christians in other places? And their growth in faith and love would have to consist in part of some kind of nonassimilative integra-tion which would neither arbitrarily break down all the cul-tural differences nor allow the diverse elements of the body to wither and die, or be stunted due to the lack of proper circu-lation of witness and testimony through the whole body.

This is the ultimate reason for missions. God has allowed a gorgeous diversity among the butterflies, the leaves, the flowers, and the human families of mankind. If He does not intend to reduce the number of butterflies and flowers to a single model, He may not intend to eliminate all the ethnic, racial and linguistic differences in the world today. If He doesn't, then there is (and always will be) a powerful case for special mission organizations to facilitate the intercultural contact and to provide the lifeblood that will enable the whole body to flourish through interdependence, rather than to languish in fragmented isolation or to be stultified in a monotonous uniformity.

The theological imperative means that we condemn national churches to stultification if we frustrate their right and their duty to enter into serious mission. This ominous stagnation can occur to missionless churches in the Celebes as easily as it can develop among complacent nonmissionary minded Christians in a Detroit or London suburb. This is a theological dimension that has nothing to do with arithmetic or demography.

THE BACKGROUND OF THE IMPASSE

At least two assumptions may contribute to the widespread blindness about the need for younger missions as well as younger churches. One of these arose years ago in what is now called the ecumenical camp. The other, which leads almost precisely to the same conclusion, is a pattern of thought common among the most fervent Evangelicals.

Ironically, the first assumption began to develop at that time in history when the older historic denominations' mission efforts were staffed and run primarily by people who would be considered clearly evangelical today. It was D. L. Moody who launched John R. Mott into the explosively powerful Student Volunteer Movement, for example, and it was these early evangelical student leaders and their followers who, in country after country around the world, organized the missionary councils. By 1928 there were twenty-three. By 1948 there were thirty, and virtually every "mission field" country of the non-Western world and even of the sending countries had its missionary council or Christian council. Note that in only three of these was there any reference to "churches" in the title. They were missionary councils or "Christian" councils, but *not* councils of churches. This means that in India, for example, both national churches and *foreign* mission societies were originally represented in the national Christian council. Also, as a minor element, there already were indigenous mission societies of certain special types, such as quasi-nationalized offices of the American Bible Society or of the YMCA. The development of younger *churches* was the focus of attention, and apparently it was almost automatically supposed that *missionary societies* could only come from abroad. This fact later became a booby trap. Western mission societies themselves usually took the initiative to withdraw from these councils (in order to let national churches "run their own show") and, as a well-intentioned but tragic parting shot, they often even recommended either directly or indirectly that only *churches* should be allowed as members in the councils they left behind.

This fateful step assured the free sway of authority by national leaders, but it also swept the American Bible Society and the YMCA *and all future indigenous mission societies!* The National Christian Council of India in 1956 determined that "only organized church bodies are entitled to direct representation in the Council."[2] As a result, many Christian councils actually changed their names to "councils of churches." Still other councils, as that of India, for example, changed their nature (as above) without changing their names.

However, it is not as though everyone simply forgot about the need for mission work to be carried forward by personnel and funds from within the new nations and the younger churches. By this time in history it was felt that all missions should properly result from the direct initiative of *church* organizations as such. The move to exclude all but churches from these new councils did not, it was thought, do any more than eliminate *foreign* missions. Missions sponsored by national Christians, it was assumed, would quite naturally and normally be represented in the meetings of those new church councils by the appropriate respresentatives of the churches themselves. Thus the unquestionable principle stressing the autonomy of the national church was implemented in such a way as to exclude without a hearing the cause of the voluntary society. The reason the records do not show any great tussle at the time is partly because of the confusion of the two issues and of the predominant urgency after 1945 of getting the foreigners out of the picture. It also resulted from the fact that by this time most of the larger and older voluntary societies had already severed ties with these councils, and were thus not present to voice any opinion as to the structural implications of the new development. This leads us to the second basic assumption which has caused blindness among present-day Evangelicals about the need for younger missions.

There is no disguising the fact that a great deal (perhaps by now it would be fair to say the bulk) of mission efforts has been and is the work of people who normally call themselves Evangelicals. Evangelicals have expressed their missionary interest both inside and outside the older denominations. Every move by the older denominations to decrease foreign mission efforts has resulted in proportionate transferral of personnel and funds to newer "more mission-minded" denominations (and their mission boards) or to interdenominational missions, old and new. Thus, the average missionary overseas has tended to be either a strong Evangelical working within an older denomination (and thus believing that churches as such can and should send missions) or increasingly he is likely to be a missionary working for an interdenominational society, in which case he commonly believes that while older, perhaps liberalized, denominations back home can't be expected to send many missionaries, certainly the new churches overseas (started from scratch by evangelical fervor and developing with close dependence upon the Word of God) will surely be as missionary-minded as the missionary himself.

Thus, by 1972 we see that on every side, whether liberal or

conservative, there is a nearly unanimous assumption that the autonomous mission society in the mission land is either wrong and shouldn't exist or that it will be necessary only as an emergency measure someday in the future when younger churches follow the path of older United States denominations and "go liberal."

CONCLUSION

It is painful to add one more reason for blindness about the need for younger missions. True passion for the lost today is relatively scarce, even among missionaries. You don't have to be very daring to be a missionary today. As one missionary put it, "Circumstances have changed so much that it takes more courage to go home to the States than it does to go overseas." In the case of the United Presbyterians, for example, a young seminary graduate can very likely get a higher salary by going overseas as a missionary (if there is any budget for him at all) than he can by starting at the bottom rung of the ladder in church life back home. In general, American missions are a very elaborate end product of a massive century and a half of institutional development. The early missionaries were generally poor people who went from a poor country. But it did not take them long to build up institutions and vast land holdings—in some cases little empires—and in all cases a vast array of paraphernalia unimaginably beyond the ability of the national churches to duplicate.

Thus, even in an economic sense, the missionary from a well-heeled country is his own worst enemy should he ever want to promote a bleeding, sacrificial outpouring in foreign missions on the part of Christians in the national churches of the Third World. They literally cannot "go and do likewise."

Let us envision for a moment the young United States mission candidate. He may have to scrounge around for the wherewithal to buy his family a car, a camera, and a washing machine (just the "bare necessities" of the US life-style). Once on the field he will make expensive plane flights to the capital city for necessary medical help from real medical doctors. Even the most pitiable, poverty-stricken new missionary appears quite wealthy to the national Christian of most mission lands. For example, he may purchase just a few native trinkets to dress up his home for the benefit of the occasional tourist from America. What he buys for this purpose may appear in the national's eyes to be a shockingly trivial use of items which are to him culturally functional and essential, and may even cost him a year's savings!

Quite obviously missions, United States style, are out of reach to the Third World churches. National churches are as unlikely to be capable of following the life-style of United States missions as they are able to own as many cars per family. The economic gap is so great that the only possible solution is for autonomous younger missions to enter the picture on their own and be able to do things their own way. This may or may not mean they will set up their own promotional office in Wheaton, Illinois. In any case, it will be a whole new ball game.

We may end the century somewhat in the way foreign missions first began (in Protestant hands), with German candidates going under Danish auspices supported by British funds. Entirely new patterns may develop once the ingenuity and creativity of the younger churches reign free. One thing is clear: We cannot promote second-generation churches without promoting second-generation missions. The great new fact of *our* time must be the emergence of Third World *missions*. This is the next phase of missions today.

NOTES

1. The word *plant* is not ill-chosen. To say *establish* would be presumptuous by contrast. *Plant* means precisely that you take into your hands life which is beyond your power and help it to take root and grow by a process which is beyond your power. *Planting* is a delicate but very much needed task in which man assists God.
2. Harold E. Fey, ed., *The Ecumenical Advance: A History of the Ecumenical Movement,* vol. 2, 1948-1968 (Philadelphia: Westminster, 1970), p. 98.

Unquestionably, one of the most courageous developments in the world of evangelical missions today has been the recent restructuring of the Latin America Mission. At this writing the developments are still too experimental for conclusions to be drawn, but Horace L. Fenton, Jr., who has been intimately involved since the process began several years ago, has described in fascinating detail the behind-the-scenes dynamics of the situation. This chapter is a document which will become the basis of discussions on the subject of church-mission relations for years to come.

8

LATINIZING THE LATIN AMERICA MISSION

by HORACE L. FENTON, JR.

How can a foreign mission lose its foreignness? This is the essence of the problem which every missionary organization faces today. It is at the root of church-mission tensions, and an adequate answer to the question must be found if the world is to be effectively evangelized. Foreignness is an increasing liability in the work of the Lord, and our allegiance to the Great

HORACE L. FENTON, JR., became General Director of the Latin America Mission, Inc., in 1965 upon the death of R. Kenneth Strachan, after many years of experience as a mission administrator and Presbyterian minister. He holds the B.A. and D.D. degrees from Wheaton College, and the B.D. from Princeton Theological Seminary. Dr. Fenton's provocative articles on missions and related subjects have appeared frequently in such magazines as *Eternity, Evangelical Missions Quarterly, Christianity Today, International Review of Missions,* and others, as well as in the LAM house organ, *Latin America Evangelist.*

Commission may prove to be only lip service unless missions learn how to become more thoroughly rooted in the culture which they seek to serve.

The restructuring program which has been instituted recently in the Latin America Mission represents one attempt to grapple with this problem. If our experience in this area—both our victories and our defeats—can be of help to sister organizations, we shall thank the Lord, and this chapter will be successful.

THE BACKGROUND

A bit of history is essential. Seen against such a background, the changes which are being made may seem drastic, but they are certainly not sudden. They have historical antecedents, dating back over a period of years. Many different elements prepared the way for the new structures which are now emerging.

It is obvious that the leadership of the late Dr. R. Kenneth Strachan, general director of the mission from 1951 to 1965, set the stage for these changes. For years he had urged the rest of us to look forward to a time when the Latin America Mission might become a missionary arm of Christ's church in Latin America. More specifically, he insisted that the mission must work in close partnership with the Latin American church. To that end he led us in a number of steps which helped to make such a partnership a reality.

More than twenty years ago, the mission opened its membership to qualified Latin Americans, insisting only that they meet requirements similar to those demanded of North American candidates. A number of Latins thus became full members of the mission, and soon assumed places of responsibility and leadership.

An endeavor was made to put mission institutions on a true partnership basis under the leadership of boards composed of both Latin Americans and North Americans, with the Latins assuming an increasingly greater responsibility for decision-making.

As a result, Latin Christians were given the opportunity to manifest and develop their gifts of leadership and to gain valuable experience which would prepare them for even more influential roles later. Even before Dr. Strachan's death, our division of evangelism was largely made up of Latin personnel and was under Latin leadership. The same was true, to a lesser extent, of other aspects of the work.

It was soon evident that these steps toward partnership with the Latin church greatly increased the effectiveness of the mission's work in Latin America. Yet it became increasingly apparent as the years passed that much more dramatic and radical steps must be taken if, in reality, the mission ever was to become a missionary arm of the Latin American church.

It was clear that, in spite of everything we had done, the Latin America Mission remained a North American organization. This was evident in its top leadership, its decision-making elements, and its basic image, both in Latin America and in North America, in spite of continued earnest efforts to lower the North American profile in the mission. Yet it was all too obvious that in certain basic senses we remained what we had always been: a North American organization carrying on its work in Latin America. Two consequences of this fact are worthy of mention here.

In the first place, while membership in the mission continued to be open to Latins, it was plain that only a limited number of such brethren would thus unite with us. Given the rise of ethnic self-consciousness in Latin America and the increasing sense of Latin solidarity, they could hardly be expected to join us in great numbers. Why should they become a part of an admittedly North American organization? Why should they run the risk of having to become "gringo-ized" in order to become members of the Latin America Mission?

A careful assessment of the situation showed that we would never become a truly Latin American organization just by adding Latins to our staff, especially when the number of such recruits might diminish with the passing of the years.

Second, under the circumstances pictured above, it was evident that the Latin America Mission could not possibly be a missionary arm of the Latin American church. How could the church in Latin America, increasingly conscious of its own growth and power, accept a North American organization as its chosen instrument? How could Latin American Christians be asked to contribute personnel, funds and leadership to a group which too obviously was governed from abroad and which might therefore still seem to be an outpost of a North American empire?

Dr. Strachan's vision of our serving the Latin American church was still a worthy one, but it could not come to pass within the existing organizational structures.

NEW THINKING AT THE TOP

The board of trustees of the mission began showing a growing awareness of this situation and of the need to do something about it. In recent years they had increasingly delegated their legal powers to field authorities and had shown a remarkable sensitivity to the complexity of the missionary situation. They fully recognized the need of a readiness to make changes at every level of the work in order that the gospel of Christ might be more effectively communicated in Latin America.

This sensitivity to the needs of the field was produced in part by the firsthand contact which board members have maintained with the work in Latin America. Most of them have visited the fields. Field leaders, on their trips to the States, have often been given extended periods of time at board meetings to update the trustees on the Latin American scene. Consequently, the board has kept in vital contact with the fields.

Some members of the board have in recent years had unusual exposure to the dramatic changes that are taking place in Christ's church in Latin America. In mid-1970 the board president made a trip to Costa Rica to confer with the general directors of the mission about the leadership needs of the work. As a result of these discussions, the overall picture came more clearly into focus and the board became thoroughly acquainted with some of the problems which were demanding attention.

Another board member spent a month in Costa Rica in August, 1970, on the staff of Inter-Varsity's Overseas Training Camp. He returned to the States with a deep conviction which he shared with the board, that, given the wonderful group of Latin leaders God has provided, there was a real need for the board of trustees to reexamine its own role and to turn over much more of its authority to field leadership, and especially to Latins.

These matters became an increasing preoccupation with the board, and they discussed them at great length, not only among themselves but also with individual missionaries who were competent to give help in assessing the situation.

Meanwhile, the general director had asked the board to divide his responsibilities. He was convinced that he ought not continue to be responsible both for the overall administrative supervision of the work on the field and for a ministry to the churches and to the mission constituency in the United States. He therefore asked to be relieved of one or another of these aspects of his work.

Sensing the wisdom of such a division of labor, the board prayerfully sought a new general director. Several men within the mission were obviously good prospects for the post. Under Kenneth Strachan's leadership, a team concept of administration had been set up, with the result that a number of men had been thoroughly trained for administrative responsibility.

However, it soon became apparent to the board that merely to name another leader was no solution to the basic problem, which was in reality structural in its nature.

Thus a variety of factors had combined to make it plain to everyone concerned that new and even drastic steps were called for, that our whole organizational setup needed to be restudied, that with the help of God the mission must somehow become more fully rooted in Latin America.

THE JANUARY CONSULTATION

In October, 1970, the board of trustees decided to call a consultation to be held in San José, Costa Rica, in January, 1971. It is worthy of note that the board took the initiative in this matter. Subsequently, several Latin leaders stated that they were deeply grateful that the consultation had its origins with the board and was not something demanded by dissident elements in Latin America.

It was decided that about fifty people would be invited to the consultation, the majority of them Latins. Not all would be members of the mission; some were business or professional men in Latin America. The Latin America Mission of Canada would also be represented, as would the Latin America Mission of Mexico. In addition, the various field-based ministries of the mission would send their delegates.

It was arranged that the consultation would immediately be followed by the annual sessions of the interfield council, so that the council could legally implement the recommendations of the planning groups.

There was much work to be done beforehand. Latin American and North American leaders were asked to prepare position papers, dealing with the historical background of the mission, the evolution of its organizational patterns, its present situation, the evidences of need for change, and the various structural options that might be open for us. These papers were circulated beforehand in both Spanish and English so that all delegates were given a full background for the consultation.

The meetings themselves constituted an interesting phenomenon—altogether apart from the results produced. The delegates had gathered from a number of different countries, with varying ethnic and cultural backgrounds. For three long days they grappled with the issues at hand, sometimes bewildered by the complexity of them, more often amazed at the way the Lord gradually seemed to lead toward consensus.

North Americans were coming to know Latins in a new way, and Latins were developing a new understanding of the North American outlook. Deep feelings were manifested by both groups; while there was no bitterness of a personal nature, there were a few occasions when we were more conscious of heat than light!

Nevertheless, a wonderful spirit of fellowship prevailed. There was an increasing sense that we were being guided by God toward a better understanding of the problem and toward His provisions for its solution. There were occasions of special blessing as, in a deep sense of our need for wisdom, we cried out to God.

Individual differences of opinion were respected, but there was a growing measure of agreement and a conviction on the part of all that we were moving in the right direction.

In addition to the options that had been suggested in the position papers, a number of other varieties of structure were considered. Ultimately we had ten different possibilities before us. After long discussions, one of these was favored above the rest. Yet it was recognized that there were features in several other alternatives that might well be incorporated in this one, and subcommittees went to work on the necessary changes.

In time the basic outlines of a new structure emerged. While much detailed work remained to be done, at least there were specific recommendations to make to the interfield council to guide them in the grueling task of filling in the gaps.

When the council met in the succeeding days, it invited all the consultation delegates to sit in on the sessions, and also extended a special invitation to all members of the mission family to come as observers. It was determined that from the beginning everyone concerned would have the fullest possible opportunity to know what was going on in one of the highest legislative bodies of the mission, especially since each individual was vitally involved in the changes.

Next, the basic ideas were put into writing. Two continuing committees were appointed. One was to prepare a constitution for the new organization. The other committee was to take care of all additional elements involved in making the transition from one type of government to another. The council finally adjourned, weary in mind and body, but buoyed up by a strong feeling that the will of the Lord had been discerned and acted upon.

A NEW CONSTITUTION

The next step was drawing up the first rough draft of the new constitution. Out of the consultation and subsequent interfield council sessions had come the conviction that a new community of Latin American Evangelical Ministries should be set up. Membership in this community would be granted to entities of three different categories: international ministries of the Latin America Mission which were moving toward autonomy; federations formed of the local ministries in various countries (associations of churches, schools, the Bible Home, etc.); and the supportive organizations (for example, the Latin America Mission, Inc. of the U.S.A. and the Latin America Mission [Canada] Inc.).

Delegates from these entities would make up the general assembly of the new community, meeting twice a year to discuss their common interests, to coordinate their promotional and other activities, and to strengthen each other in the work. Apart from the prerogatives that they voluntarily relinquished in order to make such a general assembly function, the member entities would be fully autonomous, answerable only to their own boards. However, each member entity would be required to subscribe to the doctrinal statement of the community, which was identical to the doctrinal statement of the Latin America Mission.

Moreover, while each would have its own budget, all would adopt a standardized form of accounting, in accordance with the recommendations of the community. In the member entities, the leadership would be in the hands of Latin Americans wherever possible.

The business of the community between its semiannual meetings would be carried on by an executive committee elected by the general assembly. The period from October, 1971, to January 1, 1973, would be a transitional time for which special interim procedures would be provided as the move was made from the old structure to the new.

Under the new setup the Latin America Mission, Inc., of the U.S.A. would be one of the member entities. It would have responsibility for recruiting and preliminary screening of candidates, for raising funds, and for intensifying and extending the ministry of the mission in the United States, working with both Spanish-speaking and English-speaking groups.

The role of the board of trustees would be very different under the new setup, but still crucially important. However, each member of the community would decide the nature of its own work and the means for accomplishing it.

The constitutional process was a long and arduous one. The first working draft was prepared and circulated not only to all the legal bodies of the mission but also to all its ministries. Besides, each missionary was given a copy of this rough draft. A series of small-group meetings was set up to evaluate and criticize the proposed constitution. Individual missionaries were urged to study the document carefully and to give their reactions, pro and con, in writing. As a result, thirty-eight single-spaced typewritten pages of suggested additions, modifications and deletions were received!

The constitution committee went to work once again, weighing carefully all of these suggestions, and making many changes in the original document. A second working draft was prepared, and this was circulated widely at the various levels within the mission. It was clearly understood that further reactions and criticisms would be welcomed.

Additional helpful material resulted from thoroughgoing discussions of this revised version, and once again the drafting committee went to work. In August, 1971, an enlarged session of the interfield council met, charged with producing the final draft of the constitution. Once approved by the council, this draft would be submitted for action to the other legal bodies of the mission—the board of trustees and the field committees of Costa Rica and Colombia. In addition, the document was submitted to the Latin America Mission of Mexico and the the Latin America Mission (Canada), Inc., as well as to all ministries that seemed likely to become members of the new community.

The understanding was that if any of the legal bodies had continuing concerns with regard to details of the constitution, these concerns could be expressed in amendments to be submitted to the January, 1972, meeting of the general assembly. Thus, further delay in the acceptance of the basic document could be avoided and proper provision made for entering into the new structure, on a transitional basis, as of October 1, 1971.

Within a period of weeks this final draft of the constitution had been approved by all legal bodies of the mission. In each case it was accepted as it stood, with suggested amendments to be considered at the later date.

SOLVING THE COMMUNICATIONS PROBLEM

The problem of internal communications was recognized to be one of great importance. At first there was a wide range of reactions within the mission family to the proposed changes, due in part to the fact that information was inevitably limited at that time and that no one could give an exact picture of what the ultimate organizational pattern would be.

This period of uncertainty and ignorance understandably produced a number of tensions and strong reactions with regard to the new plan. Some missionaries felt definitely threatened by the change; having been given a divine call to serve in Latin America, they were afraid that now their usefulness might be limited or terminated in the near future. Others openly expressed fears that there might be doctrinal deviations under such a setup, or that Christian public in the United States and Canada—perhaps misunderstanding the changes—would reduce their support of the work. Some thought they saw the possibility of a power struggle within the mission, with Latin Americans and North Americans arrayed against each other in it.

The series of group discussions and individual interviews previously mentioned were set up to deal with these things, and to communicate as fully as possible the nature of the contemplated changes. In addition, mimeographed memos and bulletins were widely circulated to all concerned, keeping them constantly informed of developments. Open expression of concerns and fears was urged, and the leadership of the mission made an earnest effort to deal with all of them.

Consequently, much of the suspicion and of the serious questioning that had arisen was dissipated. Some concerns were seen to be without foundation; others, more legitimate, were dealt with in the revision of the constitution. There was an increasing sense on the part of many that we were moving in the direction that God had pointed out. Some had lingering doubts about the speed at which things were changing. Others had questions still unresolved. But gradually it was very evident that God was bringing us all to a much greater spirit of unity than had previously existed. Today there is a large measure of unanimity in the mission family as to the rightness of the steps that have been taken.

External communications were seen as very important also. It was essential that our mission's constituency and others who were in the leadership of missions or of churches in the homeland should be kept well informed about what was happening. These people are our partners in the work, and we needed their prayers and their sympathetic counsel. A new film, presenting the need for change and the steps which are being taken, was prepared for use by discussion groups in North America. News releases to the secular and religious press, articles in our own magazine, and extensive correspondence were used to acquaint our friends with the lessons we were learning from the Lord and with the steps that we were taking in an endeavor to do His will.

THE COMMUNITY BEGINS TO MOVE

Once approval was given to the constitution by the interfield council in August, 1971, the council, on an enlarged basis, immediately moved into a provisional meeting of the general assembly. This had to be provisional because the other legal bodies of the mission had not yet had the opportunity to vote on the new constitution, but it was necessary that a beginning of the new structure be made without undue delay. (As one of our leaders aptly put it, "When you're riding one horse and mean to shift from his back to that of another horse, you don't dare lose too much time in making the move!")

So, on a conditional basis, the new community got under way. Officers and an executive committee were elected. The first president of the community, elected by acclamation, is Dr. Jorge Taylor, a Panamanian, a member of the Latin America Mission, a graduate of our Latin American Biblical Seminary, a member of the faculty of that institution, and the holder of an earned doctorate from Michigan State University. Dr. W. Dayton Roberts was named general secretary of the community.

There are nine members of the executive committee plus four alternates, and of the total number it is interesting to note that eight are Latin Americans.

The approval of the other legal bodies having been obtained by October 1, 1971, the transitional period was begun on that date, and the executive committee began the implementation of various aspects of the new constitution. Meanwhile, Dr. Roberts visited the United States, Canada, Mexico, Panama and Colombia in the interests of the community. He also spent much time helping the member entities to prepare themselves legally and otherwise for functioning under the new structure.

Budgets of the new entities were hammered out and prepared for presentation at the first official general assembly meeting in January, 1972. Statutes were drawn up for the internal government of the community and of its member entities, and other essential preparations were made for the full functioning of the community.

It is relatively easy to draw organization charts, to modify existing structures, or to theorize about new forms of government. But the real issue is whether the changes will make us more effective in fulfilling our God-given call for the evangelization of Latin America.

BLESSINGS AND BOOBY TRAPS

In a sense, of course, it is too soon to evaluate what has happened. All of us who have been involved in the restructuring program are well aware that pitfalls and booby traps still lie ahead and that we could very well miss the plan and purpose of God even at this late date.

This is not, therefore, a time to make reckless claims. However, one would have to be utterly ungrateful to God to fail to notice some very encouraging things that have been happening as a result of the new structure. Already there are many indications available that the blessing of God is upon what has been done and that some of the goals, which were theoretical only a few months ago, are beginning to be achieved.

It has been most encouraging to watch the closing of the ranks of our missionary personnel as the direction of God's leading became more apparent. We are united behind the changes, even though as individuals we may have continuing questions about details of the new structure.

Another significant result is the conviction, especially as expressed by some of our Latin brethren, that it is now evident that we are not engaged in window-dressing and empty talk when we speak of giving authority and responsibility to Latin

Americans. In our mission and in other organizations there has been a surfeit of such talk in times past; now we are beginning to see some action.

It has been encouraging, too, to note how the Latin leaders in the various ministries which are becoming autonomous under the new setup manifest an increased sense of legitimate pride in a work which is now theirs in a new sense. Already they are helping the Latin American church to become partners in the new enterprise through financial support, the provision of personnel, and by earnest prayer backing. This can only lead to a stronger sense of stewardship and of partnership in the work of Christ in these lands.

Latin leaders continue to express their appreciation for the contribution made by North American missionary personnel and for the help of the mission's constituency in the United States and Canada. Our Latin brethren are perfectly willing to take the place of leadership and responsibility which is rightly theirs, but they are not seeking in any sense to declare their independence from the church of Christ in any other place.

THE RIGHT TO SCREEN MISSIONARIES

They want more missionaries from North America, but they rightly make it very plain that they want something to say about the screening of missionary candidates and their ultimate assignments. And they remind us, directly and indirectly, that a very special type of missionary is needed to fit into the new organizational structures that are coming into being.

It is very evident to them and to us that strong financial help from North America will be needed for a long time to come. Increasingly, the Latins themselves will be participating in the financial undergirding of the work; but given the anticipated expansion and the rising cost of carrying on the various ministries, it is both inevitable and legitimate that North America should continue to have a sizable share in this aspect of the work. Indeed, if Latin America is providing the work with real leaders, why should not the most affluent countries in the world provide financial resources to enable these leaders to carry on the ministry God has given them?

It is already apparent that the expansion of the work under the new setup will provide multiplied opportunities for the de-. velopment of new Latin leadership, which might not have emerged had not the changes been made. The rise of this leadership is in itself an answer to the prayers of God's people through the years.

We are grateful too for the interest expressed by the leaders of other missions in what we are doing. Many have written for additional information concerning these recent developments, and we have been glad to supply it. We are well aware that as a service mission our setup is somewhat different from that of other organizations, and none of us believes that our structure is necessarily an exact pattern for anyone else.

However, to the extent to which the new setup is biblically based and is in keeping with the changing situation on the mission field, the experience of the Latin America Mission may provide stimulus and encouragement for other organizations. And we shall be thankful to God if this is the case.

Generally speaking, the response of the Christian public in North America has so far been very encouraging. Many pastors and laymen have expressed the strong conviction that the Christian public needs to be given a more adequate picture of the situation on the mission field today and how this can best be met. The Christian public, by and large, will be responsive to creative thinking in dealing with this situation; for too long we have underestimated their capacity to do so.

There has been some misunderstanding in certain circles— perhaps because we have not communicated our story adequately. Some have thought that the Latin America Mission was going out of existence; some have feared that the direction we have taken means the end of the missionary era, or a reversal of the indigenous emphasis of years gone by. Again, we are reminded of the importance of more adequate communication as we move ahead in our restructuring, so that such false ideas may be laid to rest. Meanwhile, we are thankful that there has been a relatively small degree of misunderstanding on the part of Christian people.

We are well aware that our task of reorganization is far from complete. We could still miss the plan of God for us in any number of ways. Yet our hearts have been encouraged by a growing conviction that we have been kept within His will, at least as far as the general direction of the changes is concerned. We have an equally strong conviction that He means us to continue to move ahead along these lines and to work out the implications of the steps that have been taken, with a deep sense of dependence upon Him for wisdom and strength.

When the apostle Paul laid upon his fellow believers the admonition, "Brethren, pray for us," he was not engaging in pious talk. His appeal for help in prayer was undoubtedly based on his recognition of the size of the task that confronted him and on his awareness of demonic opposition. A somewhat similar burden is ours as we move ahead in our endeavor to eliminate the foreignness of the Lord's work in Latin America and to see it directed by our brethren in Christ in those lands.

The task will not be easy; the opposition will be great; our own human fallibility is all too evident to us. Nonetheless, we are confident that God will lead and guide—and doubly confident as we know that our brethren are praying for us to this end.

*The Christian and Missionary Alliance has gained
a well-earned reputation of being an organization
that knows where it is going and how it intends
to get there. The development of their strong Vietnamese church has been the subject of many high-
level discussions in the world of missions, but
rarely has the story of its relationship with the
mission been told with the detail Grady Mangham
gives us in this chapter. Of special interest
to readers will be the frequent references to the
international Asia Conference where the constructive cross-fertilization of ideas and experiences
resulting from the personal encounter of Asian
churchmen from several countries might be considered as a model for others to follow.*

9

DEVELOPING CHURCH RESPONSIBILITY IN VIETNAM

by T. Grady Mangham, Jr.

Church and mission representatives in Vietnam celebrated the sixtieth anniversary of Protestant witness there in 1971. The long process of Christian development has made the Christian and Missionary Alliance Church of Vietnam an excellent example of how tensions between mission and church have been dealt with.

T. Grady Mangham, Jr., is Area Secretary for Southeast Asia and the Middle East for the Christian and Missionary Alliance. Before assuming these responsibilities in 1967, he served for twenty years as a missionary to Vietnam, engaged primarily in evangelism and church-

HISTORY OF THE WORK

The first resident missionary began the C&MA work in Vietnam in 1911. Thirteen years later, in 1924, the first national conference was held. By 1927 the churches had organized into a national body. That year the first national committee was elected, and the following year a church constitution was ratified. In 1930 this fledgling church recognized its own missionary obligation to the ethnic minorities in the Central Highlands, and sent its first "missionary" to work alongside those from overseas who were pioneering among the tribal groups.

Another step of major significance was taken in 1959 when the churches established among tribal Christians in all parts of the country were accepted into the national church organization as a separate district. More recently, the church's missionary interest extended beyond the borders of their own country when they sent their first "foreign" missionary couple to Laos in 1962.

The Evangelical Church of Vietnam (Hoi Thanh Tin Lanh Viet Nam) is organized with a president and six district superintendents as full-time administrators. There are 368 local churches with a total of 51,000 baptized members (Doan Van Mieng's estimate). These churches are served by 131 ordained pastors, 128 unordained ministers, and 85 catechists. Seventeen trained workers of the church make up the Protestant contingent of the Chaplains' Corps in the Republic of Vietnam's military services. Nationals serve as directors of the Bible and Theological Institute at Nhatrang and the Bible schools for tribal students located at Dalat and Banmethuot. The church operates 72 schools, both elementary and high schools. Five

planting. As Chairman of the C&MA work among the tribal groups of Central Vietnam, he traveled widely throughout the area. Mr. Mangham, a graduate of Nyack Missionary College, serves also on the Board of Directors of the American Leprosy Missions, Inc., and as Vice-president of the American Council of the Ramabai Mukti Mission.

orphanages are under the church's direction. A leprosarium program, centered in Banmethuot and reaching into four provinces, is jointly administered by the Christian and Missionary Alliance and the church. The church also cooperates with the Mennonite Central Committee in administering hospitals at Nhatrang and Pleiku. A small printing press in Saigon was purchased and is operated and maintained entirely under the supervision of the church.[1]

God has raised up capable and dedicated leaders for this emerging body of believers in Vietnam.

THE MISSION'S STANCE

"The Christian and Missionary Alliance has as its principal missionary objective the winning of adults to Christ and the establishing of churches in all places were converts are won."[2] This is the very first statement in the book, *Policies and Procedures.* You will note the objective is twofold: winning men to Christ, and establishing churches wherever there are converts.

Various methods or principles have been used by missions in seeking to attain that objective. Variations on the different policies will be found from country to country and from culture to culture. In 1927 The Christian and Missionary Alliance adopted as an official policy some of the concepts which are now referred to as the "indigenous church method." Webster's dictionary defines *indigenous* as "produced, growing, or living naturally in a country or climate; native."

The Missionary Atlas states:

> The indigenous church—a church truly rooted in the country where its members live—is the aim of Alliance missions. Made up of mature, instructed believers and trained pastors, such a church is a verile, witnessing, independent body. It is not the transplanting of an organization as it is conceived in our own land, but the expression of the transforming power of the gospel in the culture of the people and in accord with the New Testament pattern. This is accomplished through teach-

ing the Word and depending upon the Holy Spirit to bring illumination to believers.[3]

The historic position of the C&MA holds that evangelism and church-planting can best be accomplished by maintaining the mission as an organization separate from the developing church in each country.[4] This position has been formalized as follows:

> It is recognized that church and mission are essentially distinct. The mission is an organization composed of representatives from the homeland supported by or through the Society and functioning under the direction of the Society. . . . In its relationship to the indigenous church, the mission is an organized body of friends who stand ready to help when needed. Beyond the ministry of the local church the mission must continue to function in a widening outreach. . . . The mission is not to regulate church activities and the church is not to regulate missionaries' activities except in those cases where missionaries have been assigned to some form of church-related work by the conference and at the request of the church.[5]

SPECIAL FACTORS

There are at least three factors of major significance in Vietnam's church history against which the entire picture must be drawn. Each has affected the work in its own way. It is not our purpose to analyze them critically, but it should be said that each has had both detrimental and salutary effects.

DISRUPTIONS OF WAR AND POLITICAL CHANGE

The disruptions of war and political change are the first problem. World War I, which occurred just three to seven years after the initial missionary occupation, brought some disruption. This is surprising, since no fighting took place in that part of the world. However, the problems arose from the fact that some of the missionaries had German names, giving the French colonial rulers a pretense to hold them in suspicion.[6] There was, of course, a great deal more disruption during the period of World War II. Even before Pearl Harbor, the Japanese army had made the Indochinese peninsula a part of their design for imperialistic conquest. As the threat of full-scale war became more ominous, some missionary personnel moved to the Philippines where they expected greater security. Those who remained at their posts were eventually interned and held as prisoners of war until hostilities ended.

The end of that war ushered in a period of great political unrest and military activity for all of Indochina. The flames of nationalism had been fanned to white heat. Tragically, the leadership in that period of revolution was dominated by Communism. This beclouded the issue for Christians on the local scene as well as for leaders seeking solutions at the international level. Fighting continued and increased until the signing of the Geneva Accords in 1954. A period of relative peace ensued.

By 1956, it became evident that (1) the Communist regime in North Vietnam would not be satisfied until its influence and control were extended throughout the entire country; and (2) the almost one million refugees who had left home and possessions rather than live under a Communist-dominated government in the North, together with a growing percentage of the population in the South, would not submit to such a takeover without a fight. No final solution is yet in sight.

Coupled with these periods of prolonged warfare have been significant political developments. The work began during a period of colonial rule by the French (1911-1945). The war for independence lasted nine years (1945-1954), ending in the division of Vietnam at the 17th parallel. Since that time, mission work and known church history have been confined to the Republic of South Vietnam under free and often favorable conditions.

ONE MAJOR PROTESTANT CHURCH

The second important factor is that only one major Protestant church organization exists in Vietnam. This resulted from the fact that, until recent years, the C&MA was the only Protestant mission working in Vietnam, with the exception of a few Seventh-day Adventists.[7] Within the last few years, other mission groups have come to establish their work, but in almost every instance the leaders of the Evangelical Church have extended an invitation for these to work cooperatively rather than to raise up separate or rival church structures. The "support" missions have accepted the invitation. Others have chosen to develop their churches independently.

It is of interest to note that *all* of those who have come officially to carry on church-planting work are within the conservative, evangelical sector of Christendom. Liberal theology and ecumenical pressures have come only from outside the country and from some involved in relief and social-service activities.

CHURCH'S ORGANIZATIONAL STRUCTURE

The third significant factor in Vietnam is the unique organizational structure of the church. It embraces not only the churches among the ethnic Vietnamese, but also those of the diverse tribal groups. Still it encourages a measure of identity among the tribal peoples by uniting all of them in a district following ethno-linguistic lines rather than geographic ones. This has several important implications: (1) Tribal representatives serve on the national church committee. If the tribal churches were totally integrated into the geographic districts where they are located, there is little chance that they would be elected to the national committee. (2) A district organization exists where all members of the conference are tribespeople. This permits and encourages the development of leadership among the tribespeople. (3) Local churches abound where the tribespeople can worship and praise the Lord in their mother tongue. This means that in some cases there are several churches in one town, each of which uses a different language. It also means that a Vietnamese church and a tribal church located in the same town will, nevertheless, belong to two different church districts.

MISSION-CHURCH RELATIONSHIP—HOW IT WORKS

Now that we understand something of the church in Vietnam and policies that have guided the mission, we should now turn our attention to the specific tensions to see how these have been dealt with. We need to see the composite picture of mission-church relationships as they have developed in Vietnam today. We will outline these in seven principal areas.[8]

SUPPORT OF WORKERS

In the very early years of the work, Dr. R. A. Jaffray "pointed out the necessity of a strong stand on self support."[9] His program of reducing mission subsidy 10 percent for each ten new believers in a given church fellowship seemed to work well during those exciting early days of rapid expansion. By 1927, when the organization of the church on a national level was carried out, there were eight self-supporting churches. The work went forward with much blessing, and by 1941, 75 percent of the 121 congregations had become self-supporting.

At that time Japanese troops began to pour into Indo-China in compliance with the "Joint Defense Pact" imposed by the Vichy government of France.[10] Thus began the first ordeal by fire of the Vietnamese church. Representatives of the church were notified shortly after the outbreak of war in the Pacific that beginning February 1, 1942, there would be no more subsidy from the mission. Had any local church or committee been in the habit of looking to the mission for its running expenses, this announcement might have proved most disastrous. The effect, however, was just the opposite. Within a few weeks, in the southern district it was reported that "by dint of some doubling up and a far-sighted policy on the part of the self-supporting churches," no place of worship would be closed. In the more economically depressed central and northern areas of the country, the situation was not quite so bright. A number of churches there did have to close.[11]

Allied attacks against the Japanese in Indo-China, the rise of the nationalist front, the proclamation of the independence of the Democratic Republic of Vietnam on September 2, 1945,[12] and the resulting warfare as the French sought to re-establish their colonial control, brought great suffering, loss of life, and destruction of property to the Vietnamese people. The church did not escape. When missionaries were released from internment and others returned from the United States, a difficult situation confronted them. Moved by the suffering and poverty resulting from continual fighting in areas throughout the country, the mission gave generous amounts for relief, for the rebulding of destroyed churches, and for subsidies to pastors in affected areas. As fighting continued, this became an established pattern.

When the mission felt it was time to move back toward the principle of self-support, relationships became strained. When the mission announced that, beginning in 1955, financial support in the form of subsidy would be gradually reduced, tensions naturally arose.

It was at this juncture that the first Asia Conference of C&MA churches was held in Bangkok in 1955. One of the major agenda items dealt with self-support for the churches. Reports of success in attaining self-support in some Asian countries were presented. Thailand indicated,

> There are now sixteen churches which have self-supported pastors. . . . The spiritual leadership of all other church groups is by Bible school-trained self-supported laymen. . . . The adoption of the self-support program has been an en-couragement to tithe and has contributed substantially toward the incentive to give offerings to the Lord.[13]

Indonesia reported,

> In the Sesajap District there are 51 churches, each support-ing its own pastor; in the Belitang District there are 15

churches, each supporting its own pastor. . . . In both of these districts, the basis for self-support was, and is, tithing which was taught to the Christians as soon as they believed. . . . It is important that missionaries and national pastors be themselves fully persuaded that self-support can be attained from the beginning and there must be the determination to put it into effect.[14]

The Philippines reported,

There are now 38 couples and 27 single workers on full self-support. . . . Many volunteer workers called lay preachers, who support themselves by farming, pastor local churches. The fact that the national church has made self-support a requirement for voting membership in the conference made such a membership a test and a triumph.[15]

Periods of lively discussion followed these reports. The delegation from Vietnam was much impressed when they realized that other Asian churches had moved ahead of them in teaching the Christians to accept their responsibility of supporting their own pastors. These brethren returned to Vietnam with vital information to be shared with fellow workers. It was not long afterward that the president of the Vietnamese church informed the mission that, rather than follow the suggested program of gradual cutback in mission funds, the national committee had decided that all mission subsidy for pastors should be terminated immediately. Since then, the church has continued a pattern of steady growth on a fully self-supporting basis.

The Second Asia Conference was held in Saigon in 1958. Rev. Le Van Thai, president of the Evangelical Church of Vietnam, gave a report indicating that all churches had become self-supporting. The question was then posed:

"Mr. Thai, at Bangkok you said the relationship between the Vietnamese and the missionaries was rough. Is it still so?"

Mr. Thai answered, "Praise the Lord, it is gone."

When the question was asked, "Why is it gone?" Mr. Thai

replied, "Because we stopped talking about money. The church's aim and objective are higher. Now we are looking to the Lord for help through the Vietnamese themselves and we have taken a step of faith."[16]

CHURCH BUILDINGS

Included in the self-support concept practiced by the C&MA is the idea that the local church once planted should make its own decision as to the type of building it needs. It should be responsible to build commensurate with its own abilities.[17] During the period of early growth in the church in Vietnam, this did not seem to present a problem. However, after World War II and the period of disruption which followed, many church buildings had been destroyed. Financial assistance was then provided by the mission to help rebuild these structures. It became an easy assumption that funds should also be provided for building new churches and/or rebuilding all the older ones. This became a new point of tension between the mission and the church.

During his stay in Saigon at the time of the Second Asia Conference, Foreign Secretary Louis L. King was invited to a special dinner where representatives of the Vietnamese church were also guests. A discussion came up about the matter of church buildings. President Thai stated that it was almost impossible to begin a new church in a major city because of (1) the high cost of property, and (2) building codes requiring the expenditure of funds in excess of the capability of small Christian groups. Another difficulty was that of securing loans locally, and the exceedingly high interest rates. Dr. King expressed his willingness to consider any feasible proposal that would help the church expand its base in the major cities. This discussion led to further consultation.

Before the conference was concluded, R. M. Chrisman, area secretary for Asia, said, "There are opportunities and needs for financial assistance which challenge the faith of our entire Society. . . . As God enables, we shall continue to support these and other related projects." Among other things, he listed "church building programs in large cities where land costs, building restrictions, and larger than normal accommodations are needed, thus making the cost far more than the national church or local congregation can meet."[18]

Details for this new program of assistance were to be worked out a few weeks later when the following action was taken by the foreign department:

> With regard to giving financial help towards the opening of new churches, it was voted:
>
> a. That financial help be given only to those churches which are in the capitals of provinces and in port cities.
> b. That this program apply only to the opening of new churches.
> c. That there be an existing group of Christians who are supporting their worker.
> d. That The Christian and Missionary Alliance grant to the Evangelical Church of Viet Nam an [unspecified] amount to be used by them as a revolving fund for church building projects.
> e. (1) That the local church raise one-third the cost of the project.
>
> (2) That the local church be loaned up to one-third the cost of the project from the revolving fund administered by the National Church organization (per "d" above).
>
> (3) That The Christian and Missionary Alliance give, from funds in New York, one-third the cost of any church project.[19]

Set up initially as a pilot project applicable only in Vietnam, this policy has now been adapted (with appropriate refinements) for implementation in all of our overseas work.

BIBLE SCHOOL

Early in the history of missionary work in Vietnam (1919), a center was developed for the formation of catechists and pastors. John Olsen, a man richly endowed as linguist, scholar, teacher and writer, was appointed director of the school. Under his dynamic and at times authoritarian leadership, the school took on his character, as did the man who served for years as his associate, Ong Van Huyen. So well had the foundation of the school been laid that when, at the outbreak of World War II, the missionaries were interned and financial support from the mission was completely cut off, the school continued to function under national leadership through the spring of 1945. By the fall of that year, however, "the school had to be closed, not so much because of lack of funds, as a result of political upheavals."[20]

The school was reopened in 1948, with thirty-five students in attendance under the codirectorship of John Olsen and Ong Van Huyen.

The policy book states, "Our Bible schools can best be conducted as cooperative projects under the joint administration of the church and the mission." Provision is made for a governing board on which "the President of the church, the head of the school, and the mission chairman should be members by virtue of their office." It is further stated, "It is desirable that the recognized head of the school be a national."[21]

The joint committee, as one of its functions, serves as the governing board for the Bible school.[22] It has responsibilities in the area of property, finances, personnel and policies. When the school moved from Danang to its new location in Nhatrang, the joint committee approved of the acquisition of property and decided that it be acquired in the name of the church, not the mission. When funds were made available by the mission for construction, the joint committee approved the building plans. It was decided to commit the building project to the church, and to channel the funds directly to them. For a total of $170,000, buildings were erected that could never have been duplicated by the mission at that price.

The joint committee receives budget requests from the school annually. It reviews the budget and passes on requests for financial assistance to the mission. The school is still subsidized by mission funds. Our view is that this is another area where financial assistance may legitimately be provided to the church without undermining the indigenous nature of the church itself. Mission funds are designated for the operational budget—not for support of students during their on-campus study program. An auditor's report is prepared annually by the school, submitted to the joint committee.

Personnel needs of the school are processed through the joint committee. A consensus is reached as to the individuals who can best fill the requirements. If they are nationals, a request is given to the national church committee to release them for appointment to the school. Should a missionary be desired, a similar request goes to the mission. In every case, a decision is not reached unless there is unanimous consent. The actual appointment to the school will be by the joint committee. A missionary thus assigned falls into the category of "those cases where missionaries have been assigned to some form of church-related work by the conference and at the request of the church."[23]

I have spoken only of the school at Nhatrang, but the same principles apply for the two Bible schools located at Dalat (Koho tribal area) and Banmethuot (Raday tribal area) where nationals (tribesmen) have been appointed as directors of these institutions.

CHURCHES IN TRIBAL AREAS

Beginning in 1929, personnel of the mission was located in areas where frequent contacts were made with tribal groups. These people, in those days called "Moi" (Mawee) which means "savage," were little understood, but they were recognized as a part of the unfulfilled task. Converts were made in a number of locations, and churches were planted. Exploited by the French plantation owners and despised by most Vietnamese, these people responded readily to the gospel. No formal organizational patterns for these churches were established until 1952. Prior to that date, all of Indochina had been under one mission administration. In 1952 when the French granted a measure of autonomy to Laos, Cambodia and Vietnam, they set up a separate government agency for the tribal interests called "Population Montagnard du Sud" (PMS). The mission followed their example, establishing separate mission conferences for the oversight of the work in Cambodia, Laos, Vietnam, and the tribes of Vietnam. Soon after, plans were initiated to organize the churches among all of the tribal groups into the Tribes Church of Vietnam. A president was elected and a constitution was drafted.

It became increasingly evident that the Vietnamese national committee was not sympathetic to the establishment of such a separate organization. For a number of years, the Vietnamese Christians had shown a keen interest in a ministry to the tribespeople. As early as 1930, some had expressed concern,[24] and by 1932, Vietnamese workers had joined the missionaries in carrying the gospel to areas difficult of access.[25] As the tribal Christians, encouraged by the mission, moved ahead with plans for their own church organization, a triangle of tensions developed. The agelong animosities between the tribal people and the Vietnamese missionaries often came to the surface. The Vietnamese brethren frequently felt that the foreign missionary took the part of the tribesman in any misunderstanding which developed. The foreign missionary at times felt resentment against the Vietnamese co-workers and the more aggressive, more highly organized church which they represented.

At a meeting to discuss this entire issue in Saigon in February, 1959, the following consensus emerged: (1) the Vietnamese church had never officially recognized the legitimacy of a separate tribal church organization; (2) Rev. H'Sol, president of the Tribes Church, expressed surprise that the Tribes Church was "separate"; and (3) the mission had made a mistake to foster the idea of a separate church organization for the work among the tribes people.[26] Two actions were recorded by the joint committee as follows:

1. Moved that we confirm the fact that the Vietnamese Evangelical Church in all of Viet Nam is one Church, organized and based on the constitution of the Vietnamese Evangelical Church, both in the mountain areas as well as other regions, except where cultural and living conditions will present differences in the organization of evangelical effort.

2. Moved that we request the American and Vietnamese missionaries who take part in the above organization to unite to find a means whereby it would be possible to lead the Tribes Church in accordance with the constitution of the Evangelical Church of Viet Nam, except those articles which the Tribes Church is not able to put into effect, in which case we simplify certain of the conditions until they are able to follow them fully.

This paved the way for a request by the tribal churches to be accepted as a separate district in the Evangelical Church of Vietnam. Official action was taken at the annual conference of the church, establishing this district and recognizing the former Tribes Church president as the district superintendent and, as such, a member of the national committee of the church.

MISSION PROGRAM OF THE CHURCH

In 1930 the church in Vietnam began to express its missionary responsibility to the more primitive tribal groups living in the interior. The Rev. Le Hoang Phu reports,

> By the end of 1930, the Evangelical Church had 104 congregations . . . that same year the national conference undertook a new task: a missionary enterprise among the tribes. One of the pastors "felt the urge of the Spirit to go as a missionary" to one of the wild tribes that inhabited the mountains and jungles of the country. The conference decided to appoint him and to support him and his family in this new ministry.[27]

Interest in this mission project grew as reports were taken

to the Bible school at Tourane (Danang). The national church conference of 1942, faced with the imminent withdrawal of the foreign missionaries following the outbreak of war in the Pacific, took significant steps to maintain the missionary outreach of the church.

> The first full-fledged missionary convention, held during the conference, with Vietnamese missionaries serving ten tribes, received enthusiastic response and support from the delegates; and significantly, six of the twenty-five motions of this conference concerned missionary work among the tribes: organization of an annual missionary conference, support of the Vietnamese missionaries by special offerings taken regularly from all local churches, missionary messages to be delivered by local pastors at least once every quarter, etc.[28]

In 1946, because the churches were under severe pressures economically as a result of political and military developments, the mission undertook the full support of the four families continuing in this missionary ministry. In addition, interest grew for expanding the work into other tribal districts. The missionaries had relaxed the emphasis on self-support because of special conditions in the country, and funds were easily available from North America through appeals for support of national workers. By 1957, fourteen families had engaged in "missionary" ministries, but primarily supported by foreign funds. How could the commendable missionary passion of these brethren be related more realistically to the churches from which they had come? The national church committee was happy to recognize them as their representatives among the tribespeople, but it was reluctant (1) to assume responsibility for administering their work, or (2) to make a serious attempt to raise financial support for them.[29]

Much negotiation went on between mission and church representatives. One of the major points of tension was resolved when the tribal churches became a part of the national church organization. At this point, the brethren of the national committee began an intensive effort to stir missionary interest throughout the churches, challenging the Christians to accept the financial obligations which this brought with it.

In July, 1961, the Third Asia Conference of C&MA churches met in Zamboanga, Philippine Islands. The foreign department had drawn up some stated objectives for this conference. One was,

> To press further the missionary responsibility of the Asian churches. . . . The approach would be by presenting the following:
>
> 1. Papers from each delegation on the subject, "The Unevangelized Areas and the Unfinished Task in The C&MA Fields."
> 2. Address on "The Biblical Basis for the Missionary Responsibility of Every Church."
> 3. Papers from each delegation on the subject, "Our Missionary Program—Its Strengths and Weaknesses."[30]

The report from Hong Kong fell like a thunderclap among the assembled delegates:

> About ten years ago, an overseas evangelistic band was organized in Hong Kong. We expected to send some graduates from our Alliance Bible Seminary to Indonesia, Viet Nam, and Cambodia, but due to the difficulty of securing visas for Indonesia, none were sent there, and only six were sent to Viet Nam and Cambodia. Now there are two beautiful and suitable Alliance churches erected by Chinese Christians in Cambodia and Viet Nam. In fact, now the graduates . . . are scattered in many countries of South East Asia. . . .[31]

The report from Japan was even more electrifying;

> In 1958 . . . Miss Mutsuko Minomiya felt the call [of God] to go to Brazil as a missionary. . . . It was next to impossible for a single lady to obtain permission from the government to go to Brazil . . . the large sum required for passage and other necessities presented no small problem. God in a wonderful way made it possible for her to obtain a passport and the

financial need was abundantly provided. In April, 1959, we sent her as our first missionary to Brazil.[32]

These reports, coupled with the message by Dr. Louis King on "The Bible Basis for Missionary Giving," resulted in a deep moving of the Spirit on the hearts of all who were present. The findings committee of the conference reported,

> We wish to express our admiration of the Japanese and Hong Kong initiatives in sending missionaries actually to far off foreign countries. We recognize that every church small or large can launch into a foreign missionary program and that while our immediate field should not be neglected, we should launch out into foreign missionary work even before our own field is entirely evangelized.[33]

The Vietnam delegation to that conference returned home with a new vision and a new challenge. They enthusiastically shared their reports with the church committee at the national level. The new impetus and interest set two things in motion simultaneously. First, the national committee moved quickly to appoint a couple to serve as "foreign" missionaries in Laos. Their work assignment was threefold: ministry to the Vietnamese minority in Vientiane, join the North American missionaries in possible ministries among the Lao people, and reach the Black Thai refugees who had moved out of North Vietnam when the Communist government was established there. Second, the national church conference held in June, 1963, was to be a great missionary convocation.

What a memorable and moving experience that 1963 conference was! All of the initiative and planning were in the hands of the national committee. I attended at their invitation to participate in the spiritual ministry of the church, as well as to observe its functioning in self-administration, a long-established pattern.[34] Seldom in my entire life have I been so deeply moved as during those days of conference. I felt we all were experiencing a historic transition when the missionary passion which had so characterized the C&MA in North America was ignited in marvelous fashion in the church in Vietnam. Missionary giving increased dramatically. Young people offered themselves for service wherever the Lord might call them and the church might send them. Missions, both in the central mountain and plateau areas of their own country as well as beyond their national borders, has been a live issue with the evangelical church since that time.

Subsequent agreements between mission and church have resulted in all of the "specialized workers" sent to work among the tribespeople coming under the support system of the church. These men and their wives are known as missionaries in a very real sense, for their ministries are among people who speak a different language and whose cultures differ greatly from their own.

SEARCH FOR RENEWED EVANGELISTIC FERVOR

In 1965 there was a deep longing on the part of many in the church and in the mission for God to do something new. At a joint committee meeting, one of the younger pastors asked, "What new program does the mission have to propose or talk to us about at this time?" There was nothing of significant note. How could one be expected to have new plans and programs when the military situation was so shaky, and the future held out little promise for improvement? We would continue with the regular programs!

The church had known a long history of blessing and success in its evangelistic efforts. By the late 1930s there had been some periods of remarkable growth through people movements and expansion through kinship ties. Then in 1938 the ministry of Dr. John Sung of China "made such an impact on the church that years and decades later, many Christians and preachers still remembered his flaming Bible messages and referred to his meetings as the turning point of their life and ministry . . . the impetus given to evangelism and evangelistic activities was felt everywhere."[35] As a result of the 1938 revival, prayer groups and witness bands were organized across the land. Those who joined the witness band pledged themselves to spend a part of one day every week witnessing for Christ. After many years, this became mere routine for some, though for others it was still a vital exercise.

But in 1965, almost thirty years later, there were stirrings in the hearts of a number of people for something new from the Lord. Reports had come of Evangelism-in-Depth programs carried on in some Latin American republics. Would something of a similar nature be possible here? A special committee on evangelism was appointed by the mission at its annual conference. After several months of reading, study and prayer, this committee was convinced that any program simply developed by the mission and passed on to the church was doomed to failure. The final recommendation was for a spiritual-life retreat for all pastors and missionaries (men only). It would be a time of sharing concerns, of seeking God's face as brethren, and of seeking to deepen fellowship with one another. If it pleased the Lord that out of this gathering should be born a new program for evangelism, all would rejoice.

That conference held in March, 1966, was another highlight. God came down in our midst! Hearts were melted, confessions made, misunderstandings settled, the deep movings of the Spirit in the hearts of many were attested! An important preliminary step had been taken in preparation for a saturation evangelism program later to be born in the hearts of two men.

The Fourth Asia Conference was held in Hong Kong in June, 1966. The Vietnam delegation was particularly prepared in heart to hear the firsthand report from Maharashtra, India, of the saturation evangelism program recently concluded there. A report was also brought to the conference by the area secretary for Africa, G. C. Klein, regarding "New Life For All" crusades in some African countries. The summary statement of the conference said, "Your committee calls upon every delegation to endeavor to implement this program within each country."[36]

At the next joint meeting of the church-mission committee

in Vietnam, much time was given to discussion of evangelism. It seemed that Evangelism-in-Depth, translated into Vietnamese, would not express all that was felt by those most deeply interested. After experimenting with several names, it was decided that "Truyen-Dao Sao Rong" (Evangelism Deep and Wide) would be best. Some months later the program itself began to emerge as God particularly laid it upon the hearts of Doan Van Mieng, president of the church, and Franklin Irwin, missionary. Word from Vietnam in late 1971 states,

> Our Evangelism Deep and Wide Conference at Dalat with five leaders from each district was extremely blessed. . . . There was a wonderful spirit of love and unity in the burden to bring salvation to Vietnam. It was especially good to see that they feel this is THEIR program and not one handed them by the mission. These men will be training pastors in various seminars during the month of December in preparation for the program of 1972.[37]

CONCLUSION

Other subjects could be discussed to illustrate the outworkings of a mission-church relationship that has resulted in dynamic church leadership under the hand of God. But from the examples given, several general principles can be distilled:

1. Firm policies were clearly spelled out, and the missionaries were expected to adhere to them.

2. Well-defined channels of communication were always open between leaders of the church and mission.

3. A readiness to negotiate those items not considered an encroachment on the rights, privileges and responsibilities of the developing church characterized all involved.

4. A continuing emphasis on evangelism and church-planting as the responsibility of both church and mission was maintained.

5. A forum was provided in the Asia conferences where a developing church in one country could become an encouragement and an example to churches in other countries. In this

regard, I am reminded of what Paul said when writing to the believers at Thessalonica, "Ye were ensamples to all that believe in Macedonia and Achaia" (1 Th 1:7).

NOTES

1. "Ky Niem 60 Nam Tin-Lanh Truyen Den Viet-Nam" ("Report of 60 Years of Evangelical Ministry in Vietnam") (Saigon, 1970).
2. *Policies and Procedures of the Foreign Department* (New York: The Christian and Missionary Alliance, 1970), p. 7.
3. *Missionary Atlas, A Manual of the Foreign Department of The Christian and Missionary Alliance* (Harrisburg, Pa.: Christian Pubns., revised as of June 30, 1964), p. 3.
4. Louis L. King, "A Presentation of the Indigenous Church Policy of The Christian and Missionary Alliance" (Paper read at a missionary conference held in Charlotte, N.C., in 1957).
5. *Policies and Procedures,* p. 99.
6. Phu Hoang Le, "The Evangelical Church of Viet Nam During the Second World War and The War of Independence," (Master's thesis, Wheaton College, Wheaton, Ill., 1967), p. 27.
7. Ibid., p. 4.
8. *See also* King, "Mission/Church Relations Overseas" in *Missions in Creative Tension,* ed. Vergil Gerber (South Pasadena, Calif.: William Carey Library, 1971).
9. I. R. Stebbins, "The Indigenous Church of Viet Nam."
10. Phu Hoang Le, p. 42.
11. Ibid., pp. 43-44.
12. Ibid., p. 57.
13. *Report of the Asia Conference* (Bangkok, Thailand, 1955), p. 82.
14. Ibid., p. 85.
15. Ibid., p. 74.
16. *Report of the Second Asia Conference* (Saigon, Vietnam, 1958).
17. King, "A Presentation of the Indigenous Church Policy."
18. *Report of the Second Asia Conference.*
19. Board of Managers minute no. 6/58 (Board of Managers meeting, Apr. 8-10, 1958), p. 2.
20. Phu Hoang Le, p. 43.
21. *Policies and Procedures,* p. 7.
22. King, "Mission/Church Relations."
23. *Policies and Procedures,* p. 99.
24. Phu Hoang Le, p. 30.
25. "Ky Niem 60."
26. Letter written by R. N. Ziemer, Feb. 24, 1959.
27. Phu Hoang Le, p. 30.
28. Ibid., p. 38.
29. Letter written by J. H. Revelle, Feb. 26, 1959.
30. *Report of the Third Asia Conference* (Zamboanga, Philippines, 1961).
31. Ibid.
32. Ibid.
33. Ibid., Findings no. 4.
34. J. H. Revelle, Chairman's Narrative Report for 1958.
35. Phu Hoang Le, p. 32.
36. *Report of the Fourth Asia Conference* (Hong Kong, 1966).
37. Letter written by T. H. Stebbins, Nov. 17, 1971.

*Certain risks are inevitably involved in the process
of turning a work over to the nationals. But,
as all missionaries know, they are risks that must
be taken if the new church is to develop in a
healthy way. With commendable transparency,
Melvin Hodges has described some aspects of
the turnover process that he knows from firsthand
experience with Assemblies of God work in
Latin America. Contrasting the polarization which
occurred in one case with the harmony of the
other will provide the reader with valuable
insights into principles of missionary work.*

10

POLARIZATION AND HARMONY

by MELVIN L. HODGES

The Assemblies of God has missionaries working in all of
the countries of Latin America. National organizations in all
the countries are found in different stages of development.
While we cannot claim that there have been no problems in the
area of missions and church relationships, yet, as a whole, rela-

MELVIN L. HODGES has been Field Secretary for Latin America and
the West Indies for the Assemblies of God for eighteen years. Prior to
assuming that position he served as a missionary to Nicaragua and El
Salvador for fourteen years. His duties include coordinating the work
of his church in twenty-six countries where the Assemblies of God
count 278 missionaries and some 11,000 national ministers. Mr.
Hodges' book, first published under the title, *The Indigenous Church,*
and then in revised form under *Growing Young Churches,* is a standard
textbook in evangelical Bible colleges all over North America. He is
also one of the coauthors of *Church Growth and Christian Mission,* edited by Donald McGavran, and has published numerous articles on
missions in leading evangelical publications.

185

tionships have been harmonious and fruitful, and some pit-falls have been avoided. It seems evident to us that policies developed after much experience have contributed significantly to this trend.

First, all Assembly of God missionaries have been oriented to aim for the goal of a self-governing, self-supporting indigenous church in each country.

NATIONAL-MISSIONARY EQUALITY

In order to attain this goal, a national organization has been formed early in the history of the work in each country, with a constitution which places missionaries and national pastors on the same level of privilege. Election to official positions is limited only by the ability of each worker to meet the requirements of the constitution and to secure the backing of fellow workers. In several cases, national organizations have begun with as few as four or five churches. Quite logically, the missionaries fill posts of leadership in the beginning, since they have brought the work into existence, and the younger workers who are pastoring prefer that a missionary take this responsibility. In this position, the missionary teaches by example in the same manner that he has led the way in the development of other areas of church life. It is specifically desired that nationals fill all posts for which they are eligible. Often in the beginning certain limitations of the constitution, requiring a stipulated degree of experience in the ministry for certain offices, are temporarily suspended to allow new workers to participate. This helps avoid a missionary-dominated organization. Admittedly, this procedure is somewhat risky, but we have not been disappointed in the outcome.

Usually our missionaries, attuned to the political climate of the country and being aware of the advantage of national brethren making their own decisions, seek to be relieved of their administrative posts as soon as possible. In a few cases they have insisted on this even before it seemed that the national ministers were actually ready for the change.

Since there are no restrictions on nationals filling executive positions as soon as they have obtained sufficient maturity and experience to command the respect of their own brethren, there is a minimum of feeling that the missionary is smothering national initiative. This greatly mitigates against a "power struggle" between missionaries and nationals. In most cases, the transition to complete national leadership has been achieved without serious tensions.

PATTERN OF PROGRESS

However, since people are still people, some risks are involved. Usually before national leadership is attained with a corresponding partnership participation on the part of the missionaries, a certain oscillation between extreme positions is experienced. The progress has been more or less as follows:

1. The work is originally developed with missionaries prominent in leadership.

2. A national leadership develops in this situation, and usually, if relationships between missionaries and national pastors have been wholesome and cordial, the first national superintendent will be someone close to the missionaries who has worked well with them.

3. Often, if the national superintendent is too much of a follower and depends too much on the missionaries, some dissatisfaction is likely to develop against him on the part of the more aggressive national leaders. They may complain that although a missionary is not superintendent, he is actually running the field through the superintendent who is more or less of a puppet.

4. The reaction against the national superintendent in this case may develop to the point that someone with more radical tendencies is placed in the office. At this stage, some of the nationals may be a little overconfident and the missionaries may feel that their ministry in the country is threatened. They may even feel unwanted. This is where maturity, understand-

ing and patience on the part of the missionary must be exercised.

5. At this juncture, one of two developments may transpire:

a. The strong nationalistic leader may push his point of view too far, and a reaction against his policies may result. Being young and without too much experience, he may push his point of view so far that the more conservative element begins to assert itself again. The leader may find himself without sufficient following, and the post may go to someone else; either a missionary may be returned temporarily to the office, or, a more moderate national leader, who can avoid polarizing his position, will be placed in control. This latter creates a position whereby missionaries can work out a partnership relationship with the national church and enjoy fruit and growth for a long period.

b. The nationalistic leader may quickly learn that the work is more difficult than he had anticipated, and modify his extreme position. If he comes to the conclusion that the missionary is not a threat to his position of leadership, a better understanding may be reached and he may come to the missionary for counsel and guidance in difficult questions.

Happily, many of the fields have avoided the problem of extremism, so the transition to complete national leadership has taken place in a tension-free atmosphere. So much depends upon the personalities involved; the greater the maturity and leadership among both nationals and missionaries, the smoother the transition will be. To illustrate these principles, we will examine two Latin American fields without identifying the countries or workers involved.

POLARIZATION IN REPUBLIC X

In Republic X, missionary work was begun in a period when the importance of indigenous church principles was neither fully understood nor widely practiced. Consequently, the work in this country did not follow the pattern as explained above. In the beginning, missionaries dominated the work completely. Even with the rise of national leadership, the missionaries found it difficult to give recognition to nationals who did not have equal training and background.

In spite of this lack of understanding, relations for the most part were cordial and national leadership began to develop. A Bible school was established which trained national pastors, and the work prospered. However, as the missionaries kept a rather firm control on the work, an element in the national leadership began to seek more independence.

In due time, a young missionary came out to the field who favored the national church leadership. He began to encourage the leaders to assert their prerogative. As a result, this young missionary was made superintendent of the field with strong backing from the nationals.

The inevitable happened. A polarization sprang up in the missionary family, some standing with the young missionary superintendent and the national leadership, and some holding out for the status quo with missionary leadership in control.

The field entered a tumultuous period of tension. Finally, the national leadership demanded to have a greater voice in the Bible institute and to have a say as to who the director would be. This was resisted on the part of some of the missionaries involved who felt that the Bible school was the missionaries' particular domain and that a move toward national leadership in this area was a "rebellion" against the missionaries.

The national church leadership was strong enough to find the necessary support, and they voted a national brother in as director of the school. They invited the missionaries formerly in charge to remain as teachers.

At this point the matter perhaps could have been resolved peaceably if the missionaries could have acceded to this desire. It was likely that the missionary would have been placed back in the school as director within a couple of years if he had been willing to go along with this new arangement. However, these missionaries considered the matter as a personal affront and a repudiation of their missionary ministry. They decided, rather, to change fields and go elsewhere.

In the meantime the Bible institute under national leadership ran into problems. Because the new director was not prepared for his responsibilities, he made serious mistakes. The nationals then returned a missionary to the post. However, it was a missionary who had shown understanding with the national leadership in the time of crisis.

Much the same thing happened in the superintendency, although there was not as much resistance here. When the young missionary who had stood with the national leadership through the crisis retired from the field, they elected a national to take his place. However, after a couple of years, they returned a missionary to this post for a period of two or three years. Then a national was chosen as superintendent once again.

At the present time a national is superintendent of the work, and a qualified national is in charge of the Bible institute. Missionaries work in the Bible institute and have developed a partnership with the national church. The time of tensions is over, and it now seems that missionaries and national church relationships will be harmonious and fruitful in the future.

From this experience we can learn two important lessons:

1. When missionaries cling too tightly to the privileges of their position, they lose more than they gain. Missionaries do well to remember that their principal calling is not administrative, but to plant and strengthen the church. Missionaries do not have to fill certain ecclesiastical posts in order to be effective for God.

2. If basic attitudes are right, extreme positions will moderate so that the church can move along in a more normal fashion. Understanding, patience and love on the part of a missionary will help hasten this process.

It is my conviction that the two things which cause the most tension are the handling of money and holding too tightly to administrative authority. There is always a place for a missionary who has a spiritual ministry and love in his heart for the people.

HARMONY IN REPUBLIC Y

The development of the Assemblies of God in Republic Y can be considered a good case study of normal relationships.

The work there was started when revival in a neighboring country spilled over the border and three or four small rural churches were started in that area. Late in the '30s a young missionary was appointed to nurture this small but promising work. When there were five or six small organized churches in the country, the first conference was called and the work organized.

The missionary continued as superintendent for a period of years. In the meantime he was joined by other missionary helpers, although there have never been more than four missionary families on the field at one time.

After a few years, the first national superintendent was elected and the work continued to develop. The missionaries spent their time teaching in the Bible institute, in visiting new fields, and encouraging new congregations.

The work has now had two national superintendents. The present superintendent has been in office for more than fifteen years. There are two Bible schools and the churches number over 300, with approximately 12,000 believers. Some 200 students attend the Bible schools. Twenty-six new churches were added last year.

The relationship of missionary with national is normal and harmonious. Small irritations have occasionally developed, but these are smoothed out in the presbytery where missionaries and nationals meet. Missionaries serve as counselors on the general presbytery, but hold no executive office. Missionaries usually direct the Bible schools at the request of the nationals, although the nationals are increasingly occupying more positions on the teaching staff.

Missionaries are respected, honored and loved. National pastors consider it a great honor for a missionary to visit their churches. Requests are sometimes received that more missionary couples should be sent.

In the more than thirty years that this work has developed, there has been no missionary-national crisis.

Perhaps one reason for the good relationship has been the low ratio of the number of missionaries to the number of pastors. The larger the number of missionaries on a field, the more likelihood that the nationals will feel threatened by their presence.

Even more important, these missionaries have all been firm believers in the policy of developing national leadership. Missionaries have been glad to see nationals develop in their ministry and administrative capacities. The nationals, in turn, respect and seek the counsel of the missionaries.

*The development of a new African missionary-
sending society of some 100 missionaries with an
annual unsubsidized budget of over $20,000
is one highly visible indication that the Sudan
Interior Mission has been doing some things right
in West Africa. In this chapter Ian Hay describes the principles upon which the SIM, one of
IFMA's largest missions, related to the African
church in a way that stimulated healthy church
growth and indigenous missionary outreach.*

11

THE EMERGENCE OF A MISSIONARY-MINDED CHURCH IN NIGERIA

by Ian M. Hay

At Green Lake '71 the four hundred delegates urged mission societies "to discover forms of church-mission-church relationships that allow for the fullest scriptural expression of the missionary nature and purpose of the church."[1] This chapter will attempt to suggest some guidelines which have proved useful in Africa and which may be useful elsewhere.

IAN M. HAY is North America Director for the Sudan Interior Mission. He holds the B.A. (cum laude) from Bryan College and the M.A. (summa cum laude) from Columbia Bible College Graduate School of Missions. Mr. Hay has thirteen years of experience as a missionary in Nigeria, both in church-planting among the Gbari people and as the Field Secretary for the Sudan Interior Mission for West Africa. He serves as President of the Evangelical Missions Information Service, and is a board member of the Interdenominational Foreign Mission Association and of Bryan College.

Fellowship and Flexibility

There is strong scriptural evidence to show that a break in fellowship within the body of Christ will hinder the development of the body and the working of the Holy Spirit. "Can two walk together except they be agreed?" Peter warns that the prayers of a married couple will be hindered if their fellowship is broken. Is this not also true in regard to church/mission relationships? If the mission organization and the church which has grown up as a result of that mission's operation are not walking in fellowship and harmony, the growth of that church will be hindered. Its evangelism and missionary outreach will be lost.

One of the significant factors producing church growth is the relationship between the new church and the mission agency that was used of God to bring it into being. The mission must be big enough to plan for changes in relationship which may alter its working patterns without considering such changes as defeat.

Missions, like all organizations, must be dynamic if they are to be viable. They must face change realistically. This has always been true. Our times make it even more so now.

Books seem to be tumbling off the presses telling of the rapidity of change and its effect on modern man. One of today's best sellers begins with this warning:

> In the three short decades between now and the twenty-first century, millions of ordinary, psychologically normal people will face an abrupt collision with the future.[2]

Technocrats are not alone in their concern. Mission and church leaders are well aware that the pace has accelerated. The individual missionary must ponder just how these rapid changes affect his personal relationship with the national church.

Changing Africa

Nowhere is this more evident than in Africa. The facts of

political change are well known; they have been phenomenal. The altered course of history will continue its march in a new direction. The old colonial days are long gone. Those "winds of change" of 1960 have reached hurricane velocity now! The Christian faces a kaleidoscopic future. The greatest contemporary change in Africa is the fact of the existing church with its very remarkable strength and growth.

Any study of the relationship between church and mission must allow for such changes. At each stage of the growth of the church the relationship will differ. Disaster awaits those missions and individual missionaries who either will not or cannot adapt. The luxury of maintaining the status quo is no longer an option. Yesterday's relationships, correct as they may have been in their time, do not suit today's situation.

The following is an analysis of the growth of one church association and the relationships which now exist with a foreign mission society. Specifically, we will describe the relationship between the Sudan Interior Mission and the Association of Evangelical Churches of West Africa.

The Background

The Sudan Interior Mission began its work in Nigeria in 1893. The story of the early struggles, of the death and defeat, is well known. It took twelve years of hard labor before the first church came into being.

By 1950 the first stage of SIM pioneering in Nigeria had almost ended. The leaders sensed the end of the era of the mission's maintaining authority and sole organizational responsibility. The time had come for the churches, separated as they were into geographical tribal units, to be brought together for fellowship and strengthening. Prior to this the individual church groups which had developed around "mission stations" were only faintly aware of the existence of other such groups. Travel and communication had been difficult, if not impossible. But this had all changed. Many factors had now come together: Nigeria was approaching independence, nationalism was growing, and remarkably rapid church growth was beginning. These all demanded more cohesion for the church. As a minority group in animistic and Islamic cultures, the churches needed to know each other and to share their faith in Christ. At this time SIM organized the first general conference of church leaders.

In May, 1954, forty-five years after the first ten converts had been baptized at Egbe, Nigeria, elected representatives of 337 churches met there to officially recognize the existence of a new autonomous church body. The Association of the Evangelical Churches of West Africa was born. David Olatayo, first president of ECWA says,

> We the members of the organization known as the Association of Evangelical Churches of West Africa were formerly adherents of the Sudan Interior Mission.
>
> But by the grace of God the work has grown. We formed ourselves into a church body, drew up a constitution and registered with the government of Nigeria in 1956. Our organization consists of local churches, local councils, eight district councils, a general assembly and our own missionary arm.[3]

THE NATURE OF ECWA

ECWA is an association of theologically conservative and strongly evangelical churches. It has a congregational-type structure with autonomy for the churches and a general assembly to coordinate activities, a structure which seems to fit well in the African culture out of which it has grown. The first paragraph of the constitution explains the purpose of the organization:

> To maintain a society for the support of public worship of God the Father through Jesus Christ, our Lord, to minister in the Word of God and to promote evangelism.[4]

The founding of ECWA was the fulfillment of early SIM

policies. It is the outgrowth of the church-planting methods instituted by the pioneers and firmly established by godly African leaders. "Looking beyond the preaching of the gospel, Dr. Bingham (pioneer and founder of SIM) and the leaders of SIM saw their ultimate goal—the establishment of the church in Africa."[5]

The early missionaries of SIM had entered Nigeria when serious thought was being given by most mission strategists to what later was to be called "indigenous church principles." From the beginning the writings of John Nevius and Roland Allen were studied and applied to the Nigerian scene. All missions in West Africa owe a debt to Henry Venn, general secretary of the Church Missionary Society during the nineteenth century.

Venn is a "legendary figure in Protestant Missions. He exerted a powerful influence in shaping the common pattern of the missionary enterprise through the nineteeth century, an influence that continued in a considerable measure right down to the middle of the twentieth century."[6] The work of SIM in Nigeria which resulted in ECWA was profoundly affected by Venn's ideas. The work was founded and maintained along those principles as adapted to fit the local scene.

Moses Ariye, ECWA pastor and evangelist, recorded the story at the church's tenth anniversary in 1964:

> Right from the beginning, the SIM has been working towards an indigenous church, so all the churches they started have been self-supporting. That is what it has been right from the beginning. ECWA is an association formed out of the work of SIM in Nigeria. These churches were begun by the SIM or by converts of the SIM.
>
> ECWA is a government recognized group, registered exactly ten years ago. Each church is self-governing in itself, but we associated ourselves together because of our common origin and interest.
>
> The SIM doesn't actually exercise any authority at all in

ECWA. We only have SIM as an advisor. Someone, such as the Field Director, has a chance to sit on the general church council, but they are advisors. . . . The Africans are actually running the work.[7]

ECWA has come a long way. Having passed through the early stage of foreign missionary evangelism and church-planting, she has developed into an organizational entity. Following her birth and subsequent partnership with SIM, she has seen remarkable growth and response, as these statistics reveal:

Year	No. of Churches	Sunday Attendance	Communicants	Pastors and Evangelists
1908	1	unknown	10	0
1954	400	50,000	14,700	583
1964	900	300,000	21,000	650
1970	1400	400,000	60,000	1700

ECWA MATURITY AND MISSIONARY OUTREACH

ECWA has grown to be a responsible, mature church. It could be described in Beyerhaus' words as follows:

one which reaches out, not only after support, protection, instruction or even inspiration, but also in mission and service, in discipleship modeled on its Lord—who came not to be ministered unto but to minister—making its own contribution to the world-wide task of building up the Body of Christ in love. Giving as well as receiving.[8]

Perhaps the best illustration of ECWA's maturity is seen in the growth and development of its missionary arm. Such a development is the final proof that a church is really functioning as such, that it has grown to maturity. The missionary fulfillment of the commission of Jesus Christ has not been completed until the "all things that I have commanded you" have been communicated with understanding and response. Douglas Webster said,

> The surest sign that the gospel has taken root in a new culture is the growing up of missionaries from that culture to reach out further still. The gospel is received in order to be retransmitted. Missions are integral to genuine Christianity. . . .[9]

Louis King emphasized the same point at Green Lake '71 in this way:

> The quality of their spiritual life and experience should be seen in their own evangelizing power. Hence the so-important thing is not the process whereby the mission operates and evangelizes, but rather the character of the spiritual life and experience of the church, which if healthy will lead into evangelism itself. The objective is the creation of a witnessing church in which the Holy Spirit will achieve Christ's purpose in winning lost peoples.[10]

Missionaries have always passed on this emphasis if they have been in any sense faithful to their own calling. On October 8, 1866, Henry Venn sent the following message to the Christians of Africa:

> But while we thus entreat you as children of the light, to walk as before God, worthy of your Christian profession, the thought at this Season uppermost in our minds is the responsibility resting upon you as a Native-Christian Church, in the midst of a heathen land, to cultivate and exercise a Missionary spirit. . . . We wish, dear brethren, this day to lead you faithfully to enquire how far YOU are remembering your duty to *yourselves!* Shall ENGLAND remember Africa, but AFRICA forget *herself?*[11]

AFRICAN MISSIONARY WORK

This emphasis has been a major part of SIM strategy. The development of the Evangelical Missionary Society in Nigeria is a prime example of how a foreign mission and a national church work together.

The EMS was begun by the Sudan Interior Mission. In 1949 (five years before the beginning of ECWA) the SIM West Africa Council organized an effort to help the church fulfill its responsibility in foreign mission, to go beyond its own borders, to cross cultural lines in witness. The mission council outlined the following at that time:

1. Instruction in personal responsibility for the salvation of others is to be intensified in the teaching of the Word of God.

2. Information portraying the need of areas outside of their own Jerusalem and Judea is to be given to educate the churches in the foreign missions concept.

3. It is recommended to all churches that one Sunday a month be set aside for foreign missions and an emphasis is to be given on the receiving of offerings to support that work.

4. An organization to be known as the African Missionary Society of the Sudan Interior Mission is to be set up so that the churches can cooperate in a corporate endeavor.

5. This missionary organization is to be governed by a group of African church leaders in partnership with SIM representatives chosen by the Field Council of SIM.

6. An SIM missionary is to be set apart to be full time secretary of AMS.

7. Financial responsibility for the African Missionary Society is to be entirely African.

8. The rules, principles and practice of the society are to be formulated by its own council and approved by the SIM Field Council.[12]

These minutes show that the initial thrust of ECWA's foreign missionary arm came through SIM. In those days the basic control was foreign and missionary, not church. This quickly changed, however.

In 1952 many changes were made when the church organization emerged. The governing council of the African Missionary Society was reorganized, with African representation now made by the different church districts. The AMS council also appointed two Africans to work full time with the SIM missionary secretary.

In 1953, seventeen church leaders met with four mission representatives to review and reassess the AMS and its relationship to SIM and to the new church organization which was coming into being. A year later ECWA was organized and registered with the Nigerian government. At that time the AMS was integrated into the new church organization, passing from SIM control to the control of ECWA. The AMS council became completely African, with its representatives chosen by the church districts of ECWA. The SIM secretary shared the responsibility of the work with an African appointed by the AMS council.

At this time SIM and AMS entered into a comity agreement. Areas of the unevangelized sections of Nigeria and neighboring countries were allocated to one or the other.

By 1958 the appointment of the SIM missionary as secretary was withdrawn, for the time had come for complete national leadership. At first the AMS council was reluctant to accept this view, so it was agreed that for a period of time a representative of the SIM would continue to serve as an adviser to the council and meet with them in their sessions. The SIM was firm in its conviction, however, that an SIM missionary should no longer bear responsibility for AMS. An African secretary was then appointed by the church and AMS council.[13]

In 1964 the name of the mission was changed to Evangelical Missionary Society. The society was a part of ECWA since its founding in 1954, but it was autonomous as far as administration was concerned. In 1970 the church accepted complete responsibility for the administration of the EMS program as part of its evangelistic and missionary outreach. The growth of this missionary outreach can be seen in the following chart:

GROWTH OF THE EVANGELICAL MISSIONARY SOCIETY
OF ECWA

Year	Personnel*	Income to EMS from ECWA
1950	27	$ 1,534.28
1951	?	1,749.60
1952	?	4,889.80
1953	?	5,846.40
1954	?	6,696.99
1955	?	7,451.28
1956	?	6,897.59
1957	53	6,797.79
1958	55	7,270.98
1959	56	7,974.40
1960	60	8,884.20
1961	65	10,691.20
1962	65	13,103.74
1963	75	12,228.33
1964	85	13,472.50
1965	85	14,772.06
1966	87	17,923.84
1967	87	19,095.82
1968	91	18,858.96
1969	93	20,631.72
1970	97	20,682.79

*The numbers represent the heads of families only. All are married and have families. The wives are also considered missionaries, but are not counted here.

LESSONS FROM THE PIONEERS

The present working relationship between SIM and ECWA is one of partnership. As one African leader put it, "We believe in hand-in-hand ministry of the missionaries and the nationals. We Africans believe in this, especially in Nigeria. . . . We believe in cooperative effort."[14]

Partnership does not describe what the relationship has always been. Changing times and the growth of the church have brought this. The tie between mission and church in days gone by was different. In the same way, the relationship which exists now may not be best for tomorrow. Here is where flexibility and adaptation are needed. To make this work, right attitudes are imperative. As George Peters said at GL '71, "Partnership of equality and mutuality is as much an attitude, a relationship, a philosophy, a way of missions, as it is a pattern of legislation and administration."[15] In each generation, missionaries are called upon to find the best way to relate to the church for the ultimate good of the church. That is the goal. All too often, however, since they are human, missionaries react in ways which may be detrimental.

Rooted in Nigeria's history is the story of relationships between missionaries and the people. A generation before the SIM pioneers went to the "interior" of Nigeria, other missionaries had been at work in the coastal areas. Those missionaries had strong influence. This has been carefully recorded by J. F. Ade Ajayi in his book, *Christian Missions in Nigeria, 1841-1891.*[16]

Professor Ajayi's analysis of the effect of missions on the country is penetrating. The evidence of missionary influence in politics and involvement in trade makes fascinating reading for those trained to avoid these pitfalls. He states that missionaries and traders were interdependent, a relationship that made for strange partners.

SIM pioneers learned from those experiences and sought to avoid the pitfalls. The fact remains, however, that the attitudes of paternalism and colonialism were part of their makeup. The missionaries were men of their times. Though they did avoid the political and economic ties, the mission/church relationships which existed were paternal. The missionary was the father, the African Christian his son. This obviously affected the relationship which grew up between church and mission. For over fifty years the paternalistic pattern was dominant.

It is easy for those of us living in the late twentieth century to be critical of the past generations' failures. Our vantage point in history perhaps does permit broader vision. The tragedy is not so much what happened in the past; it occurs when we who work today try to maintain those same types of relationships, or when we are so busy confessing the sins of our forefathers that we fail to note the errors we ourselves are now making. The next generation will not fail to point them out to us!

The failures of the early missionaries so evident in history only serve to emphasize that what has been done in Nigeria is God's work despite man's foolishness. Missionaries are human. In spite of them God used their witness to His glory. One can but praise Him that what has been established in Nigeria, emerging from feeble beginnings, is a strong church which will stand and grow.

Today's Relationship

Today the relationship existing between ECWA and SIM is one which fits the desire of ECWA leaders for a close working tie. Byang Kato, past general secretary of ECWA, expressed this at Urbana '70 when he concluded his address:

> Does the national church want missionaries? The answer is emphatically positive. These are days of harvest in many fields. The net is breaking. We are beckoning to you to come and join us, draw the net. We are not inviting you to come and be the boss. Neither are we calling you to come and serve us. But we want you to come, realizing that our Lord Jesus Christ is the master of the harvest. We are all going to be partners under the Lordship of Christ, for we are "workers together with him."[17]

In the bond between ECWA and SIM each recognizes the other as a separate entity. Three categories are noted in the work:

1. factors which pertain to the church alone
2. factors which pertain to the mission alone
3. factors which pertain to both

This has worked well in practice. The principle for success is based on complete openness with good communications at all levels. This communication has been made possible by mutual representation at the highest level of mission and church councils and by the establishment of joint committees to develop policies which affect both church and mission.

The rationale for this type of relationship has been summed up by SIM General Director Raymond J. Davis:

> The primary objective of ascertaining and maintaining the proper relationship of church and mission as separate organizations is the recognition of Christ as the Head of the church. When looking to him as the progenitor, sustainer, and ultimate glory of the church, there is not only no need for the church to look to any other for complete provision of all that she may need, but in the measure in which she does look to another is the Holy Spirit ignored and grieved. Therefore, the church will best look to Christ for her spiritual life, her guidance, her material resources. The freedom and liberty of oneness in fellowship and separation of organization, releases both men and material possessions for the continual expansion of Christ's kingdom in obedience to the Head of the church.[18]

PRACTICAL IMPLICATIONS

ECWA is an autonomous church which has taken over large areas of work which once were handled by SIM. Elementary and secondary schools, dispensaries, and Bible schools are now controlled by a virile church. Some missionaries of SIM assist the church in some of these programs where there is still need. In the major areas of Nigeria in which SIM worked, there are churches which are self-governing, self-supporting and self-propagating. This being true, what is the place of SIM? What methods and resources will be used in the future and for how long? These questions must be answered realistically. How they are answered will affect relationships. Perhaps the thinking of SIM will assist others working in similar circumstances.[19]

EVANGELISM

There are still multitudes that have not accepted Christ and large numbers that have not heard or had an adequate understanding of the Christian message. In this sense there is a big job yet to be done. Who is responsible for continuing this witness? Is SIM responsible for this? Is it a dual responsibility, or should the church assume this with mission assistance in specified areas? Present SIM policy favors the third option for the following reasons:

1. *The church has the resources of personnel.* The growth of the church shows this. The implementation of the New Life for All saturation evangelism program has mobilized this reservoir of manpower. In contrast, SIM has only a handful of people increasingly restricted by government visa policies. The mission task can only be supportive.

2. *The church has the knowledge and organization for the task.* Carefully planned development by joint ECWA-SIM evangelism and church-growth committees has produced a well-organized church with a large number of trained leaders. This organization goes to the grass-roots level, with evangelism committees in district and local church councils.

3. *The church has the rapport and acceptance of the people.* The church does not have to cope with the problem of foreignness. With the local church representing Christ, the presentation of the gospel is indigenous. Africans are presenting to Africans the Saviour who died for Africans.

In accepting the fact that the continuing program of evangelism is mainly the responsibility of the church, SIM considers the following to be its pattern for evangelism as long as such help is needed:

1. *Help organize and set up evangelistic programs.* The success of the New Life for All program was in a great part due to the fact that it was a combined effort of missions and churches. The missionary personnel involved were not many, but they were able to provide much of the know-how in the setting up of the program and in the preparation of the needed materials. This type of help will still be needed for an indefinite

period, but it will be limited to missionaries with the necessary interest, ability, gifts, training and experience.

2. *Hold seminars and training courses on evangelism.*

3. *Make surveys to find areas of need and to help establish priorities.*

4. *Provide supervision where needed.* There are still some areas where the church has not developed beyond the need of some help that can be given by missionary staff. This requires a high degree of mobility and a willingness to serve a group of churches.

5. *Provide financial help.* Financial help is needed in areas of administration, technical help, supply of literature, radio, transportation, etc. In the administration of the New Life for All program, 90 percent of the main office expenses were met from outside sources and 10 percent from the church, whereas on the local level, where evangelism actually took place, 95 percent of the finances came from the church. This type of financial help will still be needed in certain areas of the evangelism program.

TRAINING LEADERS

The training of leadership for the national church is the major area of responsibility for SIM. It must be remembered that this is part of the Great Commission. Leadership training follows solid biblical principles and is Pauline in origin. Care must be taken to share in this responsibility as long as it is beneficial to the growth of the church.

Much of the educational program of SIM is already in the hands of the church. Ten years ago the staff of postprimary institutions was 80 percent missionary and 20 percent national. Today this is reversed, and the missionary percentage will continue to decrease.

The SIM responsibility continues in the following ways:

1. *The training of lay Christians.* As we contemplate the rapid growth of the church in Africa, the importance of a well-trained laity to augment the full-time leadership of the church

cannot be overemphasized. This training will be done by Christian education in the churches, theological education by extension, teaching of religious knowledge in government schools, and local assistance to pastors.

2. *The training of full-time Christian leadership.* SIM missionary personnel is still needed to assist the training of leadership at the Bible college and seminary levels, for much of this program is still beyond the ability of ECWA. SIM will continue to provide funds and personnel for developing and operating the seminary until the church is able to do it.

PROBLEMS

In any kind of relationship as complex as that which exists between ECWA and SIM there are bound to be problems. Eugene Rubingh in his helpful analysis of the growth of the church among the Tiv in Nigeria has a whole chapter which he calls "The Problematics of Partnership." He says that these problems "comprise the particulars of the joint journey of Church and Mission and illustrate the unvarnished confrontation of ideas in conflict on that journey."[20]

There is little room in this study to analyze the problems in any depth. They can only be alluded to, but they should not be ignored.

MEMBERSHIP

One of the major problems facing the church in Africa is the wide divergence between adherants and members. ECWA is well aware of this. At a recent council they viewed the problem this way:

> Bible teaching is needed in our churches: The Problem:
>
> 1. Many who attend church are not members.
> 2. Most of those who attend church never enter any class for Bible instruction.
> 3. During the next two to five years we should expect a large increase in new converts. Our average attendance will double.

4. Many professing Christians do not really know the Lord. They have shown their readiness but we must lead them on carefully to full life and commitment.
5. The above-mentioned condition of the church leads very quickly and easily to three evils:
   a. backsliding into old ways of life.
   b. bringing of pagan practices into the church.
   c. some will turn to false cults.

The remedy is:

1. To teach the whole of our church attenders the fundamentals of Bible knowledge—what is God's purpose for man, his plan of redemption, and how he is working it out in history.
2. To apply this teaching to their daily lives.
3. To do this in the quickest possible way and by the most effective and efficient means.[21]

Recognizing with ECWA the great need in this area, SIM's aim is to help in every way possible to meet this problem.

FINANCE

The problem of finance always looms large in any discussion of church-mission relationships. SIM practice, as has been seen, has been rigid in following indigenous principles. This has applied to finance. However, SIM recognized that the financial needs of a rapidly expanding church cannot be ignored. There are legitimate areas of help. The problem is to locate that fine line between worthwhile and needful assistance without at the same time taking away from the church its own sense of responsibility. Any semblance of economic imperialism or colonialism will harm, not help, the church.

The quantity which each partner brings to the relationship varies at different stages in the development of the church. There are legitimate times for the SIM and its supporting constituency to give financial aid to ECWA in the same manner in which Paul collected funds when the church in Jerusalem had need. To meet this problem SIM has set up the following guidelines:

a. Funds may be applied only to projects which have been approved by the Mission-Church Councils in joint agreement.
b. Requests for approval of projects must come through the proper church administrative channels, and funds must be administered through the same channels.
c. No funds may be used for the direct maintenance of pastors or evangelists in established church areas, unless they are engaged in a project for which the church cannot assume financial responsibility.
d. Support for projects will not be of a nature that the continuation of the church would be endangered if the support were removed.
e. Capital investment funds will usually be approved on the basis of some relative investment by the churches.
f. Funds to meet recurring expenses will be planned, wherever possible, on a diminishing basis, in order to stimulate the increased giving of the church toward the project.[22]

Generally the help will be for such things as financing certain institutions, such as the seminary, or for scholarships for advanced training of leaders.

John Janzen, a Christian anthropologist, has warned,

Whenever generosity of giving, teaching, and helping is of an unconditional character, the recipient must be able to return the gift of some equivalent in order to remain his own respectable self. Otherwise he will begin seeing himself as inferior to the giver; his personal sense of worth is downgraded and instead of being grateful he will be bitter. This set of forces is very much misunderstood in many mission programs today.[23]

INTERPERSONAL RELATIONSHIPS

Perhaps interpersonal relationships are the basis for the greatest problems. "People problems" outweigh all others in our efforts to walk together. George Peters pinpointed this at Green Lake:

> Christianity is basically a religion of life and relationships. Relationships are of deeper significance than organizational structure and identity. The struggle for the preservation of organizational identity must not be permitted to disrupt the spiritual relationships whatever our rights may be.[24]

During the transition stage as ECWA developed there was a tendency to carry things to extremes. In the early days of ECWA, many in SIM bent over backward to help ECWA find its role and place. At times this went too far, so that often church members accused the missionaries of being remote and out of touch. This has been recognized. Now missionaries are encouraged to become associate members of the church and to be active in their local churches.

Some missionaries have been unable to cope with the changing times, while others have not agreed with the structure of ECWA as it developed. On the other hand, there have been instances of ECWA leaders acting in wrong ways toward their brethren in SIM. ECWA is aware of this. As one African wrote, "There is need for SIM and ECWA to understand each other's problems. Lack of this understanding is responsible for the doubts and suspicion that form barriers between them."[25]

INSTITUTIONS

A right solution for large institutions bends the mind of any mission/church strategist. There are institutions which have been legitimate for the mission to operate, but it is debatable whether these same institutions should be a church responsibility. Is is fair to burden a young church with the financial and administrative load of a large hospital, or the management of a large chain of bookstores? Should these be under the church or under a separate board of governors within the Christian community? There are no easy answers. Right solutions to these problems must be found by ECWA and SIM. How they are answered today will affect tomorrow's type of relationship.

Henry Lefever has recognized the problems in all these relationships:

> Great efforts have been made in the course of the last generation, that is in the immediately recent past, to see a solution of the problems raised by the developing autonomy of the churches which have arisen as a consequence of the work of foreign missions. It is not surprising that there should be such problems: they are the expression in the life of the church of those perennial and universal tensions in the life of the family. A satisfying solution in each case, in church and family, requires the grace of the Lord Jesus Christ and understanding of personal relations in the light of the Holy Spirit.[26]

CONCLUSION

Henry Venn spoke of the day when a mission society would complete its work:

> Regarding the ultimate object of a Mission, viewed under its ecclesiastical result, to be the settlement of a Native Church under Native Pastors upon a self-supporting system, it should be borne in mind that the progress of a Mission depends upon the training and the location of Native Pastors; and that, as it has been happily expressed the *"euthanasia* of a Mission" takes place when a missionary, surrounded by well-trained Native congregations under Native Pastors, is able to resign all pastoral work into their hands and gradually relax his superintendence over the pastors themselves, till it insensibly ceases; and so the Mission passes into a settled Christian community. Then the Missionary and all Missionary agencies should be transferred to the "regions beyond".[27]

There will always be plenty of work to do. SIM is not concerned with its "euthanasia" as a society but is concerned that we end with a strong, mature, responsible witness for Jesus Christ in Nigeria. As long as ECWA needs SIM to accomplish that goal, the two will seek new ways of sharing the burden.

NOTES

1. "A Green Lake '71 Affirmation," in *Missions in Creative Tension,* ed. Vergil Gerber (South Pasadena Calif.: William Carey Library, 1971), p. 383.
2. Alvin Toffler, *Future Shock* (New York: Random House, 1970), p. 11.
3. J. H. Hunter, *A Flame of Fire* (Toronto: Sudan Interior Mission, 1961), p. 246.
4. *The Constitution of the Evangelical Churches of West Africa* (Jos, West Africa: ECWA, 1956), p. 3.
5. Hunter, p. 240.
6. Max Warren, ed., *To Apply the Gospel* (Grand Rapids: Eerdmans, 1971). p. 7.
7. Moses Ariye, "Pastor Moses and the Miracle," *Sudan Witness,* June 1964.
8. Peter Beyerhaus and Henry Lefever, *The Responsible Church and the Foreign Mission* (Grand Rapids: Eerdmans, 1964), p. 190.
9. Douglas Webster, *What Is a Mission?* (London: Highway Press, 1958), p. 13.
10. Louis L. King, "Mission/Church Relations Overseas," in *Missions in Creative Tension,* p. 183.
11. Warren, p. 72.
12. Sudan Interior Mission, "West Africa Council Minutes" (Jos, West Africa, private papers, 1949).
13. Raymond J. Davis, "A National Missionary Movement" (Paper presented to the IFMA/EFMA Retreat, 1964).
14. Ariye.
15. George W. Peters, "Mission/Church Relations Overseas," in *Missions in Creative Tension,* p. 224.
16. J. F. Ade Ajayi, *Christian Missions in Nigeria 1841-1891* (Evanston: Northwestern U., 1965).
17. Byang H. Kato, "The National Church: Do They Want Us?" in *Christ the Liberator* (Downers Grove, Ill.: Inter-Varsity, 1971), p. 170.
18. Raymond J. Davis, "Mission/Church Relationships," Furloughing Missionary Seminar Study Papers (New York: Sudan Interior Mission, unpublished papers, 1971), p. 58.
19. William G. Crouch, "The Future Ministry of SIM in West Africa" (Jos, West Africa: Sudan Interior Mission, 1971).
20. Eugene Rubingh, *Sons of Tiv* (Grand Rapids: Baker, 1969), p. 167.
21. Evangelical Church of West Africa, Minutes (Jos, West Africa, private minutes, Oct. 1969).
22. Sudan Interior Mission, *Manual* (New York: Sudan Interior Mission, 1970), pp. 28-29.
23. As quoted in Levi O. Keidel, Jr., "The Peril of Giving," *World Vision Magazine* (Nov. 1971), p. 8.
24. Peters, p. 195.
25. Nigeria School Supervisor (name withheld) (Paper circulated to ECWA and SIM leaders, 1967).
26. Beyerhaus and Lefever, p. 13.
27. Warren, p. 28.

The "syndrome of church development" is a dan-
ger inherent in missionary work that has not
been stressed in evangelical missiological writings
in recent years. C. Peter Wagner in this final
chapter contends that if this syndrome can be
avoided both the mission and the church will be
healthier. He proposes that ultimate mission
objectives be stated, not so much in terms of
the church, as of the "fourth world," and gives
some specific recommendations for implementing
these principles.

12

MISSION AND CHURCH IN FOUR WORLDS

by C. PETER WAGNER

Few readers are likely immediately to understand the significance of the term "four worlds" in the title of this chapter.
It may be one of the first times it has been used in print, since
the "fourth world" is a relatively new term currently being
popularized by a small circle of missiologists.

C. PETER WAGNER is Associate Professor of Latin American Affairs
in the Fuller Theological Seminary School of World Mission and also
Executive Director of the Fuller Evangelistic Association. Before as-
suming these responsibilities he spent sixteen years as a missionary in
Bolivia under the South America Mission and the Andes Evangelical
Mission, most recently as Associate General Director of the AEM.
Mr. Wagner holds the B.S. from Rutgers University, the B.D. and
M.A. from Fuller Theological Seminary, and the Th.M. from Princeton
Theological Seminary. Some of his most recent books include *Latin
American Theology, The Protestant Movement in Bolivia, A Turned-On
Church in an Uptight World, An Extension Seminary Primer* (with
Ralph Covell), and *Frontiers in Missionary Strategy.*

"Third World" is now in common use, however, and is found in several of the other chapters in this book. Although some think the concept is condescending (which are the "first" and "second" worlds, anyway?), it nevertheless is quite useful. It refers to those countries, most of which are below the thirtieth parallel north, populated by the black, brown and yellow races, and struggling against almost impossible odds toward an elusive goal sometimes called "development." Africans, Asians and Latin Americans, together with some minority groups closer to home, share a world view which has many common elements. They feel that history has been unkind to them, that they have been exploited by colonialist and imperialist ambitions of the more affluent nations, that current world policy has cleverly stacked the cards against their attaining a truly just portion of the world's goods, and that present international trends are widening, rather than closing, the gap between the rich and the poor nations.

The Third World nations have to a large extent also been those called "mission fields" and evangelized by Christian missionaries from the first two worlds. When missionaries speak loosely about the "national church" they usually mean those newer churches which are emerging in the Third World. Some missions have stated that their goal has been to plant churches, *indigenous* churches if you will, in the Third World. It is the contention of this chapter that this stated goal, while perhaps innocuous on the surface, is nevertheless in the final analysis truncated. It is good as far as it goes, but it does not go far enough.

By articulating the goal in terms of the church alone, missions may end up betraying their own nature. In the beginning, most missionary visions are focused on the world from which disciples are to be made rather than on the church, which at the very beginning does not yet exist. By their nature missions fulfill their mission primarily in the world. In chapter 1, Jack Shepherd rightly stresses that the proper missionary formula is God-church-world. We must grant that one of the noble, and indeed necessary, results of a successful mission in the world is a church. But if the missionary task is considered accomplished because a church now exists, the original missionary vision has been lost. Note that the *final* element in the formula is the *world*. Disciples are made, not in the church, but in the world.

At this point, the term "fourth world" may be helpful. The "fourth world" embraces all those peoples who, regardless of where they may be located geographically, have yet to come to Christ. In that sense, the fourth world is the top-priority objective of missions.

This pushes the statement of the goal of missions one notch further than the indigenous church. The indigenous church may become a great and dynamic instrument for the continued push toward the fourth world, but it is an unfortunate fact that in some cases it has instead become a hindrance to the discipling of the fourth world.

Therefore, the proper objective of a mission is not merely the establishment of a church, but ideally of a *missionary* church which is in turn moving into the fourth world. If the mission has somehow been unsuccessful in transmitting its own missionary vision to the new church, it has not lived up to its best potential and highest calling.

STUNTED OBJECTIVES STUNT GROWTH

Much more conscious effort needs to be dedicated to clarifying today's missionary objectives than missionary strategists have been willing to invest in the past. To consider the church as an end in itself rather than an instrument for "making disciples" in the fourth world is to adopt a stunted objective. Stunted objectives will sooner or later stunt the fulfillment of the Great Commission.

The primary objective of missions needs to be distinguished from secondary or intermediate objectives. What are some of these intermediate objectives? As we list them, let us state clearly that just because they are intermediate, they are neither bad, inferior nor superfluous. If you live in New York City and want to drive to Pennsylvania, for example, you have to go through New Jersey. While you are moving through New Jersey you are glad to be there, but you are not satisfied with staying there if your goal is Pennsylvania. New Jersey is only an intermediate objective.

Some intermediate missionary objectives include a larger number of workers, an increased budget, more activity in sending and receiving churches, excellence in ministerial training, spiritual revival, culturally relevant liturgy and music, translation of the Scriptures, distribution of certain quantities of Christian literature, wide dissemination of the gospel message through the mass media, the manifestation of social concern, etc. As *intermediate* objectives, all the above and many more good things that missionaries and churchmen do can be very useful in accomplishing the *ultimate* objective of making disciples. If this distinction is kept clear, possibilities of continual, healthy church growth will increase.

A mature church is often another helpful instrument toward making disciples. Certainly, once disciples are made they must gather together in congregations (whether inside or outside of the institutional or more traditional churches is not relevant here) in order to share the *koinonia* or Christian fellowship so necessary for Christian nurture and qualitative growth. But while the church *should* be a help toward the task of reaching into the fourth world and making disciples there, it often is not. In this sense the church can be thought of as the automobile that takes you from New York City to Pennsylvania. If it is in good mechanical condition, it is a great help; but if the carburetor plugs in Jersey City and the transmission goes out in Newark, the car turns out to be a hindrance and you realize you would have accomplished your objective of reaching Pennsylvania better if you had taken the train.

JESUS PEOPLE

As everyone knows, some churches have plugged carburetors, so to speak. They are ineffectual in reaching the fourth world and need to be bypassed. One does not have to go to the Third World to find examples, although they abound there as well. Right here at home we have a abundant supply of churches which have become introverted and centripetal. They give little thought and energy to the task of reaching the fourth world. In the 1960s, for example, a large segment of the fourth world gathered together on the West Coast of the United States in the hippie movement. Most of the "national churches" (the U.S. "establishment" in this case) were either hostile, indifferent, or incapable of reaching this curious fourth world group in an effective way. They didn't know what to make of the psychedelic drugs, the free sex, and the Eastern mystical religions.

Because the "national church" could not or would not make disciples among these street people does not mean that the Spirit of God allowed them to be forfeited. He raised up agencies outside the established church (call them "missions" in our context), such as the World Christian Liberation Front in Berkeley and the Jesus People Movement in Los Angeles. These new "missions" did not worry about protocol, comity, or the agenda of the established church. They moved ahead with such evangelistic methods as coffee houses, street meetings, *Hollywood Free Papers*, baptisms in the ocean, and Christian communes, which predictably were little understood by the establishment. They wore beads, let their hair grow out, played guitars and went barefoot. As a result, many of the "national churches" did not even want these "missionaries" to attend their services. They said, in effect, "Missionary, go home!" Here, right at home, we witnessed "creative tensions" between the mission and the church.

Although many United States churches still have not accepted this freewheeling new missionary movement, the trend —at least on the West Coast—is toward reduced tensions and more mature recognition of the all-important fact that the supreme task of both establishment and counterculture is winning the fourth world. Therefore, a mutual appreciation is developing, based on the recognition that God can use each of the groups to make disciples in different segments of the fourth world.

CHARISMATIC MOVEMENT

Just one more example from home base before returning to the Third World. Let's move from the counterculture to the middle class.

During the 1960s the United States "national churches" were to a large extent in the doldrums. They were plugged-carburetor churches which were not fulfilling the Great Commission even in their own communities. Again, the Spirit of God raised up a force of "missionaries" which did not meet the approval of most "national churches." In this case the majority of these "missionaries" were good church members who had become frustrated and restless because of the introversion, nominality and ineffectiveness of their churches. They did not form a counterculture; they formed a "charismatic movement."

This charismatic movement startled the leadership of the established churches in much the same way that missions startle the leadership of some of the newer churches in the Third World. They could not understand why these "missionaries" held their meetings in living rooms rather than in church halls. They were revolted by some of the unusual liturgical practices of the charismatic movement. They questioned the validity of baptisms in private swimming pools. Some churchmen shouted "Missionary, go home!" so loudly that their churches split. But others, more wisely, made the adjustments necessary to harness the pulsating spiritual vitality of this new "mission" for the renewal of the church and the evangelization of the fourth world.

These contemporary examples of church-mission tensions, of course, are not unusual in the history of Christianity. Anyone who turns back the pages of church history with this in mind can notice that it has been a recurring pattern. God has been raising up Jesus People and charismatic movements under other names through the centuries. The Waldensians and the Lollards, the Pietists and the Methodists, the Conservative Baptists and the Assemblies of God, the Student Volunteer Movement and Campus Crusade, the Christian and Missionary Alliance and the Sudan Interior Mission—all are examples of "missions" which formed because their own churches had become ineffective for winning certain segments of the fourth world.

It must be recognized that sometimes the carburetor can be repaired and a stalled church can once again become effective in the fourth world. Most Evangelicals in the United States are aware of the "evangelism explosion" in James Kennedy's Coral Ridge Presbyterian Church in Florida and of the "body-life evangelism" of Ray Stedman's Peninsula Bible Church in California. Churches like these complete the picture I am attempting to paint. Some churches are effective evangelistic instruments, while others are not.

BACK TO THE THIRD WORLD

This brief flashback into our own homeland church-mission tensions is designed to clarify our thinking concerning parallel church-mission tensions in the Third World. Across the board, Christian churches in the Third World are no different from those at home. Some will effectively reach the fourth world; some will not.

But missions, if they are true to their nature and their calling, *must* keep their objective as the fourth world. This must be the starting point of church-mission policies. The effective evangelization of the fourth world must remain, Gibraltarlike, the objective of missions.

Effective evangelism of the fourth world will make multitudes of disciples and baptize them into the church. But as long as there are more people to win out there in the fourth world, these churches that have been formed under the blessing of God do not constitute the final objective. If the whitened field holds ten thousand bushels of wheat, a five-thousand-bushel harvest is not enough. The harvesters would be foolish to allow the fascination of five thousand harvested bushels tempt them to shut down their combines and begin to manufacture bread, spaghetti and breakfast food before the harvest is completed. The Lord of the harvest would call them "wicked and slothful servants."

This is why missions which turn from evangelism to church development do poorly. True, the church needs some help. The wheat that has been harvested needs to be stored in elevators if it is to be preserved. The newborn infant needs milk and its diapers changed. Missions which neglect this basic nurture are irresponsible. But missions which allow the emerging church to absorb so much attention and energy that the push into the fourth world is slowed down or stalled are worse than irresponsible. They are unfaithful to their calling from God.

Let the Natives Evangelize

"We now have a national church," some missionaries say. "Let the natives do the evangelism. We will now teach the Bible to the Christians, help them raise better crops, improve their hygiene, train their pastors, and teach them modern evangelistic methods. Since they speak the language better than we do, since they know the culture, since they are the right color, they now become responsible for the fourth world. We have done our job." In other writings I have called this severe fallacy in missionary strategy the "syndrome of church development." I would not keep stressing it if my experience had not confirmed that it is such a widespread and devastating error in the thinking of both contemporary missions and national churches.

Missionaries who fall into the syndrome of church development are often rather deluded. They unwittingly operate under the false assumption that they can do almost everything better than national Christians. They feel they can preach better sermons, they can organize more active church programs, they can lead choirs and play instruments better, they can teach Sunday school classes better, they can build better buildings, write better tracts, teach better seminary classes, they can start youth camps and youth centers, they can write constitutions and administer denominational offices with supreme efficiency. On top of all this, they are free—the church doesn't have to pay a cent for all this service. Sometimes, in fact, the missionaries are able to obtain sums of outside money that enlarge the church treasury rather than take from it.

But these missionaries, somehow, don't feel they can evangelize better than nationals!

The above may border on a caricature, but it is close enough to much current missionary mentality to raise a warning flag for discerning missionaries and churchmen. All the different activities involved in the syndrome of church development are good in themselves, and at one time or another a missionary may help the church by participating in them. But they are only temporary. A mature church can handle all of them. As men like Roland Allen and Henry Venn saw years ago, the less the mission gets involved in these internal affairs of the church, and the quicker the church itself assumes responsibility for these things under the Holy Spirit rather than under the missionary, the better for both mission and church. But even when the ideal is reached and the new church fully and effectively handles all its own internal affairs, neither the church nor the mission is relieved of its responsibility toward the fourth world.

SETTING PRIORITIES

Whereas for a time this concept was neither articulated nor accepted in evangelical missions, some hopeful signs of progress are appearing. In a remarkable editorial entitled "Our

First Priority," Joseph McCullough of the Andes Evangelical
Mission reflects the trend in his own group:

> Evangelism, once again, will be the primary thrust of the
> Andes Evangelical Mission. Reaching the unreached has
> always been our objective as a pioneer mission. But somehow
> with the growth of a strong national church, we began to
> think that the responsibility for evangelizing belonged to this
> church. Our task would be to carry on the training program
> of Bible schools, seminaries, and other church-supporting
> ministries such as literature, radio, youth centers, camping,
> Bible conferences, and so forth. . . .
>
> In a new way, however, we believe the Lord would have us
> direct our attention and efforts to direct evangelistic oppor-
> tunities. As missionaries we need to set the example and pace
> for the national churches and pastors. Our responsibility is
> to keep moving out to the cutting edge of the work. As new
> churches are planted, we will continue to break new ground
> rather than limit our efforts to organizing and training.[1]

One might ask whether missions like the Andes Evangelical
Mission have the *right* to establish such priorities. Should they
not have asked the national church to make the policy statement? Should not the nationals decide whether they want doctors, radio broadcasters, seminary professors, primary school
teachers, chicken farmers, basketball players, Bible translators,
airplane pilots, printers—or (perhaps) evangelists and church
planters? Are not missions which seem to go above the head
of the national church in setting their priorities in the fourth
world arrogant and domineering?

No more so than the Jesus People movement which moved
into the West Coast fourth world without seeking the advice
and consent of the established churches their parents belonged
to. Nor than the horseback circuit riders of the Wesleyan
movement who perhaps "arrogantly" penetrated the British
fourth world without the approval of the national (Anglican)
church. The fact that some of our present-day missionary organizations do the same thing cross-culturally does not alter

the principle that when God raises up a group of His servants and gives them the missionary vision of making disciples in the fourth world, this vision is never required to be brought under the control of the established church, no matter whether this church is found in the first, second or third worlds. The Protestant effort in Latin America, for example, began and flourished despite the protests and persecutions of the Catholic established church.

Having said this, however, it is necessary to point out immediately that the best of all possible situations is complete harmony both in thought and action between church and mission. This seems to be the situation, for example, that Ian Hay describes in chapter 11 of this book. Both the Sudan Interior Mission and the Evangelical Church of West Africa have kept their vision fixed on the fourth world. As a result, the harvest in West Africa is being gathered with top efficiency.

WEST CAMEROON

As all missionaries are aware, this kind of harmony between church and mission does not always develop. Take a recent situation in neighboring West Cameroon, for example. The remarkable good growth of the West Cameroon Baptist Church, beginning in 1950, stalled with a plugged carburetor in the period 1955-60. One of the reasons was an overenthusiastic policy of indigenization on the part of the mission. Apparently losing its vision of the fourth world, the mission thought that the withdrawal of missionary personnel engaged in evangelism and church-planting would hasten the indigenization of the church. Evangelism became the responsibility of the church, no longer that of the mission. With indigenization taking higher priority than the fourth world, the syndrome of church development was in full swing. Commenting on the situation, Lloyd Kwast says, "This complete withdrawal from evangelism by the mission was without doubt an excessive move and hurt the growth of the Church."[2]

Earlier in this book, Robertson McQuilkin has stated that

"the church universal has an obligation to all people outside of Christ and may not attempt to discharge this responsibility by delegating it to representatives who are not fulfilling it."

At Green Lake, Louis King warned strongly against what we are calling the syndrome of church development. He stated that as a *first principle* in mission/church relationship, "missionaries refrain from accepting administrative functions in, and forego imposing their plans upon, the church."[3] Without using the term "fourth world," King asserted that "the mission's relationship with the church is primarily at that point in which the church is engaged in witness and mission to the non-Christian world outside its door."[4]

George Peters adds his voice to reinforce these principles. He believes that missions, properly conceived, are neither mission-centered nor church-centered. While they are "church-based" they are also "world-faced." One of his diagrams presented at Green Lake represented the mission of the church as a bow shooting an arrow called "missionary thrust" toward the world. The two equal sections of the bowstring were labeled "sending church" and "receiving church."[5] On the church-development syndrome, Peters says,

> The energies of the sending church must not be spent in perfecting church structures, drafting constitutions, exercising church discipline, and superintending institutions. The goal of missions is not the structural and institutional life of the church community, but the proclamation of the gospel to those who do not confess Jesus Christ as Lord and Savior.[6]

SECONDARY ISSUES

Once the matters of the fourth world as the primary objective of missions and the syndrome of church development are cared for, the other issues involved in mission/church relationships really become secondary. The New Testament gives us no inspired structure for mission/church relationships. Fusion, modified fusion, dichotomy, modified dichotomy, unilaterality, functional partnership, parallelism—all are options with more or less validity according to the circumstances and according to the degree they help or hinder the fulfillment of the Great Commission.

Certain geographical areas of the world, certain ethnic temperaments, certain historic backgrounds, certain backlogs of failures or successes in mission/church experiments, certain ecclesiastical conditions, or a myriad of other circumstances might combine on one field in such a way that fusion of mission and church is the most acceptable alternative. But an entirely different combination of these same factors might recommend parallelism on another field.

It is a mistake to commit a mission to a certain preconceived principle of relationship with the national church without regard to the local circumstances. By doing this, a mission can all too easily forfeit its opportunity to evangelize. Some missions, committed to an inflexible policy of indigenization, have disbanded their missionary organization and assigned their missionaries to the newly formed national church. There is nothing wrong with this procedure per se, if by doing so the total outreach to the fourth world becomes more effective. But if the church loses its own evangelistic vision and tells the mission that it prefers radio technicians and community development experts to evangelists and church planters, the mission should reconsider the relationship. If contracts have been signed and the church is stubborn, probably the mission will have to look for other fields if it is to continue faithful to its call to make disciples of all nations.

In a widely circulated article, Donald McGavran warned the delegates to Green Lake not to "betray the two billion." By the "two billion" McGavran means what we mean by the fourth world. He said that "church-mission relationships have little importance in themselves. They are important chiefly if they enable effective discipling of men and ethne to take place."[7] Pragmatic considerations, based on the biblically centered imperative of fulfilling the Great Commission, will determine the best mission-church relationships for a given time and place.

ASKING THE RIGHT QUESTION

Is the day of the missionary over? Now that there is a strong indigenous church in Upper Zax, are there any more missionaries needed there? Do the Upper Zaxonian Christians want any more missionaries?

These are all *wrong* questions, but they are frequently being asked in church circles in the sending countries today. Sometimes they cause confusion and unnecessary tension between missionaries and their sending churches.

All should be clear that the day of the missionary will not be over until the present age ends. When Christ gave the Great Commission to make disciples of all nations, He added the reassuring promise that He would be with His servants to the end of the age (Mt 28:20). This was not only a promise but also an indication of the duration of the Christian mission. Missions must continue until Christ returns.

The bulk of this chapter has been dedicated to the issue raised in the second hypothetical question above. The existence of a strong national church in Upper Zax, in the United States, or in West Africa does not regulate the need for more or fewer missionaries, unless the missionaries have fallen into the syndrome of church development. We will not labor this any further.

The third question, however, needs more clarification. Some Third World churchmen are visiting the United States and setting up qualifications for the kind of missionaries they would like, and they are getting the ear of sending churches. One man in particular from Latin America, whose name is not important here, has said that the church he represents wants only those missionaries willing to participate in the changing of Latin American social structures and in the liberation of the Latin American man. He wants social revolutionaries, not evangelists.

By reacting to this attitude, I do not want to give the impression that I oppose the Latin American social revolution. In other writings I have declared myself a supporter of it. Nor do I want to give the impression that it is in any way wrong for this man and other Latin churchmen to participate in the revolution to the degree their consciences direct them. I do contend, however, that neither he, nor his church, nor the pope himself has any right to say that a Spirit-filled missionary, called of God to preach the gospel of Christ to the fourth world, to turn men from darkness to light and baptize them into the church, should not fulfill his calling.

If he is talking about the kind of missionary who has felt led to "help the church," whose objective is the Third World church rather than the non-Christians of the fourth world, who has fallen into the syndrome of church development—in that case he and his colleagues have a perfect right to tell any missionary to go home or stay home. Let the members of any church or denomination decide what is right for the internal functioning of their church. Let them set up personnel requirements and accept only workers they desire and approve. But if the Third World churchman has lost his vision for a world without Christ and without hope, if he no longer is concerned that people who die without repentance and faith go to an eternal punishment in hell, if he is more burdened for the salvation of society than the salvation of souls, he of all people is least qualified to decide whether *evangelistic* missionaries should fulfill Christ's command to make disciples in the fourth world, even when that part of the fourth world is in his own country. The source of the missionary mandate is the triune God, not the church. The final accounting will be given before the judgment seat of Christ, not before some ministerial council or ecclesiastical assembly.

This is why asking whether the Upper Zaxonians want any more missionaries is not the right question. The right question is: Are there any men and women in the fourth world in Upper Zax who need Christ, who are receptive to the gospel, and to whom missionaries from Lower Bovima (the hypothetical sending country in this case) can effectively communicate? If the answer is yes, they must go, unless, of course, there is a high degree of assurance that the Upper Zax church will indeed take care of that fourth world in terms of reaping all the harvest there before it is too late.

WHERE HAVE WE GOOFED?

This doesn't mean that anyone should thumb his nose at the church. Harmonious relationships, I repeat, are the best of all possibilities. But we do learn from history and from men like Martin Luther, John Wesley, William Carey and A. B. Simpson that the establishment should not be allowed to stand in the way of fulfilling God's will. Remember the Jesus People?

It is a sad but true fact that many Third World churches do not have a vital burden for the fourth world. How could this have happened? There are three major causes:

1. *A lack of missionary teaching.* For some strange reason, missionaries have not made it a point to teach missions to the emerging churches. Chua Wee Hian once said, "Most of my missionary friends confess that they have never preached a single sermon on missions to the young churches."[8] Exceptions to this are described elsewhere in this book, especially with the Sudan Interior Mission in Nigeria and the Christian and Missionary Alliance in Asia. But the general rule holds, and missionaries should correct this serious omission as soon as possible.

2. *A lack of missionary example.* If missionaries have decided to "leave evangelism to the natives," no wonder the natives have little evangelistic burden. Missionaries should set the example for the church if they expect the church to develop the proper vision for the fourth world.

3. *Nominality in the church.* While two of the three causes of the lack of missionary vision in some newer churches can be traced to the missionaries themselves, a third relates directly to the church. Especially when the second generation comes

into leadership, nominality is likely to set in, just as it has done in so many churches in the sending countries. The only cure for this is a renewed vision under the supervision and power of the Holy Spirit.

CONCLUDING RECOMMENDATIONS

In conclusion, I would mention five recommendations to missions which desire to maintain the best relationships with the churches they are involved with, and at the same time not betray their own true nature. This is a fine and difficult line to walk. Mistakes are inevitably made; tensions inevitably arise. But hopefully they are *creative* tensions, and when they are resolved, both mission and church have benefited.

1. Maintain as the guiding principle for mission policy effective discipling of the fourth world. Jesus came to seek and to save the lost, and missions must not deviate from that. Although constantly tempted to stay behind with the ninety-nine, they may not do this as long as there is one more lost sheep to find and fold.

2. Do all possible to transmit the vision for the lost to the emerging church. From the very beginning teach the newborn babes in Christ that part of their commitment to the Lord is to use their gifts in the effective fulfillment of the Great Commission.

3. Avoid the syndrome of church development. Do not become unduly involved in the internal development of the church. Trust the new believers to the Holy Spirit, give them responsibility early in their Christian experience, allow them to develop their own relevant patterns of church organization, liturgy, leadership, finances and training.

4. When structures need to be developed, choose the structure of mission-church relationship on pragmatic grounds. Make whatever arrangement will best make disciples in the fourth world.

The ideal structure combines resources from mission and church in a concerted effort to win the fourth world for Christ;

together they are discipling peoples and multiplying churches for God's glory.

The second-best situation occurs when the church has no resources to offer but gives the mission her moral support as the mission continues to move into the fourth world with the gospel.

The last resort is necessary only when the church is obstinate and opposes the mission's ministry to the fourth world. In this case "we must obey God rather than man" as long as people in the fourth world are waiting for Christ.

5. Help each emerging church or denomination develop a missionary sending program of its own. This, when successful, completes the cycle of world evangelism. The new church spawns a new mission. The full sequence, as Ralph Winter has already pointed out, is not mission-church, nor even church-mission-church, but rather, church-mission-church-mission. No mission should feel that its task is accomplished, even as far as the emerging church is concerned, until that church has become an active missionary church.

NOTES

1. Joseph S. McCullough, "Our First Priority," *The Andean Outlook* (Plainfield, N.J.), Fall, 1971, p. 7.
2. Lloyd E. Kwast, *The Discipling of West Cameroon, A Study of Baptist Growth* (Grand Rapids: Eerdmans, 1971), p. 148.
3. Louis L. King, "Mission/Church Relations Overseas," in *Missions in Creative Tension* ed. Vergil Gerber (South Pasadena, Calif.: William Carey Library, 1971), p. 181.
4. Ibid., p. 175.
5. George W. Peters, "Mission/Church Relations Overseas," in *Missions in Creative Tension*, p. 230.
6. Ibid., p. 208.
7. Donald McGavran, "Will Green Lake Betray the Two Billion?" *Church Growth Bulletin* (Palo Alto), July 1971, p. 152.
8. Chua Wee Hian, "Encouraging Missionary Movement in Asian Churches," *Christianity Today*, June 20, 1969, p. 11.

SUBJECT INDEX

Africa, 99, 103, 125, 137, 140, 182, 194, 195, 199
Africa Inland Mission, 47
African Missionary Society, 200, 201
Age of Reason, 106
Agents, 112
Ajayi, J. F. Ade, 203
Allen, Roland, 34, 101, 197, 223
Alliance Bible Seminary, 179
Amalgamation, 48
American Bible Society, 142
American introspection, 70
Anabaptists, 33, 34
Andes Evangelical Mission, 223
Andrew System, 125
Anglicans, 101
Animism, 99, 100
Antichrist, 109
Antioch, 10, 132
Apostle Paul. See Paul
Ariye, Moses, 197
Arnold, Patrick, 114
Asia, 99, 101, 103, 138, 140, 230
Asia Conference
  First, 170
  Second, 170-72
  Third, 179
  Fourth, 182
Asians, non-Christian, 138, 139
Assam, 101
Assemblies of God, 185, 221
Association of Evangelical Churches of West Africa (ECWA), 195-213, 225
Authority, 117, 118

Bangkok, 170
Banmethuot, 164, 165, 175
Baptists, 101, 102
Barnabas, 10, 82, 83, 121
Batak tribesmen, 100
Berkeley, 219
Beyerhaus, Peter, 27, 31, 198
Bible and Theological Institute at Nhatrang, 164
Bible school, 173
Bingham, Dr., 197
Biography, mission, 76
Birmingham, Alabama, 138

Brazil, 179, 180
British colonists, 97
Buddhism, 100
Burma, 100, 101

Cambodia, 176, 179
Campus Crusade, 221
Canada, 158, 160
Candidates, 121
  selection of, 82, 83
Carey, William, 138, 230
Celtic Peregrini, 132
Chaplain's Corps in Vietnam Military, 164
Charismatic movement, 220
China, 181
Cho, David, 126
Chrisman, R. M., 172
Christian and Missionary Alliance, 163-65, 221, 230
  Asia conferences of. See Asia Conference.
Christian Missions in Nigeria, 203
Christian Nationals' Evangelistic Commission, 106
Chua Wee Hian, 230
Church, 17-37, 115, 131-34, 137
  believers', 33
  as body of Christ, 31
  buildings, 173
  definitions of, 19-20
  development, 222
  development syndrome, 32, 222, 229, 231
  Episcopal, 125
  evangelistic responsibility of, 42
  forms of, 33
  function of, 29, 42
  general usages of the word, 23
  growth in Third World, 97
  growth, 194, 206
  identity of, 27
  indigenous, 165, 216-17
  involved, 91
  local, 36, 122
  mission of, 40-41
  /mission relationships, 48, 133, 194, 203, 212. See also Mission/ church relationships

233

SCRIPTURE INDEX

Da

NOTHING TO WIN BUT THE WORLD

NOTHING TO WIN
BUT THE WORLD

missions at the crossroad

By
CLAY COOPER
President, Vision, Incorporated
Spokane, Washington

Foreword by
MARK O. HATFIELD
Governor, State of Oregon

ZONDERVAN PUBLISHING HOUSE
Grand Rapids, Michigan

First printing   — 1965
Second printing — 1966

Library of Congress Catalog Card Number 64-8848

Quotations from *The Bible: A New Translation* by
James Moffatt, copyright by James Moffatt, 1954, are
reprinted by permission of Harper & Row, Publishers,
Incorporated.

It is impossible to make individual acknowledgments
to all whose "helps" have been conspicuously or unconsciously borrowed, or to the noble missionaries
who have provided so much of the inspiration for this
book. For materials used from unknown sources, in-
dulgence is asked. Efforts to identify will continue,
and where successful, credits are promised in subsequent editions.

DEDICATION

To the three ladies in my life:

My Mary Helen . . .

. . . whose empathy for world missions, and helpful critique of this work more than merit this tribute by her devoted and appreciative husband;

Soon Ja . . .

. . . our lovely "adopted" daughter in Korea, who wooed our hearts toward the needy children of the world;

My petite Mother . . .

. . . who is, and will always be, a part of any helpful thing I may ever do for the Saviour and for mankind.

ABOUT THE BOOK

THE READER will note that the twenty-seven chapters of this volume are inspired by specific incidents and situations recorded in the New Testament's twenty-seven books, each having relevance to foreign missions.

Tracing the missions theme through the Bible consecutively, book-by-book, produces a modern cosmorama of revelation bearing on twentieth-century crises and solutions.

The author fervently hopes that these thoughts on the various phases of the subject of missions will provoke a ready response.

CONTENTS

FOREWORD

SOUND THE BUGLE! Roll the drums! Charge!

Are we immune to these clarion calls? Has lethargy and apathy deadened the ears of would-be warriors?

Concerning our political institutions and other facets of our society, the indictments are often heard, "We are big and soft; we are rich and destitute." The author of *Nothing to Win But the World* has not excluded the Church from these indictments. The shoe may fit many *comfortable* Christians. One cannot but become agitated by these chapters.

Here, perhaps with a slightly different flavor, is a classical Christian call to evangelize the earth. The reader will know that action is overdue for Christ's followers to take seriously His admonition, "Go ye into all the world."

The author eloquently states his thesis: Communism is an enemy of both the political systems of the free world and Christianity alike. Therefore, to evangelize not only produces citizens for the kingdom of Heaven but guarantees freedom for citizens of this world.

The secular mind will see the church as an ally in the battle for freedom, and the missionary as a spiritual Peace Corpsman. The reader with "the mind of Christ" will see anew his personal responsibility to support the men and the women at the front, pushing past the frontiers of ignorance for the Lord. Each will ask himself, "What have I done to fill the need through giving, praying, going?"

This book will bring many Christians to their knees before God, for rededication to the spread of His Gospel, and will make the remaining Christians very uncomfortable.

MARK O. HATFIELD
Governor, State of Oregon

CHALLENGE

Your rice-bowl is empty, little brother;
Your hands are blue from the cold;
Your face is a map of terror and pain,
Old as mankind is old.

Men try to reach the moon, little brother,
To lasso outer space,
But would they not come closer to God
If they wiped the pain from your face?

Men launch their miracles, little brother,
They send their rockets up;
But should it not be their first concern
To fill your empty cup?

— LUCIA TRENT

PREFACE

Excerpt from
United States of America *Congressional Record*
Proceedings and debates of the 86th Congress

Extension of Remarks
of
HONORABLE WALT HORAN
of Washington
in the
HOUSE OF REPRESENTATIVES

MR. HORAN. Mr. Speaker, under permission granted to me to extend my own remarks in the *Record,* I would like to include an article written by Clay Cooper of Spokane, Washington. I think Mr. Cooper has pointed out some things that are well worth our heeding. His statement is as follows:

MISSIONS OR MISSILES — THIS WORLD OR THE MOON

The heaven, even the heavens, are the Lord's:
but the earth hath He given to the children of men.
Psalm 115:16

What a lot of talk about getting a man to the moon! Had you taken the scissors to the morning paper and clipped every article having to do with moonshots, satellites, and the communist implications, you could have had shredded newsprint for breakfast.

We are in the grip of lunarmania. Getting to the moon all but obsesses the imagination of tens of millions of people. Unless the spectacular feat is achieved soon there are going to be many, many disappointed scientists and multiplied millions of dissipated dollars squandered as well.

Perhaps we need to be reminded, in our marathon race with the Reds, of the pitfalls that lie dead ahead. We are so all-fired concerned that the Russians will out-distance us we are stampeding into a crash-spending program which could help satellite us into bankruptcy. However, this is not our most crucial concern. What is of much greater moment is that while we are striving to gain the moon, we might be losing the earth. Could not this be the Commies' fond dream?

This world is the one the Communists want. This world right down here, every hemisphere of it and every acre of it. They do not want the moon half as much as they would have us think. Why are we falling so completely for their "other world" diversionary tactics? Have we forgotten how they focused our attention elsewhere while they were carving up Korea? While we were intently parleying at Geneva, they were parceling out Viet Nam. When our eyes were glued on their created crisis in Lebanon, they were blasting away at Matsu and Quemoy, and while we were digging out from under the rubble there, the Russians were opening the Berlin front. Now they draw our attention to *worlds above* as a feint to decoy us away from this *world below* which is the real focal point of their ambition, their prime and ultimate goal.

Only God can jar us from our trance. Only He can save us from the profound state of abstraction which is causing us to follow the siren notes of Red Pied Piperism. For us to act from panic impulse is exactly what the Russians want. If they can keep us engrossed with the moon, they will have less trouble engulfing the earth. Unless we awaken to their strategy of diverting our attention from their real prize, it will be another case of "while we were busy here and there, it was gone."

Bear in mind it is not something we shoot from earth into the heavens that is going to save the world. Rather it is that Someone who came down from heaven to earth one starlit night in the long ago. Tidings of landing a man on the moon would leave two-thirds of the people of the world cold. The Good News, first told by the Judean shepherds, can charm the ears of waiting mankind. As a symbol of hope, the fiery launching pad pales in comparison with Bethlehem's manger.

It is cause for amazement to many thinking people that a nominally Christian society should frantically compete with avowed atheists in the moon-race. Let the Reds be first to reach unknown worlds. Let the known world with its known peoples and their known problems be our first concern. Why bankrupt the nation so as to plant the Stars and Stripes on the pock-marked Sea of Tranquility? The Blood-Stained Banner has yet to be lifted over more than half of terra firma! Falling victim to a celestial megalomania under the planned prodding of the Reds, while oblivious to our terrestrial mission, could prove to be a fatal mistake.

There is no Divine Commission ordering men to go to some other world. There are multiplied commands instructing us to shadow this world with the Cross. Pointing a needle-nosed Saturn into the azure holds no fulfillment for a crippled Asian leper, or for a syphilitic-blinded child in Africa, when contrasted with the needle on the end of a syringe in the missionary doctor's hand. We must be wary of frustrating the purposes of Providence by concentrating on the space race at the expense of the "race" race. I leave to the theologians and to the politicians the moral and political issues involved. But as to the necessity of ministering to the world's needs, there can be no argument.

The crux of the matter is no petition to scrap every reasonable security measure. It lies in the answer to the following questions. Shall we major in missiles and minor in missions? Shall we invest trillions for one and trifles for the other? Shall we put a man on the moon or a missionary in Martinique? Shall we waken, too late, and realize that while we were trying to gain the moon we lost the earth?

(Abridged from the *Congressional Record*, February 11, 1959)

> "And *I was afraid*, and went
> and hid thy talent in the
> earth . . ."
>
> Matthew 25:25

I

SABOTEUR

Perhaps it is time for some lyricist to parody
the nursery rhyme and start everyone singing,
"Who's afraid of the big, bad Bear."

WHEN NIKITA KHRUSHCHEV ribbed a group of Westerners, "You are as afraid of communism as you are of the devil himself," he was much too near the truth, even for a communist. Far, far too many people in the free world are becoming victims of "redphobia." Unfortunately this malady has been carried over into the Christian world.

Jesus Christ formulated His plan for world evangelization, committing Himself to provide His followers with the necessary means to the end. They were expected to be fearless in the discharge of their duties. He cautioned them to resist the single enemy agent which could partially defeat His purpose. The saboteur was *fear*.

The Saviour dramatized this point in the parable of the *talented servant* whose phobia drove him to do the queerest thing imaginable. He pictured him as a man of considerable ability, and adequately endowed to accomplish his assigned task (Matthew 25:15). Yet a baseless foreboding impelled the fellow to dig a hole in the ground where he buried his entrusted talent. Later, when faced with default his only defense was, "I was afraid." Involuntary as his fear may have seemed to him, his excuse was not valid, nor his fear forgiveable. He was castigated as an *unprofitable servant*. His privileges as

15

a bona fide broker were immediately withdrawn.

The man in the parable was meant to stand as a prototype of all future servants to whom the Lord would "deliver His goods" to advance the kingdom, and who, without prostituting them to unworthy uses, would simply do *nothing* because of some phobia. *Phobia* is defined as an irrational and persistent fear of something. It may cause one to react abnormally or ridiculously, and without reason. Claustrophobia's victims fear safe but confining places. Persons having hydrophobia dread water; those with acrophobia, heights. Medical dictionaries list 277 other phobias.

"Fear has torment," says the Scripture. Fear is a demoralizing cyclops of a monster whose eye is out, who cripples and paralyzes. Who among us has not been tongue-tied by simple stage fright? Researchers report ninety-four percent of those who first stand to speak in public wrestle with this chimerical foe. Some never conquer him completely. Fear of harmless nighttime noises can nail one as securely to his bed as if he wakened to find a burglar in the room. It may be nothing more than the rolling up of a window shade, discharged by a faulty spring. The results may be cold sweat, a quickened pulse, goose pimples, physical incapacitation. In the dark every bush can become a bear.

A competent scientist proved this in a series of tests with men in the British army. Three soldiers were asked to submit themselves to a test designed to measure the effect of their mental attitude on their physical strength. A simple gripping device was used. In their normal state, the average grip was one hundred one pounds. Under hypnosis, when told they were very *weak,* their utmost efforts registered only twenty-nine pounds. Still under hypnosis, and told they were very, very *strong,* the average jumped back to the normal one hundred one pounds, and then rose to one hundred forty-two pounds. They were actually forty percent stronger when they believed they were strong, and seventy percent weaker when they believed they were weak.

This principle holds on the higher plane. To think defeat is to know defeat. To think down is to go down. Even an apostle (Peter) began to sink when fright seized him as he walked on water. But he walked again, demonstrating that what fear can do, faith can undo. Still, here is proof that "fear brings a snare."

Christ's parable of the man with "missionphobia" is but one of the many Bible references where fear is shown to be a deterrent to the performance of the divine will in the world. Consider what it

did to Israel's conquest of Canaan. Consternation took over after
the ten spies returned to camp with fantastically blown-up reports.
They saw enemy giants so big that ordinary Israelites appeared as
mere grasshoppers. Their fears magnified the obstacles out of all
proportion to reality. The chosen people, believing the "evil report,"
refused to advance toward the promised land. A stalemate resulted.
Forty years passed before the campaign was resumed.

God spent considerable time with Israel figuratively on the
psychiatric couch. The nation had to lose its phobias, or by them
set back the timetable for their entry into the promised land. Jehovah
reasoned with them:

"If thou shalt say in thine heart [a silent admission],
These nations are more than I; how can I dispossess
them? Thou shalt not be afraid of them . . ." (Deuteronomy 7:17, 18).

The thundering of prophets' voices were heard in other eras:

"Do not call out 'Danger!'
when this people calls out 'Danger!'
Have no fear of what they fear,
never dread it.

"Put heart into the listless,
and brace all weak-kneed souls,
tell men with fluttering hearts,
'Have courage, never fear;
here comes your God . . .' "
(Isaiah 8:12; 35:3, 4, Moffatt)

". . . What man is there that is fearful and faint-
hearted? let him go and return unto his house, lest
his brethren's heart faint as well as his . . ." (Deuteronomy 20:8).

This brings us to an interesting way station. Shakespeare said,
"Hang those who talk fear." Strong language to be sure, but perhaps
not too strong when it is realized that one of the most devastating by-
products of fear is its own contagion. No one has a right to infect
others with his unreasoning alarm and dismay.

One can get a good case of the jitters just reading the religious
editorials devoted to nationalism, communism and the like. Frequently
the situation is viewed with alarm. Evil circumstances are portrayed
as having a strangle hold on the Church. Only a short time is al-
lotted to complete her work of redemption before the sky falls.

Who said so? Where is it written? A decade ago, *reliable sources* were predicting that anti-Western nationalism in India would put an end to foreign missionary work in the country within a year. Eighteen months would be the outside limit. This has proved untrue. Yet for a time and to a degree this jaundiced opinion helped retard foreign mission endeavor on the Indian sub-continent. Timid soldier-saints are ever of dubious value in the Lord's brigade.

Count devils and they seem to multiply. The time is always ideal to disregard the odds stacked against whatever is divinely willed and ordered. As long as the Prophet Elisha's frightened servant kept his eyes on the array of Syrian hordes, terror possessed him. When he caught sight of celestial combatants "round about Elisha," then it was that his master's words became meaningful:

"Fear not: for they that be with us are more than
they that be with them" (II Kings 6:16).

His faith enlivened, his phobia dissipated!

The Apostle Paul counseled people facing the tyrannies of their time, as we do ours:

"Never be scared for a second by your opponents;
your fearlessness is a clear omen of ruin for them
and of your own salvation — at the hands of God"
(Philippians 1:28, Moffatt).

Admittedly the night is dark and there are weird noises, strange ones, unaccustomed ones. But our mission is not to lie down and shake but to stand up and "shine as lights in the world" (Philippians 2:15, 16).

The interval between Christ's ascent into heaven and His return to earth to reign is to be devoted to faithful stewardship by intrepid disciples. The Master made this crystal clear in parable:

"A certain nobleman went into a far country to receive for himself a kingdom, and to return. And he
called his ten servants, and delivered them ten pounds,
and said unto them, 'Occupy till I come' " (Luke 19:
12, 13).

He let them know that "I was afraid" would prove a poor excuse for failure to do so.

They did not let Him down, these first century zealots. When threatened, they neither panicked nor froze from fright, but went right on speaking "the things which we have seen and heard" (Acts

5:20). The world was a mart, and they were willing to trade lives for souls. The "might of Hades" did not prevail.

The world is always being claimed for Christ by fearless men. John Wesley's recruiting call was, "Give me a hundred men who . . . fear nothing but God, and I will change the world." Historians agree that he did.

This generation needs only another John Wesley and his centurion band.

"And *he called unto him the twelve* and began to send them forth."

Mark 6:7

2

LET GEORGIA DO IT

The way men let women tackle the job of rescuing the race from Eden's ruin, indicates they have forgotten that Adam ate the apple too.

IN EVERY HEMISPHERE communism is peeking over the ramparts and it is little wonder. There are hardly enough men (males) stationed on foreign mission outposts of the world to man two aircraft carriers with a wartime complement.

Christ initiated His program for world conquest by hand-picking the Twelve: Simon, James and John; Andrew, Philip and Bartholomew; Matthew, Thomas and James the son of Alphaeus; Thaddaeus, Judas and Simon; all strong masculine names. Soon seventy others were recruited, making eighty-two. After Pentecost they numbered thousands. The rank and file grew. Some were seamen, others were horny-handed tillers of the soil. A physician forsook his practice, one the toll booth, another the halls of learning to enlist.

This predominant masculinity in missions was no first-century quirk. It was in line with all scriptural precedent. Men have always been God's *method*. Moses led the children of Israel out of Egypt. He was succeeded by the *man* Joshua, who employed twelve *men* to survey the promised land. The march around Jericho was made

21

by *men*. God's instrument in Samson's day was Samson. It was Gideon who marshalled 300 *men* to defeat the Midianites. The women remained in their tents.

God requisitioned the first-born sons of Israel's households with:

"You must give me your eldest *sons*. . . . Three times a year must all your *males* appear in presence of the Lord, the God of Israel" (Exodus 22:29; 34:23, Moffatt).

No such instructions were ever given concerning the women.

Who penned the Scriptures?

". . . holy *men* of God spake as they were moved by the Holy Ghost" (II Peter 1:21).

Only two books in the sacred canon bear the names of women: Esther (she didn't write it), and Ruth (a beautiful foreign missionary narrative, probably written by the prophet Samuel).

It would only be expected that Christ would rest upon the broader shoulders of *men* the greater responsibility of penetrating the pagan world with His Gospel. It would have been surprising had He not assigned the job primarily to them.

The ideal supporting role of the female may be dramatically illustrated by a thirteenth-century B.C. incident, when God's program called for the conquest of Canaan. Deborah, the only woman ever to judge Israel, recruited Barak to champion the cause (Judges 4:4-9). Refusing to head the campaign, she declared her willingness to go with him into battle, but only *with* him, not *instead* of him, or *ahead* of him.

Today it is different. Women frequently lead the way. However we have reason to believe they prefer the scriptural pattern, and resort to a leadership role with great reluctance.

Mission statistics reveal an astonishing outnumbering of males by modern Joan of Arcs who don male battle dress and march in the vanguard. On some fields the ratio may be six to one. The average bulletin listing foreign appointees is telltale. The following male to female ratio of personnel (unmarried), under foreign appointment, represents three well-known independent mission boards:

The first brochure shows *twenty-six* single women to *three* single men. The second names *forty-one* American women, with *no* male representation; and *twenty-two* to *one,* Canadian. The third paper, issued by one of the larger mission bodies in the world, pictures *forty-eight* single women and *not one* unmarried man.

It is understandable that pagan peoples should inquire of Christian missionaries, "Is your God a female god?"

Olive Howard, missionary to Ivory Coast, wrote the editor of *Floodtide* (March-April, 1963):

> "Recently, we had two new missionaries join us here—
> both women. When one of the national believers
> heard that it was two more mademoiselles we were
> meeting at the ship at Abidjan, he asked, 'Are there
> only women in God's affair in your village?' "

All too often His only representatives whom countless non-Christians observe are consecrated women. The female image is so stamped on modern missions.

No one knows where the idea ever came from, but the notion that foreign missions is a woman's domain practically permeates Christendom. Men let the women tackle the job of rescuing the fallen race as if they were unaware that Adam ate the apple too! When the issue of foreign missions is raised, seldom does the idea crease the brain of the average male that this is his area of responsibility also. To him, foreign missions is for the girls. It has something to do with lace and pink teas.

Where does one ever find a *Men's* Missionary Fellowship in the home church? On just how many foreign mission stations do men outnumber the women? Most men are merely touching this matter with the tips of their fingers. Many are not touching it at all.

American colleges and universities field more *men* on the gridiron on a given Saturday afternoon, than the American church can boast serving in Christ's foreign legion. Perhaps not more than twenty thousand Protestant missionaries are actually at their foreign posts at any one time. The male head count among these is so disproportionate as to be absurd.

Because so few see masculinity and missions at the same glance, women are obliged to serve as stand-ins and attempt the impossible . . . fill men's shoes. A classic illustration comes from the steaming jungles of Malaya. A young woman, manning a remote station alone, farewelled the visiting mission director with: "God has called a *man* to do this job out here. So far, he hasn't responded. But, until he does, I will stick here for Jesus' sake."

She recognized herself as only a willing substitute for God's plan . . . a *man!*

An English proverb bears on this point: "It's a sad house when the hen crows louder than the cock." What is sad for a house, is sad for a world. But it would be sadder still were it not for the Dorcas Societies, Ladies Aids, Martha-Mary Sewing Circles, and Women's Missionary Groups. Without them, the whole venture would be in *real* trouble.

Much of mankind's dilemma will be solved by lifting the load of world evangelization off the burdened shoulders of women and placing it back where it belongs. There are some prerogatives for which the male alone was endowed and one of them is leadership in God's army. Whenever earth's redemption goes forward apace, a predominant masculine element is in the forefront.

Today's world issues call for re-masculinizing missions. To continue the present trend becomes as ludicrous as sending a preponderately female expeditionary force in wartime, or manning subs, ships and planes with them . . . and still expecting to win. A tightly packed he-man phalanx forging ahead, making missionary plans, thinking missionary thoughts and embracing missionary problems will provide much of the solution to the present mid-century crises.

Of a perilous time in the dim past, it was recorded: "I sought for a *man* among them, that should make up the hedge, and stand in the gap . . ." (Ezekiel 22:30). Without question, this is the call of the Almighty again.

Christ is going about looking for *men* who will relate themselves to His world objectives. Those who listen can hear Him saying:

"Bring me *men* to match my mountains,
Bring me *men* to match my plains,
Men with empires in their purpose,
And new *men* with eras in their brains."
— *Sam Walter Foss*

"But tarry ye in the city of Jerusalem, until ye be *endued with power* from on high."

Luke 24:49

3

BLAST-OFF

No favorable orbit is achieved until there has been a count-down and a release of power . . . the similarity in the spiritual realm is striking.

THE YEAR was approximately A.D. 30. Ten days would be required from the beginning of the countdown to blast-off. The launching pad was an upper room in the city of Jerusalem, and the orbit was the then-known world. The missiles were men, and the solid fuel propellant was the dynamics of God Himself.

"When the day of Pentecost was fully come . . . suddenly there came a sound from heaven as of a rushing mighty wind . . . and they were all filled with the Holy Ghost" (Acts 2:1-4).

That upper room abruptly took on immense proportions as a vital, intermediate point between Calvary's atonement for the world, and ultimate "redemption of the purchased possession, unto the praise of his glory" (Ephesians 1:14).

The Christian pilgrim travels from the cross, via the empty tomb, to the Mount of Ascension. He hears the Saviour's very last command returning him to Jerusalem to "tarry . . . until ye be endued with power from on high" (Luke 24:49). When he obeys that

25

command and has received the power, he rushes from that sanctum a man with a *world* objective. Celestial City is his eventual destination, but the earth is his present arena. Paradise can wait! He is as the soldier who is eager to exchange his sleeping bag of today for laundered sheets tomorrow, but meanwhile there is a job to be done.

The Saviour took this into account when He prayed the Father *not* to take His followers out of the world (John 17:15), while also expressing the desire that ultimately they "be with me, where I am, that they may behold my glory" (John 17:24). Then He dispatched them, not to a blissful heaven, but an unblissful earth. His command:

"Preach the gospel to every creature . . . and teach
all nations, baptizing them in the name of the Father,
and of the Son, and of the Holy Ghost" (Mark 16:
15; Matthew 28:19).

This Great Commission provided sufficient authority. It lacked adequate motivation. Deprived of Pentecost, world evangelization would never have gotten off the launching pad. The immense task called for infusion of divine power. This, and this only, brought the first disciples from behind barricaded doors where they huddled in fear following Good Friday. The enduement sent them out across land and sea to turn the world upside down (Acts 17:6).

The foundling Church cowering somewhere between Easter and Pentecost could never have successfully contested the Roman sway of the ancient world. Minus the descended Spirit, there could have been no extended kingdom. No unction, no function. It was as simple as that. The Commission necessitated Pentecost. Together, they formed a compelling combination to make men invincible. The Book of Acts is proof enough.

The sacred record tells how the infant Church was empowered to the accompaniment of a sound like a violent blast of wind. Men began to witness of Christ in foreign languages they had never learned, saying whatever the Spirit prompted. Superior enablings gave them power over all foes. They are portrayed as unconquerable in every theater of operation. Unseen strength attends them. Skeptics are swayed and hard put to account for the dominion of these "unlearned and ignorant men."

What was their recourse when the movement faced stiffened resistance? They merely applied for greater resources. Luke gives the following illustration:

"When they [the disciples] had prayed, the place was shaken where they were assembled together [as at Pentecost]; and they were all filled with the Holy Ghost [again] and they spake the Word of God with boldness. And the multitudes . . . believed . . . and with great power gave the apostles witness of the resurrection of the Lord Jesus: and great grace was upon them all" (Acts 4:31-33).

In all adverse circumstances, first century missionaries simply tapped the "power from on high." It was always available.

The Apostle Paul attributed the phenomenal success of his ministry to this endowment. He wrote the Corinthians,

". . . my preaching was not with enticing words of man's wisdom, but in demonstration of the Spirit and of power: that your faith should not stand in the wisdom of men, but in the *power* of God" (I Corinthians 2:4, 5).

It can be logically assumed that the authority experienced by the Apostle Paul, and recommended to the church at Corinth, was intended by the Lord as the essential element to successful spiritual warfare for all time. The unique dynamic factor which made the first-century Church triumphant would naturally be indispensable to the twentieth-century Church.

If in our confrontation with the godless we are under-powered, we are compelled to admit the Prime Mover is not decadent. A missile may sputter and fizzle out on the launching pad, but this is no argument against the power of jet propulsion. It follows by analogy that if the contemporary Church is too weak to project the gospel light, even through the Iron Curtain, such failure is no proof against the existence of the generating Source.

One of the really significant needs of our time is the renewed awareness that the Spirit of God remains the only convicting, converting agent in the universe. He is the answer to mediocrity in missions. Satanic forces are too well entrenched and too strong to be routed with anything less potent. Our best individual and combined efforts to liberate mankind may pester and bother His Infernal Majesty, but will never devastate him. A renewal of pentecostal power will.

The ministry of evangelist Dwight L. Moody in the last century illustrates what can be done by a man filled with the Holy Spirit.

One of Moody's many biographers, Richard Ellsworth Day, sums up the evangelist's life in the words "My human best, filled with the Holy Spirit."[1] Moody began to long for the feeling of the Spirit in a measure to which he had been a stranger. There came a day in 1871 when he began praying that he might know it in full personal equation.

It was during an evangelistic crusade in Brooklyn. The campaign was poorly attended and the results small. Disappointed, Mr. Moody desperately sought God. The spare room of some friends became his "upper room" of prayer where the Holy Spirit came upon him as he gave himself completely to God. Like his apostolic predecessors, he hastened from that trysting place to lead his generation to Christ.

His personal ministry now took on gigantic proportions. Its impact made history on both sides of the Atlantic. Eventually it climaxed in Chicago when he vied successfully with the 1893 World's Fair for attendance at his evangelistic campaign. Posthumously, his influence is still molding the world. Moody Bible Institute's alumni by the thousands are contesting enemy-held ground on five continents. Much of this can be traced to an upper room in Brooklyn.

It can be regarded as axiomatic that no genuinely spiritual, progressive missionary stride has been made in the last twenty centuries apart from the "enduement of power from on high." When the Church has been inhibited by weakness and is unequal to her task of global conquest, a Voice can be heard saying, "Not by might, nor by power, but by my spirit, saith the Lord" (Zechariah 4:6). When earnest men have taken themselves to upper rooms, a resurgent Church has marched majestically forward.

In space technology, no favorable orbit is achieved until there has been a count-down and a release of power. The similarity in the spiritual realm is striking. An "A-OK" launching of the transforming Gospel to the regions beyond — hinges upon the waiting-igniting-empowering prerequisites.

The twentieth-century Church must rediscover Pentecost experimentally. To know it not merely as an event of time but as a continuing principle is, without doubt, to be imbued with sufficient reinforcement to engage the godless forces of the times, and win.

---

[1] *Bush Aglow* (Philadelphia: The Judson Press, 1936), pp. 2, 276, 279, 287.

> "The woman then left her waterpot, and went her way into the city, and saith to the men, *Come, see* a man, which told me all things that ever I did: is not this the Christ?"
>
> John 4:28, 29

4

SPONTANEOUS CHRISTIANITY

It is accepted with all credulity, this insidious "call" philosophy, as men once swallowed the theory that the world was flat.

SUBVERSIVE AGENTS continue to infiltrate unwary mankind, assisted by some accepted hallucinations which hamper the forces of good. One of the more popular notions, which accounts partially for communism's fleet-footedness compared to the snail-paced foreign missionary movement, is the whim which says, "Missionaries are a special breed. Theirs is a singular call." This is one shackle that needs to be chiseled from the Church's ankles if harassed humanity is to ever lift its eyes from its own chains and see her coming, bearing the Truth that makes men free.

Let us go back in history. See the fatigued Saviour (blessed paradox) sitting on a well curb at the end of a day's travel. No mere accident had brought Him along this route. A meeting with the woman of Sychar had been predetermined before He left Judea to come into Galilee. She was part of the reason why He had said, "I must needs go through Samaria." Geographic necessity had not dictated this routing. Customarily the Jews traveled a different way. Traditionally they had "no dealings with the Samaritans." But here Christ was to meet and impart life to one of the unlikeliest of them.

29

The woman was a member of a mongrel race standing somewhere between Jews and heathens. He would first win her and through her many more of her kind, laying the foundations of a significant soul-saving work in all Samaria. Climaxing their dialogue the woman (a water carrier) "left her waterpot," walking right away from her prized vase to carry to those yet unaware the tidings of the newly arrived Saviour.

How exquisitely natural. No one told her to go. There is no record that Christ commissioned her. She had met the Master face to face, and the living water He came to give was already springing up within her unto everlasting life. Without specific command she commenced inviting others to come and drink.

A large-scale awakening followed, remarkable for its rarity in the Lord's personal ministry. Nearly the whole city responded to the woman's invitation, "Come, see a man who told me all that I ever did." They came, they saw, He conquered their hearts. Urging Him to remain in their town He stayed for two days. Before He left, the citizenry was heard testifying to the woman,

> "Now we believe, not because of thy saying: for we
> have heard him ourselves, and know that this is indeed
> the Christ, the Saviour of the world" (John 4:42).

What happened that day foreshadowed the gathering of the Gentile world into the Church. The ripeness of the Sycharites for spiritual harvest betokened the greater ingathering of heathen hearts into His garner. The woman's motivation provided the key which would open the door to missionary service in every age.

This returns us to the unnamed woman who left her waterpot to become a missionary without special authorization and apparently on her own initiative. Her heart told her what to do. She had come to know something of Christ, and to know Him at all was to enlist under the missionary banner. No coaxing, no cajoling was needed to forsake her waterpot and become His emissary. She became instrumental at once in bringing outcasts to the Saviour. What she then did, why she did it, and what came of it, present in microcosm the whole gamut of missions.

No one seems to know where the idea originated, but somehow an insidious suggestion has crept into mission philosophy which has come to be known as "the call." It is accepted with all credulity, talked about, taught and believed as men once seriously agreed that the world was flat. It holds that without a special, sensational revelation, dream, vision or voice which can be equated with *the call,* a rank and file Christian would be guilty of rank presumption should he dare become a missionary.

Today it is openly alleged by some, tacitly assumed by many more, that any attempt to engage in foreign missions without something equivalent to a *Macedonian call* is brashness. Because of this illusion many earnest but badly informed disciples are hesitant about deliberately taking part in the global task assigned by Christ. This woman-at-the-well story helps take some of the mysticism out of missions by placing the whole matter on a sensible, reasonable, simple and operational platform.

Relating Paul's "Macedonian call," or Isaiah's "vision," or Gideon's "fleece" (Acts 16:9; Isaiah 6; Judges 6:36-40) to the Christian credential gives it a hazy incongruity. Paul's Macedonian experience was no call to *become* a missionary. It was merely a new directive to one who was *already* a missionary, involving a change of *location,* not of vocation. Certainly Isaiah's vision cannot be construed as a personal call to the foreign ministry. To lift Gideon's fleece out of its purely local setting and give it modern missionary application seems ridiculous in the extreme. Yet this is common. The woman at the well needed none of this!

It may well be asked why Luke and others accompanied Paul from Asia to Europe. They did not see the vision he saw, or hear the voice he heard. Yet this was no deterring factor. Luke wrote of it: "After *he* [Paul] had seen the vision, immediately *we* endeavoured to go" (Acts 16:10). Here is a clear-cut case of some going to a foreign country on the strength of the vision of someone else. It was reason enough to do so then. Is it not ample now?

He needs no *call* who has a *command.* Why should he wait for a *voice* who already has a *verse* indubitably involving him? It may be relevant to even ask, who needs the Great Commission? When communism drove Arthur Nyhus out of China, he took up missionary work in Japan. When the door to Free China opened, he proceeded to Taiwan. What was his motivation?

> "Even if Jesus Christ had not given us the Great Commission, commanding us to 'Go into all the world and preach the Gospel to every creature,' we would go anyway. Because when we are saved, we want others to hear what we have heard. That's the motive we call gratitude."

The unnamed woman of Samaria had that, and required nothing more.

James Gilmour, missionary to Mongolia, saw the issue in this light:

> "Even on the low ground of *common sense,* I seem to be called to be a missionary. Is the kingdom a harvest field? Then I thought it reasonable that I should seek to work where the work was most abundant and the workers fewest." [1]

Debate or rationalization should be unnecessary. An up-to-date account of just how natural missions is to redeemed man, even to Stone Age peoples (Irian Barat — West New Guinea), is offered by the late Reverend Ebenezer G. Vine. Twenty years ago, the cannibalistic tribes of New Guinea were unknown to civilization. They were locked behind high mountain ranges unaware of the outside world. It took the crash of an American Army transport plane into one of their valleys, "Shangri-La," during World War II, to catapult the savages from the Stone Age into the twentieth century. Search for crash survivors resulted in their discovery.

The introduction of Christianity to the Swart Valley by a primitive tribesman is described by Mr. Vine for the readers of this book.

Take a look at that fearsome-appearing fellow. His name is Jibitu. His wardrobe is limited to the long, yellow gourd, but remember, he has but recently emerged from Savage Stoneagedom, with its cannibal culture. Shocked at first, you'll probably see that the gourd is similar to a pair of trousers in your own culture; thus it will be bereft of offense. Even the pig tusk through his nose will be more readily understood.

Just recently, after years of evangelizing with seemingly little result, suddenly the power of God was manifested in redemption. The change was profound and far reaching. Fears of the spirit world were challenged. Old taboos lost their influence and power. A new way of life took shape.

Dramatically peace pervaded the hitherto warring tribes. Weapons of war were destroyed. Many had quietly believed the "Jesus words" the white man had shared with them. Their hearts had become possessed of a strange and unknown, settled peace. The Gospel of Christ was yielding its fruit at last.

The little Piper MAF (Missionary Aviation Fellowship) plane had just arrived at the mission station with supplies, mail, et cetera. The pilot stood by his craft chatting with the local missionary, when one of the tribesmen with his Stone Age gear strode over. He addressed the two: "White men, those people many days over the mountains, talk as we do." How he knew this, remains something of a mystery, for he was clearly indicating tribal

[1] Richard Lovett, *James Gilmour of Mongolia.*

groups 150-200 miles to the East. He continued: "Since we have understood and believed the *Jesus words,* such a wonderful change has come. We have happiness and peace we never knew before. My heart tells me to go and tell those people these same *Jesus words* that have changed us. I want to go, but it too far and too dangerous to walk. I would be killed and eaten on the way."

He was remembering the cannibal area through which he must pass to reach people of his same tongue, and he knew he would never get through. "Since I cannot walk to these people," he reasoned, "won't you take me over the high mountains . . . let me go and tell them." His wish was granted. In an hour the drone of the plane's engine was heard over the distant valley. Tribes people hurried down the trails to be at the airstrip in time to see the new visitors.

Coming to a halt at the station, the pilot is greeted by the missionaries. But see, the man from afar with the pig tusk in his nose! He appears apprehensive as he gazes upon the hordes of tribesmen! Will they welcome him — or will they prove hostile?

Look! The local Chief Tibelak strides over to the plane and extends his hand. Jibitu alights from the plane, and the Danis [primitives] swarm around him! The people listen as he speaks their own tongue. Within a quarter of an hour, hundreds of people are squatting around him. He is telling them what the "Jesus words" in his own district have done for him and many others, of the great changes wrought.

They are deeply interested, for they see in this man, one just like themselves. They come back the next night; many of them stay up through the whole night listening in rapt astonishment to the very strange news he has to tell.

Among the first to receive the Glad Tidings was Tibelak, the Chief. Deeply did he ponder these strange matters — and then, clearly demonstrating his interest and his belief in that which he had heard, he called his people together. Jibitu had been taken back to his people but the effect of his visit and of his words was profound for the transforming power had touched many. Said Tibelak, "You have heard from that man what has happened in their village and all around. They fight no more! They have peace among them. In their hearts they believe the *Jesus words* and have happiness."

With that, he issued a tribal order: "We will fight one another no more! We will be friends with the other tribes, and will not kill one another again. Bring all your spears, bows and arrows. Stack them here."

The tribal order must be obeyed. The weapons are brought in, a great armory. As darkness falls a tribal dance of gladness is staged in simple evidence of their happiness. The torches are applied to the many stacks of wooden weapons, and a vast conflagration ensues, lighting up the jungle night. Intertribal warfare is banished, and peace, hitherto unknown, begins.

A new day dawns in the Swart Valley, and it has come to stay . . . because of one aboriginal convert who, knowing nothing at all of the Great Commission, dared a flight over treacherous mountain ranges to take the Light to fellow-tribesmen "sitting in the regions of the shadow of death."

Reduced to its simplest definition, the missionary call consists of but the *need,* the *knowledge* of the need, and the *ability* to meet the need. These were the only letters credential of the unnamed woman at Sychar's well who forsook her waterpot to run and bid men "come, see the Christ." It was all the accreditation required by Jibitu, the *enlightened* New Guinea savage. Need *we* more?

"Now while Peter doubted . . .
the men stood before the gate."
Acts 10:17

5

THOSE RACIAL BARRIERS

The subtle assumption that God speaks
English with an American accent, or in
the Cockney dialect, or that He has a
Scotch burr on His tongue, is devastating.

PREJUDICE AND INDIFFERENCE have been said to be the greatest
enemies of foreign missions, and ignorance has been named as the
mother of them both.

The racially prejudiced Christian is an enigma. It is not too
surprising to find worldlings afflicted with this malady, but the believer has a Book which reveals that God ". . . hath made of *one*
blood all nations of men" (Acts 17:26). We are all actually blood-
relatives.

Prejudicial views along these lines are not new and are often
coupled with doubts. Our text portrays a prejudiced Peter as a
doubting Thomas. The complete story of his misgivings makes one
of the most fascinating dramas recorded in the New Testament and
is charged with present day application.

It was noon in the little Mediterranean town of Joppa. The
Apostle had gone to the roof-top to pray. While praying he became
hungry and contemplated the approaching dinner hour. A trance
came over him. He saw the heavens open and a sheet descending,
lowered by its four corners. In it were all kinds of quadrupeds,
creeping things, and wild birds. He heard a Voice saying, "Rise,

Peter, kill and eat." Peter remonstrated, "No, no, Lord; for I have
never eaten anything common or unclean." A second time the
Voice came to him, this time saying, "What God has cleansed,
you must not count common." Peter was not easily convinced, so
the visionary sequence was repeated two more times. It was just not
kosher. The animals in the vision — the quadrupeds, wild beasts,
and creeping things were forbidden to him by Mosaic law as cere-
monially unclean. And he was a conscientious and obedient Jew.
Ham hocks and bacon would be as unwelcome to the orthodox Jew
of today.

This series of revelations was God's unique way of convincing
a religiously and racially biased man of his obligations to his foreign
neighbors whom he downgraded and regarded generally as outcasts.
They were supernaturally timed to coincide with the arrival of three
Romans (one of whom at least was perhaps a Jewish proselyte)
who stood waiting before his gate. The Roman captain Cornelius
had dispatched them from Caesarea with the order to escort the
Apostle to his own headquarters that he might learn from him the
Way of life (Acts 11:14).

It is amazing to find Peter, a confidant of Christ, continuing
to doubt under such circumstances. Descending from the roof-top
he did not, even now, fully grasp the scope of Jehovah's beneficence
to a race not his own. His discrimination had yet to be dissipated.

Three days later Peter found himself in Caesarea preaching
Christ to the Romans, a thing he never expected to be doing. Witnessing their conversion he was amazed to discover that Jews had
no exclusive claim upon Christ. How slow he had been to fully
grasp the latitude and longitude of love.

Peter was not alone in this limited vision. His Jewish colleagues
who accompanied him to Caesarea "were astonished . . . because
. . . that on the Gentiles also was poured out the gift of the Holy
Ghost" (Acts 10:45). Even more surprising, the church leaders
summoned Peter back to Jerusalem and piously rebuked him for
going on the mission. Given opportunity to explain his unconven-
tional actions, the account he gave is replete with stimulating and
provoking suggestions for modern missions.

He commenced by putting the facts before them. "I was in
the town of Joppa in prayer." This was a tacit admission that one
could be prayerful and still not be attuned to the Lord's desire toward
the unsaved. On the other hand it suggests that a praying posture
is the most receptive attitude for the racially bigoted. Even more,

it conveys the idea that for one to *remain* in a secluded prayer sanctum, while hungry-hearted men of other races wait at his door, is the wrong thing to do.

> "I thought I heard the voice of God
> And climbed the highest steeple.
> God said, 'Go down again;
> I dwell among the people.' "

Facing the investigating council in Jerusalem, Peter maintained his ground. "I saw a vision," he declared. He told his interrogators in detail what he had seen and heard and how nonplussed he had been at the strange goings-on. He reminded the pillars of the church how, after arriving in Caesarea, he was still asking, "Why am I here?" They listened to the Roman captain's part of the dialogue, how an angel had appeared to him saying: "Send men to Joppa, and call for Simon whose surname is Peter; who shall tell thee words whereby thou and all thy house shall be saved."

Peter summed up his foreign mission apologetics with this: "As I began to speak, the Holy Ghost fell on them, as on us at the beginning. Then remembered I the word of the Lord. . . ." Recognizing that further religious discrimination on racial grounds would be an overt attempt to thwart the divine plan, he simply asked his examiners, "What was I, that I could withstand God?" Their scruples took wings. "When they heard these things, they held their peace, and glorified God, saying, Then hath God also to the Gentiles granted repentance unto life" (Acts 11:13-18).

The logical conclusions Peter arrived at were these: God is "no respecter of persons" but Lord of *all* people (Acts 10:34, 36). Earthly distinctions were now seen to be of no account to God and further vacillation by them would mean "withstanding God." Divine favoritism was recognized as nonexistent.

The slowly learned lessons of the first Christian era seem to need rediscovery in every succeeding period. Each generation assumes varying degrees of bias. The British ecclesiastics of the nineteenth century charged William Carey with rank presumption when he insisted that the Gospel be sent to the unenlightened Hindu. They contended that if and when God chose to convert the brown-skinned heathen, He would do so without the shoe-cobbler's meddlesomeness. This did not prevent Carey from devoting years of distinguished service in India or hinder him from earning the title, "the father of modern missions."

Unfortunately, there is evidence of more than a mere trace of this same antipathy among us today. It may take a more subtle form: the assumption that God speaks English with an American accent, or a Cockney dialect, or that He has a Scotch burr on His tongue. This is devastating to God's redemptive plan for man. The bias that causes Christians to overlook fraternal love and responsibility can only spell ruin to the race. Many of us could well inquire what is going to shake us loose from our predilections.

Cannot we learn from Peter's experience? Will not his roof-top vision do for us all? Shall alien men stand pounding on our door to rouse us from our highly self-satisfied, ivory-tower spirituality before we awake to the raceless scope of saving grace? We need no miracle revelation who are already under verbal injunction to make all peoples our parish.

Uninhibited childhood often teaches the prepossessed among us our best lessons. A discerning cartoonist pictures two youngsters of different color walking arm-in-arm in mutual delight, one asking and the other replying:

"What is this Brotherhood Week?"

"I don't know. It has something to do with *big people.*"

The time has come to remove every vestige of racism from our hearts. Commissioned and endowed as every disciple of Christ is, he can find no justifiable reason for contentedly loitering about in his own little national or ecclesiastical market place on the pretext ". . . no man hath hired me" (Matthew 20:1-16). The command of the Lord of the harvest is complete and final.

Go work in my vineyard today! Glean men for the
Kingdom from every kindred, tribe and nation!

> *"I am debtor* both to the Greeks, and
> to the Barbarians; . . . I am ready to
> preach the gospel to you that are at
> Rome also."
>
> Romans 1:14, 15

6

BALANCING ACCOUNTS

*It would be morally wrong to hug to
one's bosom what is meant to be shared
by all . . . a violation of the law of Universal Love.*

COMMUNISM'S pretended altruism, "To have is to *owe,* not to *own"*
and its materialistic appeal to the poorer classes is altering the course
of history for the worse. But the face of the world will be changed
for the better when Christians recognize how much they owe the
spiritually destitute and commence matching awareness with action.
Bringing the sacred rights and privileges of the down-trodden up to
parity with our own becomes a Christian obligation of the first magnitude.

At first glance, the acknowledgment by a refined Jewish aristo-
crat that "I am a debtor" may seem a little surprising. One can
hardly conceive of such a highly cultivated gentleman admitting he
owed *anything* to Greeks or barbarians or much less to Romans.
The highbred Saul of Tarsus was a self-confessed Pharisee of the
Pharisees.

The turning point came one day on the Damascus Road during
a soul-transforming encounter with Christ. At once his mind embraced the truth that Christ was indeed the long-expected Messiah.

Simultaneously he saw Him as the Saviour of *all* men. "Straightway
he preached Christ . . . that he is the Son of God" (Acts 9:20). For
this new champion of redeeming grace the Gospel could be nothing
less than a universal message. The day he was converted he began
paying the debt of love to mankind and he continued every instal-
ment until it was fully met.

Paul was filled with desire for his own race, the Jews. He professed: "I have great heaviness and continual sorrow in my heart.
My heart's desire and prayer to God for Israel is, that they might
be saved" (Romans 9:2; 10:1). He owed it to his kinsmen to be
so concerned no less than to the heathen and barbarian. This sense
of debt pervaded his every thought and action, all he did and was.
He was a man in possession of the only reprieve for a condemned
race, and his solemn responsibility was to deliver it. "Woe is unto
me if I preach not," he cried.

Ashael Grant felt something of Paul's apprehension: "I dare
not go up to the judgment till I have done my best to diffuse His
glory throughout the world."

Paul sought continually to preach the Gospel where Christ was
not already named (Romans 15:20). In one city, for a three months'
period, he spoke boldly in a local synagogue, "disputing and per-
suading the things concerning the kingdom of God." When he was
no longer welcome in the sanctuary, he occupied the rostrum of a
public forum and for two years carried on disputations five hours
a day (Acts 19:8, 10; Moffatt).

An iconoclast of the first order, wherever the Apostle to the
Gentiles found people bowing down to sticks and stones, he cried
out against the practice: "An idol is nothing. Christ is all, and in
all." Usurpers had to be deposed and Christ enthroned in the spirit
of man. Dampen his ardor? Never! His motivation? "I am a
debtor."

But Paul saw this indebtedness as not only his. It was something owed by the whole Church and he devoted a good deal of his
time packing her collective brain with the strong conviction. Argu-
ing that Christendom had built-in obligations to rescue fallen man,
he made sure its blood stream was enriched with missionary cor-
puscles. He dispatched at least thirteen epistles to Christians, persistently directing their attenticns to their responsibilities, encouraging them to take up the cause of benighted men by sending, giving,
going.

Three times Paul covered much of the then-known world to

demonstrate and plead the case. He saw the grace of God as bestowed upon the Church to the end that everyone might experience the hope of God's calling. Simply stated, the Christian's responsibility was to make all men know the unsearchable riches of Christ (Ephesians 3:8, 9). Missions was not an elective but an imperative, not an option but an obligation — a privilege and a responsibility. To direct the worshipful eyes of the world upon Christ was the goal.

Paul wrote the Thessalonians reminding them he was holding the Gospel in trust and that they were to be imitators of him (I Thessalonians 2:4; 1:6). They were more than beneficiaries. They were executors. His prayer for the Philippians, whom he hoped to find always striving for the Gospel, was that they might have a sense of what was vital and "be without offense till the day of Christ" (Philippians 1:27, 10). He reprimanded others whose missionary zeal had dwindled: "It is good to be zealously affected always in a good thing" (Galatians 4:18).

God's gifts are tools not prizes. The reconciled are to be reconcilers. The comforted are to comfort (II Corinthians 4:6; 5:18). To regard anything in one's possessions as something owned rather than loaned, is to widely miss the apostolic idea of stewardship. In whatever kind and to whatever degree given, the Spirit's gifts to the individual become the common property of all. For the Christian to have is to share. Let him confess "I ought" and he is obliged to say "I will."

Illustrations of the spiritual principle may be found in nature. Huber, the great naturalist, notes that when a wasp finds a deposit of honey it returns to the nest to impart the good news. All then sally forth to partake of the fare discovered for them. The lesson is too obvious to belabor. J. G. Holland puts it simply:

> "Open your hands, you whose hands are full. The
> hungry world is waiting for you. The whole machinery
> of Divine Beneficence is clogged by your closed hand
> and rigid fingers. Give and spend, and be sure that
> God will send. For only in the giving and spending
> do you fulfill the object of God's giving and sending."

The eighteen centuries separating the first and the twentieth have not altered the rudimentary precept, "I am debtor."

> "I have more than I can wear,
> Their feet and hands and heads are bare;
> I have more than I can eat,

They die with hunger in the street;
My life knows love of noble souls,
Their hearts are thirsty empty bowls;
I worship Jesus, risen Lord,
But they have never heard His Word.
These things let me remember when
Cries of the needy rise again."
— Anonymous

"On the first day of the week, let each of you *put aside a sum* from his weekly gains . . ."

I Corinthians 16:2
(Moffatt's Translation)

7

WEEKLY PAY ENVELOPE

Nowhere but in the budgeting of disciples of Christ will be found the solution to under-financed foreign missions, except it first be discovered in their hearts.

THE KEY to the locked door behind which the world's *have-little* people squat in destitution and hunger is in the hands of the *have-much* Christian community. It is called benevolence.

We are startled when we discover how great a part the believer's weekly envelope can play in "winning friends and influencing people" of alien extraction; winning them from communism's allurement (always promising yet never producing) to godliness which holds the "promise of life both for the present and for the future" (I Timothy 4:8, Moffatt).

The Apostle Paul's counsel on money-raising to help alleviate human suffering in other lands is classic. It recommends itself as a pattern to the churches of all nations of all time.

Palestine faced another of its oft-recurring famines. The Jews were in dire straits. The apostle devised an arrangement by which Gentile converts in Corinth and all of Macedonia and Achaia would rally to provide overseas relief. He wrote about it in substantial length, calling attention to the marked social disparity between the

43

haves and the *have-nots,* contrasting the poverty of the Judeans with the prosperous lot of the people of Achaia.

Paul made it clear he was not advocating that Jews be relieved by burdening Greeks (II Corinthians 8:13). He pled only for an equalized status. The luxuries of one should yield to the needs of another. Or lacking luxuries they would help meet their foreign neighbor's famine-created necessities from a modest store.

Paul's scheme was simple and spiritually discerning. It was voluntary too, since he merely offered it as his own counsel and not something of divine command. But it carried the assurance, "He that soweth bountifully shall reap bountifully" (II Corinthians 9:6).

Certain guidelines for giving toward the overseas fund were laid down. The contributions were *planned* and *personal,* and *proportionate* with earnings. They were also *promissory,* since the Corinthians had pledged themselves to the undertaking (II Corinthians 8:11). It was a *prudent* plan as well. To open one's hand to the needy abroad was to be loved and prayed for by grateful foreigners, a no small reward to wise investors. And from the *practical* viewpoint the project demonstrated the Christian's professed subjection to Christ. It served as *outward* proof of *inner* righteousness (II Corinthians 8:8).

The recommended program, if widely embraced and implemented today, would soon solve all the fiscal problems of the Christian enterprise. Its adoption would inject new life into the blood stream of the whole missionary venture in every economically depressed and underprivileged country on earth. It could only result in untold international good will, a major ingredient in the doing of God's will on earth.

The plan was simple. It was customary on the "first day of the week" to set aside a gift for this specific purpose. Sunday was missions day. This practice eliminated the need of special appeals for large sums periodically. Having to make do with small offerings caused by irregular, spasmodic giving was unknown.

Mission-giving was *personal* giving. Paul advised, "Let *every one of you* lay by him in store" (I Corinthians 16:2). Persons in limited circumstances as well as those in higher income brackets were expected to share. Everyone was a member of the Church's quartermaster supply.

Donations were *proportionate.* Presumably the sliding scale was used in establishing percentages for missions. The instructions were, "Give as God has prospered." Those of lesser means were not expected to share beyond their ability. Greater prosperity would mean a higher proportion to the cause. But everyone helped alleviate his foreign brother's hunger.

Giving by faith (pledging something not already possessed) made this *promissory* giving. The scriptural context would lead us to believe the Corinthians had taken the step in faith the year before, pledging if not in amount at least in intent to foreign aid. Paul wrote commendingly of their thoughtful foresight (II Corinthians 8: 10).

The *prudence* of the plan is revealed in that the fund not only fed hungry Palestinians. It occasioned many a thanksgiving to God by the receivers, and brought the Lord's bounty upon the givers (II Corinthians 9:11, 12).

It is not surprising that a method which worked so efficiently in the first century is equally effective in the twentieth. Each succeeding year finds a small but growing number of churches calling upon the membership to make "faith promises for missions." And they testify to the utilitarianism of the first-century pattern.

Following this course enabled a newly-founded, fifty-six member church in Nova Scotia (its sanctuary as yet without a permanent roof) to contribute $20,000 during one year. Some congregations aim at the $100,000 goal (and usually oversubscribe), and a few exceed a quarter of a million.

More often than not, munificence in missions contributes to success all around. It becomes a rule of thumb that the more given to missions abroad, the more prosperity is enjoyed at home; the greater prosperity at home, the greater percentage is devoted to missions abroad. It is an ever-widening circle of benefit.

What happens to the church happens to the man. In the day of meager wages, a laborer employed at $10.00 a week commenced tithing, putting aside one dollar each Sunday. His income increased to fifteen and he said: "I have been living on nine, surely I can now get by on thirteen." Soon his earnings increased to $20.00. Again he reasoned, "If before, I gave two out of fifteen, I can now give four out of twenty." On and on it snowballed until he was contributing thousands of dollars annually by using the sliding scale.

The devotee of foreign missions gives not from the motive of greater gain. Nevertheless, he cannot avoid it. He is as the benefactor described by Bunyan:

"There was a man and some did count him mad;
The more he gave away, the more he always had."

It is ironic that affluence within the average present day church should not accrue more significantly to overseas charities. Statistics are surprising. One of the smaller denominations, the Evangelical Free Church (50,000 members) tops the list in per capita giving averaging $36.40 per year. The two largest communions, each crowding a ten million membership, report an astonishing low. Recent published figures (*American Year Book of Churches,* 1962) reveal the Methodist Church averaging $1.13 and the Southern Baptist Convention, $1.90 per member per year.

Trifling as these contributions may seem, they are liberal when compared to Catholic response. Bishop Fulton Sheen laments the *twenty-seven cents* per year per Catholic in offerings for "the Holy Father's missions" overseas. A satirical cartoon in the Bishop's magazine, *Missions,* shows a plump, over-dressed dowager generously covering a soda fountain stool, and ordering: "I'll have the Double Trouble marshmallow butterscotch sundae, with whipped cream and banana on the side, and that peach syrup. But leave the pecans off . . . *I'm sacrificing them for missions.*"

The persuasiveness of precedents did much to enhance foreign missions giving in the first century. With typical resourcefulness, Paul set off the chain reaction. He wrote the Corinthians, "I have boasted of you to the Macedonians: . . . *your* zeal has been a stimulus to the majority of *them*" (II Corinthians 9:2, Moffatt). He also proposed the charities of the Galatians as examples to the Corinthians, those of the Macedonians to the Corinthians, and the benevolences of both to the Romans.

Perhaps the following contemporary example from the Orient will stir up favorable response in the Occident. Dr. Edwin Kilbourne of the Oriental Mission Society described (in a personal interview) the missionary enthusiasm of Korean believers.

> I have seen our Korean Christians weep because they had nothing more to give. They came forward, emptied their pocketbooks, then placed their pocketbooks in the offering. Taking their glasses from their eyes, rings from their fingers, clothing from their backs, shoes from their feet, they placed them on the altar and then cried because they had nothing more to give. I have known some to leave the meeting, go to their homes, get their bedding and the remainder of their clothing and bring these, saying, "Sell them for the offering." I have seen our pre-

cious native preachers, who had come to the conference from two hundred miles distant, place their return bus tickets in the offering and say, "Redeem them and give the money to missions. We will *walk* home." The Korean church knows how to give.

Only let the example of the Corinthians and the Koreans find wider acceptance among us and a new and better day will dawn for mankind.

*"I will very gladly spend and
be spent . . ."*
II Corinthians 12:15

8

FOR HEAVEN'S SAKE

*Christ warned there would be losses and
crosses, but the dangers were not to deter
His followers from invading the hostile,
pagan world.*

UNDER THE HEADLINE, "Moon Race Casualties Foreseen," the Associated Press quoted an expert in the field of astronautics as saying, "We are going to kill a lot of men in our race to the moon, but I am sure we can beat the Communists there." He called for a multibillion dollar outlay and for men who would be willing to lay their lives on the line. He warned there would be no bargain rates.

It is fascinating to compare the price tag attached to getting men to heaven. Willingness to pay and to die have always been necessary requisites. Paul did not shrink from this degree of expendability. He wrote, "I will gladly spend (all that I have), and be spent (all that I am) for you." He meant it with all his being.

The analogies are apt. Getting men to the moon is costly. Getting men to heaven is also expensive and if the price were even higher, there should be no complaint, for the superiority of the issue is obvious. There is no shortage of men offering to risk their all that the moon may be inhabited. There should be no deficit of dedicated persons willing to hold themselves expendable that heaven may be populated.

The term *expendability* has come to carry a military connotation. It speaks of "equipment and supplies to be used up or destroyed . . . most usually men" to gain an objective. In the spiritual realm this may seem a high price for fitting earth-dwellers as inhabitants of heaven. However, critics of the cost are not the missionaries, nor their supporters, nor the foreigners to whom they go, nor the appreciative government observers of the expenditure. Faultfinders are those who have never seen the benefits to be gained.

At the outset of the world-evangelizing venture, Christ warned there would be losses and crosses, but these dangers were not to deter His followers from invading the hostile world with celestial hope. Perils which Christ foretold soon came to them. Stephen, a layman, was stoned to death. James was killed by Herod. Peter was crucified upside down. Paul was decapitated. Thomas was thrust through with a spear. John was the only apostle who escaped violent death. It is affirmed he was cast into a cauldron of boiling oil but escaped by miracle without injury. Exiled to Patmos, he lived out his days under unfavorable circumstances. All held their lives to be expendable when they remembered the objectives to be gained. They "loved not their lives unto the death" (Revelation 12:11).

It was an enigma to the disciples when Christ began to teach the doctrine of expendability. Privately and patiently He explained that even He must "suffer many things and be killed and raised again the third day." From their point of view it was unthinkable! Peter rebuked Him (affectionately, no doubt), "Be it far from thee, Lord. This shall not happen unto thee." Recognizing in Peter's remonstrance a Satanic lure, Christ replied, ". . . thou savourest not the things that be of God. . . ." He then declared His followers' expendability to the cause, saying, "If any man will come after me, let him deny himself, and take up his cross, and follow me. For whosoever . . . will lose his life . . . shall find it" (Matthew 16:21-25).

Our modern unfamiliarity with this qualification of discipleship is betrayed in the following bit of fantasy carried in the January, 1954, issue of *Brown Gold:*

> I dreamed that I was in Celestial City — though when and how I got there, I could not tell. I was one of a great multitude . . . from all countries and peoples and times and ages. Somehow, I found that the one next to me had been there more than 1800 years.
> "Who are you?" I asked.
> "I was a Roman Christian," said he, "and I lived in the days of the Apostle Paul. I was one of those who died in Nero's persecutions. I was covered with pitch and fastened to a stake and set on fire to illuminate the Emperor's garden."
> "How awful!" I exclaimed.

"No," he answered, "I was glad to do something for Him Who died on the Cross for me."

The man on the other side of me then spoke: "I have been in heaven only a few hundred years. I came from an island in the South Seas, Eromanga. John Williams, a missionary, came and told me of Christ, and I, too, learned to love Him. My fellow-countrymen killed the missionary, and they caught and bound me. I was beaten until I fainted, and they thought I was dead; but I revived. The next day they cooked and ate me."

"How terrible," I said.

"No," he replied. "I was glad to die as a Christian. You see, the missionaries had told me that Jesus was scourged and crowned with thorns for me."

Then they both turned to me and said, "What did you suffer for Him? Or did you sell what you had for the money which sent men like John Williams to tell the heathen about the Saviour?"

I was speechless. And while they were both looking at me with sorrowful eyes, I awoke. It was a dream!

Losing lives, giving all (for heaven's sake) — these extremes have always appeared to some as a strange sort of squander-mania. Cynics have been known to ask in sarcasm, and sincere Christians in bewilderment, "Why this waste?" But letting go of one's self, willingness to sacrifice both person and possessions, counting gain but loss have always been considered the hallmarks of Christian soldiery.

C. Taylor Smith, missionary to Africa, was a classical example. He professed: "If I had ten lives, I would gladly lay them down in a white man's grave, to gain by the grace of God the black man's resurrection." Henry Martyn was another. Debarking the ship that brought him to the shores of India, he knelt on the sands and cried, "Here let me burn out for God."

Paul testified to having "suffered the loss of all things," having endured all things that others might "obtain the salvation which is in Christ Jesus with eternal glory" (Philippians 3:8; II Timothy 2:10). If it would have helped, he would have risked his own soul (Romans 9:3). He was willing to endure anything, to go anywhere, to pay any price for the eternal salvation of Gentile and Jew. The apostle sank his possessions and his interests in peopling heaven. "I seek not my own profit," he declared, "but the profit of many, that they might be saved." With the next breath he pleaded, "Be ye followers of me . . ." (I Corinthians 10:33; 11:1).

The record of Paul's third and final missionary journey is full of touching scenes. At Ephesus his friends wept when he told them of the hazards ahead, but they could not dissuade him from continuing on. His response to the prediction of violent death has become the credo on expendability for missionaries of all time.

> "None of these things move me, neither count I my life dear unto myself, so that I might finish my course with joy, and the ministry which I have received of the Lord Jesus, to testify the gospel of the grace of God" (Acts 20:24).

This seemed to satisfy his friends. Their good-bys were mingled with tears as they accompanied him to the ship.

The resumption of his journey brought him to Tyre. In vain the disciples here tried to warn him. Following him down to the beach they knelt on the sands and prayed. At Caesarea it was a repetition of the same. Perils were prophesied and the Christians begged him to go no farther. Unyielding he maintained, "I am ready . . . to die . . . for the name of the Lord Jesus" (Acts 21:13).

When Paul wrote that he was "in deaths oft" (II Corinthians 11:23), he was not using poetic license. His "I die daily" (I Corinthians 15:31) was no reference to the constant subjugating of his lower nature as is commonly supposed. Actually he stood in jeopardy every hour but he testified, "None of these things move me" (Acts 20:24). The big issue with him was, "Christ shall be magnified in my body, whether it be by life, or by death" (Philippians 1:20).

The question is whether we believe that today's Christians are expendable. The communists charge that we do not. They boast, "We are willing to die for our cause, but you Christians are afraid to soil your hands. This is why we are going to win the world." [1] How wrong they are!

Our generation is being repeatedly stained with martyr blood. In widely scattered places — Ecuador, Bolivia, Viet Nam and lesser known areas — devoted people are "hazarding their lives for the name of the Lord Jesus Christ." It is only that the world needs more Nate Saints, more Cecil Dyes, more Paul Johnsons, more John and Betty Stams. Nine years before the Stams were martyred by the Chinese communists on December 8, 1934, Betty penciled on the flyleaf of her Bible:

> "Lord, I give up my own purposes and plans, and all my desires, hopes and ambitions . . . and accept Thy will for my life. I give myself, my life, my all, utterly

[1] Quoted in *The Prairie Overcomer*, June, 1954.

to Thee to be Thine forever . . . work out Thy will in my life at any cost, now and forever." [2]

Every Christian a missionary, and every missionary a potential martyr. With this as our motto, the communist-threatened earth will experience a spiritual renaissance bringing heaven within the reach of every man.

---

[2] Provided by Mrs. C. E. Scott, mother of Betty Scott Stam. Published in tract form, *My Covenant With God*, by Blue Valley Blade, Seward, Nebraska.

"If any man preach *any other gospel*
. . . let him be accursed."

Galatians 1:9

9

HAVE WE A CHOICE?

*In the spiritual world, all roads do not
lead to Rome. . . . Except for one, they
all come to a dead end . . . an impasse.*

MANY "GOSPELS" are abroad, all claiming to offer a panacea for the
world's plight.

On the religious side, resurgent Shintoism and reactivated Mo-
hammedanism zealously contend for exclusive roles, while Buddhism's increasing followers aggressively recommend his *Eightfold
Path:*

Right Belief; Right Resolve; Right Act; Right Word;
Right Life; Right Effort; Right Thinking; Right Medi-
tation.

Not all philosophies competing for the world's acceptance are
religious in nature. Communism preaches a materialistic transformation of society through socialism toward a classless utopia. Militarism exalts the virtues of aggressive arms preparedness. Pacifism
advocates total demilitarization and the settlement of the world's
strifes by arbitration and appeasement. The Black Muslims cry out
for Negro supremacy over the white race.

In the middle of claims and counterclaims, baffled mankind is
asked to make a choice. The very complexity of each option, even
if it were simply a matter of electing one from among equals, would

make a preference difficult at best. But does the world have a choice?

Actually humanity has no option for there is no alternative to the Gospel of Jesus Christ. Whittier wrote, "Solution there is none, save in the heart of Christ alone." Scripture agrees. It does not hold that the message of Christianity is superior to that of other gospels. It unqualifiedly rejects the idea that there is any other. This element of exclusivism was what offended in apostolic times and sent Peter and John to jail. Commanded by the authorities "not to speak or teach another sentence about the name of Jesus," they found themselves unable to obey. They contended: "There is no salvation by anyone else, nor even a second Name under heaven appointed for us men and our salvation" (Acts 4:12, Moffatt). Christ was the only Saviour, so they actively proselytized.

Christianity's claim to its unique role in the world called for the Apostle Paul's letter to the Galatians. When some of these former barbarians began defecting to certain teachers who were proclaiming a mixture of Judaism and Christianity, the apostle took up the quill in reprimand: "I am surprised how soon you have turned to another Gospel . . . a Gospel which does not exist" (Galatians 1:6, 7, Aramaic translation).

In his argument Paul drew upon his own former way of life. He maintained that in religious scrupulosity he ranked beyond his countrymen: he was "more exceedingly zealous of the traditions . . ." (Galatians 1:14) — a Pharisee of the Pharisees. He reasoned that it took divine grace to redeem him, and that a Judaism which could not spell out salvation for a Jew could do no more for Gentile Gauls. Writing to others who seemed to be wavering in their unqualified allegiance, he pleaded with impassioned tone, "My little children . . . I travail in birth again . . . until Christ be formed in you" (Galatians 4:19). He desired them to be shut up to Christ alone, to glory in nothing but Him.

The usually tender-hearted Paul became polemical when reputed leaders dared to offer alternate hopes to sinful mankind. He took the hard line: "If any man preach any other gospel . . . let him be accursed" (Galatians 1:9). Denouncing those who were adulterating Christianity by traditional circumcision, Paul was vehement. He employed a startling image to invoke censure: "O that those . . . would get themselves castrated" (Galatians 5:12, Moffatt). He pleaded with other converts, ". . . be not moved away from the hope of the Gospel . . ." (Colossians 1:23). There was no place to move.

Salvation inhered in Christ. In Him was life, and the life was the light of men (John 1:4).

After Mahatma Gandhi died, his Hindu followers enshrined their esteem for him in the epitaph, "He Showed Us The Way." Great men through the ages have been *way-showers,* but who can compete, who else can qualify, for the distinctive claim made by Christ:

"I *am* the way, the truth and the life. No man cometh
unto the Father *but by me"* (John 14:6).

The celebrated German author, Thomas a Kempis, owes his renown of the last five centuries to his treatise, *De Imitatione Christi.* In the volume is found a spiritual axiom demanding universal acceptance:

"Without the Way, there is no going;
Without the Truth, there is no knowing;
Without the Life, there is no living."

In the spiritual world, all roads do *not* lead to Rome. They do not have the same destination. Except for one, they all come to a dead end . . . an impasse. This is dramatically illustrated in missionary Lillie Mae Gunnerman's account of an old African chief steeped in tribal beliefs. Confronted with the Gospel of Christ, he confessed: "The Jesus way is good, but I have followed the African road so long that I will follow it to the end." Later, however, as he lay dying he inquired, "Can I turn to the Jesus way now? My road stops here. It has no way through the valley."

A firm conviction that Christ was the world's only hope made missionaries out of the first disciples. Their impelling persuasion was, "He that hath not the Son of God hath not life" (I John 5:12). Life and immortality had been brought to light through the Gospel. There was no modifying this contention, no compromising this truth. Christ was, or He was not, man's Redeemer. They were certain that He was. They believed what they heard when He said: "If ye believe not that I am He [the Christ] ye shall die in your sins" (John 8:24).

On this unique plane, missions holds its great philosophical imperative. Christianity, being exclusive, must be propagated. All nations must be discipled. The "truth that makes men free" must be proclaimed to "every creature." All men must find their place in the Son.

Debating their respective religions, a Christian is supposed to have asked the Brahman priest, "Can you say, 'I am the resurrection and the life'?" The high caste Hindu's affirmative reply prompted the second query, "But can you make anybody believe it?" The disciple of Christ points to an empty tomb, an Easter morning, a risen Saviour. His religion is the only one which bases its claims to acceptance upon the resurrection of its Founder.

It must be conceded as historically true that Buddha was born, that he lived, that he taught (and taught well), and that he died. Mohammed, the father of Islam, and Zoroaster, the founder of the religion of the Parsees, lived, taught and died. All three remain dead. Jesus Christ not only was born, lived, taught and died, but He rose from the dead and is alive today.

While attending an international youth conference in New York some time back, a young American inquired of a cultured Burmese girl concerning the predominant religion in her homeland. When told, he casually remarked, "O well, that doesn't matter. All religions are the same anyway." Her kind but startling rebuff was:

> "If you had lived in my country, you would not say
> that. I have seen what centuries of superstition, fear
> and indifference to social problems have done to my
> people. We need the truth, the uplift of Christianity.
> My country needs Christ." [1]

When voices are heard declaiming against missionary endeavor, the expressed convictions of respected foreign leaders offset and overshadow all carping. Calling on Christian missionaries to intensify their efforts, S. L. Akintola, Chief Premier of Western Nigeria, has declared: "Africans can do without imperialism and all its implications but they cannot do without God and His all-embracing love and grace" [2]

Ethiopian Minister of Public Health (one time Ambassador to Great Britain and former U.N. Member) Ato Abebba Retta, agrees in essence: "I must say that the work of missionaries has not failed to gain more and more appreciation in Ethiopia, beginning with His Imperial Majesty Haile Selassie I; the Ethiopian Government, and the people." [3]

[1] *The Prairie Overcomer.*
[2] *Japan Harvest,* 1963.
[3] *Africa Now,* April-June, 1963.

Princess Wilhelmina of the Netherlands once addressed an international religious gathering: "Mankind is yearning to experience a Christianity that is real . . . it is the only true remedy that can cure the world of the spiritual, moral and social ills bringing it to ruin. All followers of Christ should join in bringing it to our world."

There is only one true and perfect religion. The Apostle Paul contended, "For other foundation can no man lay, than that is laid, which is Jesus Christ" (I Corinthians 3:11). For him, as for its present-day advocates, the Gospel was the one proven panacea for man's maladies. He spent his life spreading it and urging others to do the same.

". . . without Christ . . .
in the world."
Ephesians 2:12

10

COMMUNISM'S UTOPIA

They may well hesitate who seek to
rob humanity of its faith . . . these
men who are dependent upon the very
religion they would discard for every
blessing they know.

THE UTOPIA promised by communists is a world minus Christ. They
parody a well-known hymn:

"Once I was blind but now I can see:
The *blight* of the world is Jesus."

The truth is that a world without the Saviour would be a world without hope. This is clearly indicated in the scriptural pronouncement:
"At that time ye were *without* Christ . . . having *no hope* . . . in
the world" (Ephesians 2:12). We need only consider the despair-
ing state of people in areas where Christ is not known, to prove
the fallacy of communism's promised social bliss without Him.

A foreign missionary has written:

A great "without" has been written on heathenism. Men and
women are toiling without a Bible, without a Sunday, without
prayer, without songs of praise. They have rulers without justice
and without righteousness; homes without peace; marriage without sanctity; young men and girls without ideals and enthusiasm;
little children without purity, without innocence; mothers without wisdom or self-control; poverty without relief or sympathy;

61

sickness without skillful help or tender care; sorrow and crime
without a remedy; and worst of all, death without hope.[1]

This is the nature of a world envisioned in the goal of communism
which promises to "deGod" the world in our time.

The American poet-educator-ambassador-philosopher, James
Russell Lowell, wrote of the kind of men who would advocate such
a destiny!

> As long as these men are dependent upon the religion, which
> they would discard, for every blessing they enjoy, they may
> well hesitate a little before they seek to rob . . . humanity of
> its faith in the Saviour who has alone given to man the hope
> of life eternal, which makes life tolerable and society possible,
> and robs death of its terrors and the grave of its gloom.

The lot of mankind in a culture minus Christ can be inexpressibly
bad. Particularly is this true for childhood and womanhood. The
needless suffering of children is sometimes appalling. Weird superstitions and evil customs call for cruel rites. The evil practices of
witch doctors and medicine men add a wretchedness which, early in
life, is accepted as normal.

In Africa there is to be found among certain tribes the belief that
"the first-born is a thing of shame." The first baby is often ignored
by parents and relatives alike and left to die. In other parts of pagan-
dom, multiple births are an evil omen. One or more of the newborn
infants must be destroyed, in spite of the natural instincts of the
broken-hearted mother. Fingers may be severed from a well child
because of the death of another. Puberty rites are bestial. No ex-
planations provide answers to the superstitions perpetuated by these
practices.

Where the uplift of Christianity is not known, seven- and eight-
year-old girls may be sold on the wife market for a few goats or pigs.
The groom may be a polygamous old leper owning many goats and
pigs, and consequently many wives. It is all too common for mere
youngsters to be taught unchastity. Parents instruct them in the
misuse of their bodies. Sexual promiscuity is frequently one of their
earliest remembrances.

One of Africa's missionaries included this entry in his diary:

> I was visiting in the blind section of Kano. The conditions were
> terrible. I found little children having nothing but holes in

---

[1] Mrs. Whitfield Guinness, quoted in *Goforth of China*, by Rosalind Goforth
(Grand Rapids, Mich.: Zondervan Publishing House, 1937), p. 68.

their heads where eyes had been; with flies, and sometimes maggots, in them. I saw Moslem men herding little girls, ages nine to twelve, for illicit purposes. They cried to me but I could not help them.

In more sophisticated areas of the world (not primitive but still not Christian), childhood suffering may be different only in kind. A comparatively recent issue of one of India's metropolitan dailies tells a graphic story under the headline: *"Child Sacrificed Before Devi."* A two-and-one-half year old allegedly was offered to the imagined deity by tossing it alive into a pot of boiling oil. To the Christian mind such an act is uncomprehensible. Nonetheless, it shows the degree of the depravity possible in a society where Christ is not known, nor embraced as a compassionate Friend.

The lot of women is beyond telling in such circumstances. Non-Christian religions contribute much to the misery. One of the major ones excludes the female from prayer. Another teaches, "The sins of three thousand men do not equal the sins of one woman." Still another regards women as beings without souls. Probably the saddest stories have not been told, but from what is common knowledge it may be said that the plight of womankind in a civilization without the true God is wretched.

A Reuter's News Agency story under the caption, *"Indian Widow Dies on Pyre,"* tells of a young Bombay woman who committed the state-banned suicide ritual called "suttee" by throwing herself on the funeral pyre of her late husband. Clad in a yellow sari and with garlands around her neck, she threw herself into the flames to the clash of symbols, recitations by priests and the drum roll. *The Times of India* editorialized: "Suttee is believed by some Hindus to free the souls of both husband and wife from further transmigration and to be the noblest act a widow can perform."

It must be admitted that when men do wrong in a Christian community, they do it in spite of religion. In other communities it may be *because* of their religion. Heathen deities are often vulgar, obscene, revolting, and absurd. They can smile down on licentiousness, promising a heaven in the next world where unbridled lust may be indulged without penalties. Debauched childhood, debased womanhood, slavery and human sacrifice become the way of life where there is no diffusion of Christianity.

Mark Hopkins, the early American educator who presided over Williams College (the cradle of foreign missions), expressed this supporting conviction:

There is nothing on the face of the earth that can, for a moment, bear a comparison with Christianity as a religion for man. Upon this, the hope of the race hangs. From the very first it took its position as the pillar of fire to lead the race onward. The intelligence and power of the race are with those who have embraced it. And now, if this, instead of proving indeed to be the pillar of fire from God, should be found a delusive meteor, then nothing will be left to the race but to go back to a darkness that may be felt and to a worse than Egyptian bondage.

It should be a foregone conclusion, needing no argument or examination, that Christlessness as advocated by the communists is totally incompatible with the world's basic needs. Man's inborn capacity cries out for fulfillment. An aged African mother, who had but faintly heard the Gospel of hope, expressed this longing:

Dear white brother: my people wait a long time for the white man's God. Why do you not come and save? My tired hand will not lift up to God alone. I need help to save my people from the fire country. Soon will the earth swallow them up. Our hands hang down, our hearts are heavy. Your God is very good . . . He makes the heart beat fast like the war drum. Hope is like that. *Bring us hope.*

As long as hope remains dim anywhere in the world, the enlightened may not stand idly by, trusting that communism's announced plot to "deGod" the world will collapse under its own weight. The Apostle Paul explained his evangelizing ardor on the basis that mankind needed Christ, and that it would go hard with him if he failed to preach the Gospel (I Corinthians 9:16). The same applies to all of us.

II

SOCIAL SECURITY OVERTONES

*The Philippians were not like some who
thumb through Holy Writ, select this verse
from all the rest, and then rashly insist that
God make good. ... They qualified!*

THE LATE Franklin Delano Roosevelt in his Second Inaugural address reminded the listening nation: "We have always known that heedless self-interest was bad morals; we now know that it is bad economics." Unselfish concern for the welfare of less fortunate lands becomes the best guarantee of health and prosperity for our own country.

This principle is equally significant when applied on the individual and group level. "Those who plan the good of others prosper," is one of Solomon's timeless axioms (Proverbs 12:20, Moffatt).

Support for this statement is found in the oft-quoted, remarkable, promise-verse:

"But my God shall supply all your need according to
his riches in glory by Christ Jesus" (Philippians 4:19).

The context furnishes Biblical evidence on why the foreign-missionary-hearted become the objects of God's special provision to a degree exclusively theirs.

The pledge was given initially to Christians residing in Philippi, a colony of Rome. They enjoyed the distinction of having a series of "firsts" to their credit. Missionary initiative was among these. Theirs was not only the *first* church established in Europe; it became the first *missionary* church by allying itself to Paul's early foreign endeavors. Participation seems to have been the key.

The historical background is clear enough. The missionary journeys of Paul and his colleagues had brought them to Philippi (Acts 16:12). Here was planted the seed of the Kingdom. In spite of organized resistance, physical abuse and legal blocks, a thriving church sprang into being.

After the truth had taken firm root, Paul, true to pattern, pressed onward to the next towns without the Gospel. Keeping the supply lines open, the lately-converted Philippians provided funds and material for soldiers at the front in such quantities that Paul wrote back: "I have all and abound . . . I am full" (Philippians 4:18).

It is noteworthy that the infant church embraced the missionary responsibility immediately. Paul dated their "first day" participation from "the beginning of the gospel" among them. It is doubtful whether they had built their own sanctuary before underwriting the foreign missionary attack. Consequently Paul said they would merit special providential supply for all their future needs.

We should remind ourselves that the promise-verse begins with "But." The conjunction is a pivotal word connecting the promise with the proviso. The Philippians were not like some who thumb through Holy Writ, select this verse from all the rest, and then rashly insist that God make good. The almost-too-good-to-be-true-pledge was relevant to their case. They qualified.

God's promises are not like bank drafts which read, "Pay on demand of the bearer." Eternal vaults do not yield much to the casual comer, but will swing open to those with approved credentials. The Philippians were accredited. Their certification was that their care for Paul and his team of workers "had flourished."

Paul assured the European church that the fulfillment of this inclusive pledge was in reality but the dividend on their own investment. A paraphrase of his statement (Philippians 4:15-19), would be: "You helped me, and my God, before whom your gift is the odor of a sweet smell, will help you." (The figure is drawn from the aromatic incense burnt with the sacrifices in that old time.) Their overseas charities so pleased the Lord that they were now the beneficiaries of His bounties in return. All who met the criteria would come under the broad provisions of divine subsidy.

Giving to foreign missions has its own intrinsic value. It is necessary if the cause is to flourish. Yet beyond that the acts of the generous-hearted result in the compounding of spiritual blessings and temporal supplies to the donor. It has been said that one of the most beautiful compensations of life is that no one can sincerely try to help another without being blessed in return. It is a law of the Kingdom.

The practical question is: Can twentieth-century Christians claim the comprehensive coverage, the supply of all needs, offered by the Apostle Paul to the ancient Philippians? Yes, if they fall into the category of "fellow-laborers and true yoke-fellows" of those who are breaching the enemies' lines in faraway lands.

In assessing our position it may help to personalize the issue. Are we making it possible for missionaries to write back, as Paul did, "You have more than met my needs . . ."? Today's communications from mission fields are often appeals for more help and further reinforcement. In this light is it not reasonable to assume that our failure to meet needs abroad might be the very reason why the Lord does not supply some of our own here at home?

Foreign missionary investments are investments with guaranteed dividends. Many Christians will testify to increased prosperity in proportion to expanded missionary vision and enlarged contributions. The same assertion can be made for churches. Some about ready to close, impoverished and in debt, others with no missionary budget at all and with the pastor's salary in arrears have leaped to life on the heels of their first major missionary efforts. Once barren altars become crowded, prayer meetings gather momentum, finances cease to be a problem, and congregations grow to a size requiring larger sanctuaries. At the same time the ranks are not weakened or depleted by the departure of members leaving the home church to serve on mission fields across the world.

Americana abounds with expressions by leaders supporting the belief that the Church's vitality and her foreign outreach are inseparably joined. Philips Brooks, Protestant Episcopal Bishop of the nineteenth century, prescribed in this manner for an ailing church: "The best remedy for a sick church is to put it on a missionary diet."

George Frederick Pentecost linked the prosperity of the Church to missionary extension.

> "As the commercial and political life of modern na-
> tions depends upon the extent and persistency of their
> foreign trade, so does the life and prosperity of the
> home church depend upon the extent and energy with
> which she prosecutes her foreign missionary enter-
> prise."

Today's Arthur Mouw, veteran missionary to Borneo's wild men, believes that missions do not depend upon the Church [for survival]; the Church depends upon missions.

A Seattle parishioner candidly volunteered what would seem proof of this:

> "Our church used to give a lot to missions, but with
> all the building expenses, we no longer give as much,
> and we are not prospering. Our church attendance
> has fallen off, and our Sunday School enrollment, too.
> We are not winning as many to Christ. . . .

The symbol of a dying church has been depicted by a discerning artist. He painted a stately edifice, with high pulpit and altar, an ornate organ and stained window. In the vestibule hangs a small box with the words above it, "Collection for Missions." Just where the contributions should go, the slit is blocked by a cobweb.

No one who has tried it can deny that to engage in that which is so near the Saviour's heart is to share the same preferred status enjoyed by the Philippians of old. They invested well, if we may judge the matter on the dividends returned to them on the purely horizontal plane.

In the Sermon on the Mount, Jesus pointed out that to make His Kingdom our greatest care, would be to have food, clothing, and accouterments provided.

> "But seek ye first the kingdom of God, and his
> righteousness, and *all these things* shall be added
> unto you" (Matthew 6:33).

The Kingdom which He is building in this fallen world is to be made up of every kindred, tongue, tribe and nation. Making this enterprise our prime concern puts us in league with God who guarantees to "supply all our need according to his riches in glory by Christ Jesus." The Christian does not coldly calculate benefits to be received on the basis of beneficiaries bestowed. But no matter, the dividends follow his devotion as surely as the day creeps over the night skyline. The hand that gives, gathers!

> "There is a destiny that makes us brothers;
> None goes his way alone.
> All that we send into the lives of others
> Comes back into our own."
> — *Edwin Markham*

> "The gospel . . . was preached
> *to every creature* . . . under
> heaven . . ."
>
> Colossians 1:23

12

MISSION ACCOMPLISHED

Taking their credentials seriously, they
plunged into the seemingly hopeless task
of evangelizing the then-known world
. . . and notably succeeded.

THE LATE John Foster Dulles, after years of confrontation with militant, communistic elements of leadership throughout the earth, concluded that "the greatest need today is the vision and the spirit of the nineteenth-century missionary." He was referring to men of the stature of C. T. Studd, pioneer leader, who, when he issued a call for colleagues to reinforce the thin missionary ranks in Africa, made one stipulation: "None but forked-lightning Christians need apply."

It would seem that if the Red tide now surging over the earth is ever to ebb significantly, the Church will be forced to fight fire with fire, match zeal with zeal, sacrifice with sacrifice.

The price communists seem ready to pay for world-communization is reflected in a letter written by a former Eastern university student who went to Mexico and there became a communist. A copy of the letter to his fiancée, breaking their engagement, came into the hands of Billy Graham, who read it at the Inter-Varsity Missionary Conference on the campus of the University of Illinois:

We Communists have a high casualty rate. We are the ones who get shot, hung, lynched, tarred and feathered, jailed, slandered, fired from our jobs, and in every other way made as uncomfortable as possible. A certain percentage of us get killed or imprisoned. We live in virtual poverty. We turn back to the party every penny we make above what is absolutely necessary to keep alive.

We don't have the time or the money for many movies or concerts or T-bone steaks or decent homes or new cars. We've been described as fanatics. We are fanatics. Our lives are dominated by one great overshadowing factor—the struggle for world communism. We Communists have a philosophy of life which no amount of money can buy.

We have a cause to fight for, a definite purpose in life. We subordinate our petty personal selves into a great movement of humanity. If our personal lives seem hard or our egos appear to suffer through subordination to the party, then we are adequately compensated by the thought that each of us in his small way is contributing to something new and true and better for mankind.

There is one thing in which I am in dead earnest and that is the Communist cause. It is my life, my business, my religion, my hobby, my sweetheart, my wife and mistress, my bread and my meat. I work at it in the daytime and dream of it at night. Its hold on me grows not lessens as time goes on. Therefore I cannot carry on a friendship, a love affair or even a conversation without relating it to this force which both drives and guides my life. I evaluate people, books, ideas and actions according to how they affect the Communist cause and by their attitude toward it. I've already been in jail because of my ideas, and, if necessary, I'm ready to go before a firing squad.[1]

Paul and his associates were men of this stamp. They were bent on "preaching the gospel to every creature under heaven," and plunged with abandon into the seemingly hopeless task of evangelizing the whole world. And they succeeded! In less than one generation, the apostle from his Roman dungeon affirmed that the mission had been accomplished. The Gospel had penetrated the nooks and crannies of the known earth.

From the purely human standpoint, the first-century crusade was foredoomed to failure. Innumerable hosts, seen and unseen, physical and spiritual, were entrenched all over the world and arrayed against the first missionaries. Dungeons, stripes, crosses, imprisonments, boiling caldrons, and the headsman's block awaited those who dared defy the opposing forces.

[1] First printed in February, 1961, *Presbyterian Survey.*

But it was fruitless to harass these men of faith — nothing daunted them. They challenged tyrants to their faces, and when imprisoned, prayed jail doors off their hinges and returned again into the busy marts of life to preach as though they had never been away. Most of them died rather than defect! They took their vows and credentials seriously.

Beginning in Jerusalem, an isolated and despised part of the world, this nondescript band soon carried the transforming message across land and sea. Heathen by the scores were converted. The town squares of capital cities provided the setting for huge bonfires into which erstwhile pagans tossed their fetishes. Idols fell from their exalted thrones.

The newly converted were immediately enlisted in the forward spiritual thrust, and not many years had gone by when the ring-leaders were dubbed in faraway Thessalonica, "upsetters of the whole world" (Acts 17:6, Moffatt). Quite so; they had turned the world right side up.

In jail, aboard ship, in synagogues and homes they witnessed. On the streets, by the river's edge, among learned, ignorant, Scythian, bond and free; "in all the palace, and in all other places," Christ was manifested (Philippians 1:13)! By A.D. 60, less than a generation since their Commander-in-Chief had outlined their assignment, the job left to them was done.

Looking back over the first three decades of the new missionary movement, the Apostle Paul described the triumphant crusade in his letter to the people of Colossae. The Gospel *was preached* all over the world, he wrote (Colossians 1:23). By "was preached," he meant not merely "is being preached," but that it had been preached — an accomplished fact. This accorded with the command and the prophecy of Christ. The assignment had been fulfilled according to the Saviour's foretelling, and the cost was high as He predicted (Matthew 24:9). This is confirmed in the famous letter of Pliny, the Roman author, to the Emperor Trajan. Pliny wrote: "Many of every age, rank and sex are being brought to trial. For the contagion of that superstition [Christianity], has spread not only over cities, but village and country." So the scriptural record, "they that were scattered abroad went every where preaching the word" (Acts 8:4), is documented by profane history. The might of Hades did *not* prevail against them!

First-century Christians knew what they were about. They were not common traders in a common market, babbling about common wares. Their occupation was one of high specialization. Paul defined his mission: "I determined not to know anything among you [Corinthians], save Jesus Christ, and him crucified" (I Corinthians 2:2).

There was no doubt among the disciples as to what they were doing, or why they were doing it! Again and again they had heard Christ involve them in the discipling of nations. There could be no mistaking His intention to set them to the task of world-evangelization.

It is their sense of commission that is most needed today. Perhaps the Church is becoming oblivious to her standing orders. This could account for so much socializing and institutionalizing at the center, and so little evangelizing at the circumference. Within the framework of her charter, the Church is something more than a soup kitchen, a sewing circle, a billiard parlor or a men's club. The Ecclesia is a body of dedicated followers of Christ whose prime business is preaching and teaching the Gospel throughout the entire world. This the first disciples never forgot and went about evangelizing their world with all their power. Believers of each succeeding age would logically be expected to follow in their train.

Sacred history is studded with "forked-lightning Christians" who acted on the premise that what God had commanded it was possible to fulfill. Pessimism was not allowed to retard their forward movements. They were optimists almost to a fault. They treated as non-existent all man-made barriers. In their own time they penetrated the most forbidding doors. The whole world was their parish and they did not negotiate for something less. Their missionary maneuvers were always magnificent.

Are we able to match them? Are the obstacles in our communist-threatened world so formidable as to utterly prevent us from literally obeying the Lord's command, "Preach the gospel to every creature"? We do not face impossible odds. Fulfillment may appear impossible to the human eye, yet, if men are acting under a divine directive, God will make a way even where there is no way.

Christ appeared to be talking in riddles when He directed His disciples to feed the hungry masses with next to nothing. "What are they [five loaves and two small fishes] among so many?" they asked (Luke 9:13; John 6:9). It proved enough! When He ordered a man with a withered arm, "Stretch forth thine hand" (Matthew 12: 13), it looked impossible. But it wasn't! And when He charged a cripple who couldn't even stand on his feet, "Get up . . . and walk" (John 5:8, Moffatt), execution seemed remote indeed. But it wasn't!

Let the record show that first-generation Christians succeeded in "preaching the Gospel to every creature under heaven," and that they did it without many of the facilities and technologies that make the task easier in our day. We must confess they accomplished, without such advantages, what we are not achieving with them. They were *forked-lightning Christians*. They achieved what was expected of them. They completed what had been given them to do. They reclaimed their generation for God. They could truly say, "Mission Accomplished." So may we!

> "From *you sounded out the word*
> of the Lord . . . your faith . . .
> is spread abroad."
>
>   I Thessalonians 1:8

13

CHAIN REACTION

*What happened in ancient Greece is to
be regarded as a precedent, with believing nationals pulsatingly aware that the
Great Commission includes them, too.*

PROPHESYING VICTORY for world communism, Nikita Khrushchev
justified his optimism by philosophizing: "We are as sure of this as
we are the sun will rise tomorrow. The bacilli of communism may
enter the brains of your grandchildren. Nothing can stop it now." [1]
There are many who will agree with the reference to the *bacieli*
of communism. The accepted definition of *bacillus* is: "Any of the
bacteria, especially if *disease-producing.*"
How suitable was Mr. K's choice of words. However, his prediction will fail as others have failed before it because of a potent
antibiotic introduced into the world — *Christianity!* As vaccine pro-
tects the body from disease, injecting the Gospel into society over-
comes all plagues which would destroy the spiritual man.
A humanity-redeeming chain reaction was set off in the streets
of Jerusalem one Pentecost morning, yielding energy causing further
reactions for the blessing of mankind to this day. One significant

[1] Associated Press, May 20, 1959.

successive stage was demonstrated in Thessalonica, the capital city of Macedonia. Here the Apostle Paul paused briefly and sowed the seeds from which sprang a great multitude of believers. Immediately, the new converts became propagandists of the Gospel and "their faith was spread abroad . . . they sounded out the Word." One more national church in still another land had become a missionary hub with spokes leading in all directions: "to Achaia, and also to every place."

Because of their missionary energies, Paul held up these Greeks as a pattern for all believers. Failure to match their kind of zeal is to fall far below the expected apostolic standard. To interrupt the chain reaction is to short-circuit God's regenerating power and sabotage His saving design for errant mankind.

What happened in Greece is to be regarded as a precedent for every other land to which the light has come. History reveals that each freshly evangelized nation has received the Good News at the hands of aliens. Paul, a Jew, carried the Gospel to the Roman world. The Romans brought the message to Britain. A British Christian evangelized Ireland; Ireland sent missionaries to Scotland. This kind of chain reaction seems to be the divine order.

Christians of today need to see their faith as an expansive thing designed for export, and to understand that when it is not sent abroad it deteriorates at home. "Export or die," is a common slogan applied to the national economy, but it holds true for our Christian faith as well. Historically, the healthy church has been the missionary church. The more vigorous its outreach, the more robust it becomes.

It should be noted that the Thessalonians launched their missionary thrust at a time of formidable resistance from their own countrymen (Acts 17). But their sufferings did not prevent them from becoming the pace-setters for all others.

This early Greek church did not regard missions as a work for Jewish converts only. They joined with them in the venture. Christianity was not a *foreign* religion they would merely *adapt* to or *adopt*. They embraced it, nationalized it, and from that point on it was as much theirs as anybody's, as truly Western as Eastern, as integrally Macedonian as Palestinian. All were under the equally binding constraint to propagandize the world with the Truth.

Equal rights spell equal responsibilities. And neither race, nor culture, nor color can excuse an evasion of responsibility to preach the Gospel. The Japanese and the Sudanese, the Scot and the Hottentot, the American and the Brazilian — whoever has received the Truth is obligated to disseminate it, within the limits of his God-given talents and capabilities.

Gentile converts could not assume missions to be a Jewish monopoly. Orientals may not regard evangelism as an occidental task. The white man who leaves the evangelization of Africa to the Africans is not obeying the Great Commission. The Negro who sees missions as his white brother's responsibility is mistaken. There are no ethnic requirements, exemptions, or exceptions; no built-in national preferments, qualifications, or disqualifications. None of these are mentioned in the Church's marching orders. Out of each individual who has come to Christ for the satisfying draft are to flow the "rivers of living water," said Jesus. The evangelized are to evangelize; and when this is not done, God's race-redeeming plan is betrayed.

A hopeful trickle is at last beginning to flow from some lands other than the traditional missionizing peoples of the West, and please God, may it become Niagara-like in its proportions. Nationals are starting to leave their homelands and filter into other nations as Kingdom representatives.

A Viet Nam missions organ, *Jungle Frontiers* (1963), carries the story of the Reverend and Mrs. Nguyen-hau-Nhuong, who left their native land for neighboring Laos to take up ministry among the Black Thai Tribe.

Evangelical churches in Japan recently commissioned two missionaries to Laos. During a farewell ceremony at the pier, the father of one of the recruits made some significant comments:

> When we sent our sons to war . . . we did not expect to see them again. We did not want to see them again . . . we told them, "Do not return. Give your lives for your country." Now I am sending this young man of mine across the seas to another and more glorious conflict . . . into the service of the King of kings. Should I hope to see him again on the shores of Japan? No! I give him gladly to the service in Laos, and I do not expect to see him again on this earth.

Kenny Joseph, editor of the Tokyo publication *Japan Harvest* (1963), reports on these latest foreign missionary departures, "This raises to forty-two the number of Japanese foreign missionaries."

It would be difficult to measure the effect for good among the people of India if Japan's Christians were to commence carrying the Message to the subcontinent's four hundred million Hindus. This neutralist country has eyed with misgivings the militarism of Japan. To come to know its citizens as representatives of the Prince of Peace could have sensational results. We can only imagine what might be their achievements should Korean missionaries go to Kashmir, or Filipinos to the Muslims of Pakistan. If we are to win the world, this must become the modern trend.

Keeping the whole issue in perspective, however, it must be said that missions is more a matter of the heart than of geography. One can live for the world objective without ever crossing an international boundary. Some of the Thessalonians (of our text) were merchants on the Aegean Sea who "sounded out the word of the Lord" to those they met in their travels. The majority of them were the ordinary citizens of their town. But these too were included in Paul's favorable commendation. They fulfilled the requirements of a missionary honor society.

Our generation is studded with noble successors to the illustrious Greeks. Providentially hindered from crossing oceans, they have long arms — long enough to reach around the world. They have big hearts . . . big enough to encompass all of mankind. They make their influence felt to the earth's far end.

We are forced to one conclusion. The Christian of America to America . . . *and beyond!* The Asian to Asia . . . *and beyond!* The African to Africa . . . *and beyond!* Just let him follow the example of the Thessalonian, and Christendom will take a great leap forward toward the goal of winning the world.

14

NO IRON CEILING

There may be an iron curtain,
but there is no iron ceiling.

IT IS ARGUED that the ultimate weapon will never be invented. For every offense, there will be found a defense; for every action, a counteraction.

Perhaps we need a new look at the philosophy of prayer and what it can do to wrest half of the world from atheistic communism which has it barricaded behind ideological ramparts and literal barbed wire.

One of the most astute observations of our time is this: "There may be an iron curtain, but there is no iron ceiling." The answer to a closed society is an open heaven. Prayer becomes the ultimate power against which there is no defense; prayer is the final force in blasting open that half of the world where a billion souls lie sealed off from the missionary advance.

Christianity made its debut in a hostile world. Its propagators faced not one, but several iron curtains, including the Roman one ringing the Mediterranean. Despotism, paganism, and idolatry were only a few of the barriers.

In the vanguard were "unreasonable and wicked men . . . of no faith." But these were recognized as only obstacles and not as impasses. As mere deterrents, they only called for heavier reinforcements to demolish all the impidementa retarding the missionary advance, and to make it possible for the "Word of the Lord to run and have free course." So argued the Apostle Paul, one of the most knowledgeable of men on the science of prayer.

Paul was a man with an urgent mission. Speed was of the essence and he knew of no faster way to get the Gospel through the enemy's lines than by recruiting Christian converts into the secret service of prayer. He wrote letters to people he knew, and to those he did not know, urging prayer support. It was his permanent request, and when complied with, it seems never to have failed. He depended on it as his basic weapon.

Twice the apostle asked the same group of Christians, "Brethren, pray for us" (I Thessalonians 5:25; II Thessalonians 3:1, 2). He fully believed that the prayers of these formerly heathen Thessalonians would deliver him from the presently heathen Corinthians, and consequently would secure free and glorious spread of the Lord's word in Corinth as in Thessalonica. And these prayers were answered, for Paul successfully founded a church at Corinth.

Leaving Corinth, he encountered stiffening resistance "in the regions [still] beyond," so he sent back the common appeal to the now enlisted Corinthians, "Ye *also* helping together by prayer for us" (II Corinthians 1:11). Needing to be rescued from his enemies' connivings in Judea, and hoping to proceed to Italy, Paul wrote the Roman Christians, "I beg you . . . join me in most earnest prayer to God for me" (Romans 15:30, Goodspeed).

When Paul reached Rome as a prisoner, from his cell he dispatched a letter back to the Colossians, pleading, "Pray for me too, that God may give me an opening for the message" (Colossians 4:3, Goodspeed). To the Ephesians went the appeal to devote themselves constantly to prayer that he might have utterance and courage (Ephesians 6:19, 20). To the Philippians he sent proof of how effective prayer had been: "I would ye should understand, brethren, that the things which happened unto me have fallen out rather unto the *furtherance of the gospel*" (Philippians 1:12). Prayer prevailed!

The Pauline pattern is obvious. As soon as one hostile area was successfully taken and an assembly constituted, it was instructed to pray that still another area would be evangelized and other churches established.

Apostolic resources, practices and devices characteristically employed to overcome barriers and speed the message on its way can be summed up in two words . . . *Prayer Partnership*. It was this which made the sensational advance of the infant church possible. United prayers combined to provide an unbeatable phalanx.

It is a reasonable conclusion that had not the early Christians responded to frequent rousing calls to prayer, the Word would not have had free course so superlatively. Apart from the intercessory efforts put forth in the cottage prayer meeting in Mary's house in Jerusalem, there is little doubt that Peter would have been executed that morning after Easter. A night of intercession delivered him from prison only hours before his scheduled execution at dawn.

Supplication freed Paul and Silas from the dungeon in Philippi so they could continue their daring exploits. It forced closed continents to admit them, moved stony hearts, and startled set minds. In short, prayer accomplished what no other single factor, or combination of factors, could do. Against it, the forces opposed to the spread of Christianity had no apparent defense. Prayer was the ultimate weapon against both the seen and the unseen enemies of the Truth.

This knowledge should encourage Christians who are over-inclined to the view that the seeming standstill of one missionary venture can be attributed to unprecedented problems such as bristling nationalism and encroaching communism. Problems or no problems, prayer can again prevail. No other pattern provides greater hopes or presumes to promise so much.

Prayer's time-tested potency is told by Hudson Taylor, founder of the China Inland Mission. A missionary couple in charge of ten stations felt constrained to write the Home Secretary confessing the lack of progress. Indifference, open opposition and ignorance prevented their making headway. The situation seemed hopeless.

The suggestion was made that the Secretary try to find ten persons, each of whom would make one station a special object of unceasing prayer. With the passing of time, events began to change in seven of the ten mission stations. Opposition melted, spiritual revival came, and significant numbers of persons were converted. On the other three fields, there was still no observable change.

Again the missionaries wrote the Secretary, telling him of the phenomenon and expressing concern and bewilderment over the stalemated three.

It was not difficult for the Secretary to clear up the mystery. He had succeeded in getting special intercessors for seven of the ten stations but not for the other three.[1]

The late Dr. A. T. Pierson declared firmly: "Every step in the

[1] "Seven Instead of Ten," *Triumphs of Faith*, Vol. 77, # 4, April 1958.

progress of missions is directly traceable to prayer. It has been the preparation for every new triumph and the secret of all success."

This should encourage those who lament their unavoidably meager contributions in money. It may also hearten those whose more sizable gifts did not seem to accomplish all they had hoped, when they understand that prayer spells the difference. This does not infer that money for missions is not *relatively* important. It is only to say that prayer for missions is *absolutely* important, and that he who prays most, helps most.

This is one field of human endeavor where the proportion of prayer to money is at least ten to one (if one can express a spiritual truth mathematically). Money by itself cannot buy world evangelization—not even lots of money. On the other hand, minimal funds will probably do very little to retard the great enterprise of mercy if there is no lack of intercession. It is almost axiomatic that where there is no want of prayer there will be no shortage of money—or materiel or personnel — to round out God's saving designs for the world.

Reverting to that which has always been the ultimate weapon of the militant church can only result in a greatly accelerated foreign missions pace in the twentieth century, notwithstanding all opposing -isms, -osophies, and -ologies. J. S. Swanger has said, "Even communism has no instrument, no ingenuity with which to combat the spiritual forces of prayer."

The world is not nearly as likely to be won or lost in outer space as it is in our prayer closets. With all the evidence available, we are compelled to state no successful substitute has even been found for redeeming a generation from its tyrannies. Men have their knees. Nothing remains but to use them.

> *"Charge them that are rich . . .*
> that they be . . . ready *to distrib-*
> *ute,* willing to communicate."
>   I Timothy 6:17, 18

15

CAPITALISM IS NO CRIME

Said the Texas construction tycoon,
"When our hearts get as big as our
pocketbooks, this is going to be a
different world."

FOR A GENERATION communists have declaimed in tirade against capitalism and Christianity, equating them as twin evils and contemptuously depicting them as the embodiment of wickedness designed to keep mankind enslaved. To the Reds they are but systems of subterfuge to console the poor by promising a rich hereafter. Wars of liberation will be waged, they say, until these shackles are snapped from the ankles of the proletariat.

Long before Marx and Lenin were heard from, other voices were thundering such pronouncements as, "Go to now, ye rich men, weep and howl for your miseries that shall come upon you." The complacently rich had allowed their hoarded treasures to rot instead of devoting them to the relief of the down-trodden and the glory of the Giver (James 5:1-5).

Unfortunately, ours is a day when not all capitalists are altruistically motivated. But they should be. By divine command men are to *bestow* their riches, not *bask* in them. Heaped-up abundance, like fertilizer, does no good until it is spread. In a pile it offends. Scattered abroad it makes the earth fruitful. Riches well-gotten and well-given are a great boon to mankind. Humanitarianism in the name of Christ ought to be the rich man's trade-mark on all his doings.

In the face of the communists' depreciatory references, it is refreshing to learn of capitalists who are playing key roles in advancing God's will in the world. It is said that R. G. LeTourneau, earth-moving equipment magnate and millionaire, contributes nine-tenths of his income to Christian missions. His donations have launched immense missionary projects in Africa and South America. And why not? Is not the industrialist millionaire to live as responsibly for kingdom advance as the humblest of his plant mechanics?

Capitalists are not inherently evil, nor does money itself corrupt — only the *love* of it. Far from being intrinsically immoral, capitalism should be, it has been, and will yet be, a vital adjunct in implementing God's race-redeeming plans and purposes. Where capitalism is corrupt it is unchristian. If rich men are bad it is not because they are successful but because they are selfish. God expects men of means to be men of munificence. Whole chapters in the Bible are devoted to the accounts of nobles and princes dedicating lavish offerings to glorify God and succor men. The rich have a remarkable potential for good.

The Lord prospers some men more than others. This is as evident as it is scriptural. Honest success, prosperity and riches are gifts from God (Ecclesiastes 5:19) to be distributed and communicated, not "heaped together" (James 5:3) to make grist for the communists' propaganda mill. The divine plan has always included affluent men. The Father expects the same degree of stewardship responsibility from them as from His poorer children. He offers no dual standard of discipleship demanding less of the rich and more of the poor.

Something has been read into the narrative of the "widow's mite," and the contrasting gifts of her more prosperous neighbors, which is not there at all (Mark 12:41-44). The account has been construed erroneously to mean that God is pleased with pennies only. We can all but hear the Saviour commending the woman's sacrificial offering with "I accept not the money of the rich." It is not to be so understood.

The observation made by the Lord when He approved the widow's mite, was that the rich gave only out of their superfluity. He said nothing to indicate they could not have more acceptably worshiped with a greater portion of their wealth. The entire impression was that they could have earned the same accreditation as the poor woman had they responded in her spirit. In fact they were expected to do so, if we understand the account fairly. Jesus brushed away all ambiguity when He said:

"He who has much given him
will have much required from him,
and he who has much entrusted to him
will have all the more demanded of him."
(Luke 12:48, Moffatt)

Christ's followers do the wealthy a great injustice when they shy away from calling on them to honor Him with their affluence. It is worthy of mention that among the first to kneel at the Bethlehem cradle were the rich Magi, who presented the Child with costly gifts of "gold, frankincense and myrrh." From the homage at that secluded manger to the final chorus of worship in heaven, "Worthy is the Lamb . . . to receive power, and riches . . ." (Revelation 5:12), opulence is ever relevant to Christ and His cause.

Two words arrest our attention in this apostolic admonition to the rich — *ready* and *willing*.

"Charge them that are rich in this world, that they be not highminded, nor trust in uncertain riches, but in the living God, who giveth us richly all things to enjoy; that they do good, that they be rich in good works, *ready* to distribute, *willing* to communicate."

Paul's insistence that God has given men their wealth "richly to enjoy" infers that present enjoyment consists in *readiness* to give and *willingness* to communicate — *now*. Proof that many are not so inclined may be had by a trip to the county courthouse. Here may be found voluminous records listing the wills and bequests of persons now deceased. Astronomical sums earmarked for missions and other benevolent uses have never been touched. Attorney's fees, legal loopholes, contested wills, and technical delays have defeated the desires of the well-intentioned bequeathers — a price too often paid for not being *"ready* to distribute" while still living.

Boldly, the apostle called upon the rich to lay up "in store for themselves a good foundation against the time to come, that they may lay hold on eternal life" (I Timothy 6:19). By judicious use of earthly gain, capitalists are to amass for themselves eternal dividends. Jesus instructed men to use mammon (money), to make for themselves friends who would welcome them to the eternal home

(Luke 16:9). It is possible to so distribute riches and communicate wealth that people from the four corners of the earth will meet and greet the donors in the Celestial City. Well may the modern Midas ask himself:

"Will anyone there, at the Beautiful Gate
Be waiting and watching for me?"

Perhaps nothing will match the disappointment of the sometime millionaire at the final balancing of books, when he reflects on how his earthly gains have no credit in the legal tender of eternal values. Moth and rust had corrupted all, and no deposits were made with the Banker whose institutions everlastingly remain when all others have gone to the wall. His riches had not been used to bring temporal and eternal benefit to mankind.

Marshall D. Barnett, Texan construction tycoon, awoke to opportunity while serving as an officer in the Seabees during World War II. After observing the Church's lagging overseas enterprises, he returned home following V-J Day to harness his successful operation to missions. He prodded other leaders in business and industry with these words: "When our hearts are stronger than the pocketbook, this is going to be a different world." [1]

The luster will never fade from the children's Sunday school "birthday offering for missions," or from "widows' mites." But not until more, and still more, monied men step forward to play the Good Steward, will the communist line be proved false. Failing here, an accounting lies ahead.

Truly, millions and missions, millionaires and missionaries, should be as one in the world-redeeming venture.

[1] *A Challenge to Christianity*, Missions Unlimited, Dallas, Texas.

"But the Lord supported me and gave me strength to make a full statement of *the gospel, for all* the heathen to hear it. . . ."

II Timothy 4:17
(Moffatt's Translation)

16
DEVOTED PROPAGANDIST

The Ayore Indians of Bolivia must hear the News even though it should cost these twentieth-century couriers their very lives. And it did!

COMMUNISTS are obsessed propagators. There seems to be no limit to their misguided, self-sacrificing efforts to bedevil the world with the blighting theories of Karl Marx. One of the phenomena of the century is their intoxicated abandon.

It is reported that a panhandler, working a Florida city, solicited money from a man on the street. The stranger offered a meal instead. This was the ungrateful retort:

"I asked for money — not for food. Of course I'm hungry. My last real meal was eaten three days ago. But we need money for literature. I am a communist and we've got to keep the presses rolling."

One thing that makes a communist a communist is his fixed obedience to communism's *Fifth Commandment*: "Busy thyself with propaganda." Passionate adherence borders on the fanatical. His message is not the best news that man has to hear, but there is much to be said in commendation of his determination in delivering it.

Missionary zeal of the Christian must come to match it if the race is to be won.

The Apostle Paul was a propagandist without peer. Persistently, inescapably, one great idea preoccupied him — the thought that all men ought to be favored with the opportunity of hearing the Good News. It got up with him in the morning and went to bed with him at night. He even dreamed it! In a vision, he saw a "man of Macedonia" (Acts 16:9) begging him to leave Asia and bring the Gospel to Europe. Because he did, the Western world has been largely a Christian world.

Paul refused to adjust to the idea that people should exist in an unchristian state simply because they had never been privileged to learn of God's redeeming plan. Afoot, he carried the Message. Where he could not walk, he sailed, and even swam. When restricted in his movements — sometimes imprisoned, at other times under house arrest — he wrote letters to ecclesiastical leaders, to new converts, to proselytes and to indigenous churches, urging them to pick up where he had been forced to leave off and untiringly continue the mission of Christ to "the regions beyond" (II Corinthians 10:16).

One compelling motive drove Paul from town to town, across border after border, and from one continent to another with the message. It was that all men might come to the knowledge of the truth (I Timothy 2:4). He could do no less than maintain a "conscience void of offence toward God, and toward men" (Acts 24:16). A moral issue was involved: "As we were allowed of God to be *put in trust* with the gospel, even *so we speak.* . . ." (I Thessalonians 2:4). A trusteeship called for integrity.

In the "furtherance of the gospel," as the apostle described his mission, nothing could daunt him. Not tribulation, distress, persecution, famine, nakedness, peril or sword (Romans 8:35). While "laboring abundantly" he underwent lashings and his prison records accumulated. He was often at the point of death. Five times the Jews beat him within an inch of his life, with thirty-nine lashes. Three times the Romans beat him, once they stoned him. Three times he was shipwrecked and adrift at sea. He went through privation in town and desert. He endured sleepless nights and knew the pangs of hunger and thirst together with the rigors of being ill-clad and cold (II Corinthians 11:23-28). He fled for his life from Damascus. Enraged citizens of Antioch forcibly expelled him from their city. Despitefully used at Iconium he fled to Lystra where he was stoned. At Philippi he was denuded and flogged. He was falsely accused in Corinth. Jerusalem cried for his blood and Rome beheaded him. All these were but the means to epoch-making achievements.

Every circumstance, every incident, Paul interpreted as a stepping stone toward acquainting the world with Christ. He even explained his birth on this basis:

"It pleased God, who separated me from my mother's womb, and called me by his grace, to reveal his Son in me, that I might preach him among the heathen" (Galatians 1:15, 16).

Having preached over most of the world, Paul's last, great missionizing thrust commenced when he announced to friends, "I must also see Rome" (Acts 19:21). Notwithstanding their prophecies of bondage and death should he go, Paul pressed forward toward the capital city of the world through alternating good and bad situations. How did he construe his trial before Nero's court in Rome and the preservation of his life for a time?

"The Lord stood with me, and strengthened me; *that* by me the preaching might be fully known, and *that all the Gentiles* [present at his trial] *might hear*: and I was delivered out of the mouth of the lion" (II Timothy 4: 17).

Letters from his prison cell sparkled with assurance. They dispelled the uneasiness of his friends who might have been tempted to call the providence of God into question. The untoward things which were happening (nothing ever just *happened*) had salutary purpose:

". . . my bonds in Christ are manifest in all the *palace,* and in all other *places*" (Philippians 1:13).

Palaces and places were alike his parish, and dungeons his diocese. Throughout his life he refused to swerve from the task of proclaiming the Gospel "where Christ had not yet been named," and he pled with all who would listen to follow his example (I Corinthians 11:1). He had fought a good fight and he had kept the faith (II Timothy 4:7). His one business in life was finished. What he had said to the Ephesians before commencing his journey to Italy was true. He was still "pure from the blood of all men" (Acts 20:26).

Christians of today must not merely admire Paul in his propaganding zeal — they must imitate him. Never was the need greater for holy enthusiasm than now. This is pointed up in C. T. Studd's bit of doggerel taunting us with our lack.

> "We twentieth-century soldiers of Christ,
> Are largely composed of sugar and spice;
> Pretty and tasty and far too *nice*
> To go in for genuine sacrifice.

> " 'I'm a soldier of Christ,' says everyone;
> But somehow we're deaf to the beat of the drum
> Calling us out to take our stand
> At the foot of the Cross in some Christless land." [1]

Our present generation needs more men of the nature of Alexander Duff, who, early in his Christian experience made this determination:

> "Having set my hand to the plow, my resolution was
> peremptorily taken, the Lord helping me, never to
> look back any more, and never to make a half-hearted
> work of it. Having chosen missionary work (in India),
> I gave myself wholly to it in the destination of my own
> mind. I united, or wedded, myself to it in covenant,
> the ties of which should be severed only by death." [2]

After a lifetime of conspicuous and selfless service abroad, Duff returned to his native Scotland to plead for reinforcements. An old man now, he stood in Edinburgh and for two and a half hours held his listeners spellbound with the story of hardship and conquest. Then he fainted and was carried from the hall. Regaining consciousness he asked, "Where am I? What was I doing? Oh, yes! Take me back and let me finish my speech."

"You will die if you do," exclaimed his friends. "I shall die if I do not," he retorted. So they carried him back. The whole audience arose to honor him. Unable to stand, he sat down to continue:

> "Fathers of Scotland, have you any more sons to send
> to India? I have spent my life there, and my life has
> gone; but if there are no young men to go, I will go
> back myself and lay my bones there and let the people
> know that there is one man in Britain who is ready to
> die for India." [3]

---

[1] *Quaint Hymns for the Battlefield* (London: James Clark & Co., 1914), p. 75.
[2] Quoted in *Worldwide* (Worldwide Evangelization Crusade).
[3] *Ibid.*

The *Statement of Consecration* adopted by the founders of the New Tribes Mission is classic, and deserves broad application:

> "By His strength we take the challenge; by unflinching determination we hazard our lives and gamble all for Christ, until we have reached the last tribe regardless of where that last tribe might be, to fill in the gaps where the Gospel has not gone."

Five of the mission's first contingent of eight men were assigned to Bolivia. When it was learned they would attempt to take the Gospel to the savage Ayore Indians, they were warned by some, "You won't come back alive." But they were undismayed. Cecil Dye, spokesman for the stalwart group, wrote:

> "I don't believe we care so much whether this expedition is a failure so far as our lives are concerned, but we want God to get the most possible glory from whatever happens."

Should the venture result in martyrdom, this was their buoyant hope:

> "Perhaps more Christians at home will become more aware of their responsibility to lost men, and become less concerned about the material things of life." [4]

The seed of the Kingdom must be planted in hostile soil even if the achieving should spell massacre for the sowers. And it did! Cecil Dye and his brother Bob, Dave Bacon, George Hosback and Eldon Hunter suffered martyrdom during their first contact with the Ayores in the *Green Hell* of Bolivia. They were mercilessly clubbed to death. But what of the yield? From the blood-soaked soil of the jungle there is being reaped, even now, the first fruits of a bronze Ayore harvest.[5]

Almost as a prayer, could we recite the words: "For humanity's sake, may the propagating zeal of the Apostle Paul and the noble witnesses who have followed in his train, once again, become the dominant passion of us all."

---

[4] *Brown Gold* magazine, publication of New Tribes Mission, July, 1948.
[5] For details see *Brown Gold*, August, 1959; February, 1960; July, 1961.

". . . see that they want for nothing."
Titus 3:13
(Moffatt's Translation)

17

STRATEGY FOR WINNING

Campaigns are won or lost, depending on the quality, extent and transport of military stores provided by the Quartermaster Corps.

COMMUNISTS have shrewdly resorted to plagiarism. One suspects that they have transposed and taken out of context the scriptural admonition, "Let your abundance be a supply for their want . . . that there may be equality," and revised it into their official motto, "From each according to his abilities, to each according to his needs."

It is customary among communists for the wage earners at home to support the workers abroad who are engaged in spreading the Marx-Engles-Lenin *gospel.* Their *Ninth Commandment* urges, "Give generously . . . to carry on missionary work, especially outside the Soviet Union where the cause suffers underground." [1]

That this "commandment" is closely observed is vouched for by Herb Philbrick of *I Led Three Lives* fame. After nine years of posing as a full-fledged member of the Communist Party in America, while an informant for the Federal Bureau of Investigation, Philbrick testified:

"Communists support their convictions with their lives and with their substance. I frequently observed com-

[1] *Manual for Godless Youth,* revised edition, quoted in *The Evangelical Christian.*

rades in secret cell meetings making monthly contributions of sums much larger than the average Christian
gives to his church in a year."

Backing the Party's front men with a substantial portion of one's
earning power is the thing to do. Without swagger, a communist
in San Francisco testified:

"I work eight hours a day; eight hours I devote to sleep
and personal affairs; eight hours I give to the Party. I
give *half* of my income." [2]

Is it any wonder that with this kind of grass roots support the ham-
mer and sickle shadows half of the world?

Paul's instructions to first-century Christians living on Crete
must be reinstated today if communism's goals are to be thwarted.

"Give a hearty send-off to Zenas the jurist, and Apollos;
see that they want for nothing. Our people must really
learn to practise honourable occupations, so as to be
able to meet such special occasions" (Titus 3:13, 14,
Moffatt).

These two laymen, one an attorney, had apparently forsaken lucra-
tive vocations to become evangelists and were now without personal
income. Fellow believers on the Mediterranean island were to join
in meeting the bread-and-butter needs of the itinerating witnesses as
they went from land to land propagating the Gospel.

This sender-goer relationship was more or less epitomized by
the late Dr. T. J. Bach when he coined the little triad, "Some must
go; some must let go; some must help go." Dr. A. B. Simpson laid
bare the whole issue when he stated:

"The work of missions should demand the largest
sacrifice of our means, the best and ablest men and
women that can be engaged in it, and the loftiest
devotion, sacrifice and *enthusiasm* to sustain it."

It should be difficult for any professing Christian to explain
his do-nothing posture in the battle for mankind, or even to justify
his existence. Bishop Fulton Sheen, in his magazine, *Missions,* re-
proaches non-mission-minded Catholics with the limerick:

"A lifeguard quite handsome named Fink
Asked a drowning young beauty in mink;

[2] Quoted in *World in Focus Letter* #7, Vision, Inc., Spokane, Washington.

'Sent the missions some dough?'
She gurgled a 'No!'
He snorted aloud, 'Let her sink.' " [3]

The importance of the sender-supporter role is seen in Paul's classic statement to the Romans concerning God's design to extend His saving grace to all men. The problem of implementation lay not with potential hearers of the Good News nor with its willing bearers but with *senders*. Paul covered the issue's full sweep when he wrote:

"Whosoever shall call upon the name of the Lord shall
be saved. How then shall they call on him in whom
they have not believed? and how shall they believe in
him of whom they have not heard? and how shall they
hear without a preacher? and how shall they preach except they be sent?" (Romans 10:13-15).

If the keystone at the crown of redemption's arch is God's universal grace, the cornerstone is the one who *sends* the bearers of Good Tidings. The impossibility of a man's believing in One of whom he has not heard, creates the urgent necessity for messengers, which in turn produces the responsibility of others to *send* and *support* them. Very clearly, the redemption of the world hinges vitally upon the senders for practical implementation. Salvation's sequence rests here. As military campaigns are won or lost depending on the quality, extent, and transport of military stores provided by the Quarter-master Corps, so the success or failure of the Lord's army depends on those who man the missionary supply lines. Telltale statistics offer proof that here is missions' bottleneck.

Missionary dearth existing over much of the earth is fully at-tested with a world average of less than one Protestant missionary per hundred thousand persons. A missionary to Africa numbers his private parish at 150,000. Another estimates his at 800,000. In one Ivory Coast area a staff of fourteen workers ministers to more than half a million widely-scattered tribesmen. An aging husband-wife missionary team count their sole evangelistic responsibility in Viet Nam at a million souls. In India, 700,000 villages are without a Christian witness. One million towns and cities throughout the world have no resident Protestant missionary, according to Clyde Taylor, missions authority and statistician. Wherein lies the cause?

The ugly truth is that each year large numbers of qualified ap-plicants are denied foreign appointments because of scanty finance.

[3] *Missions,* July-August, 1957, p. 21.

Practically every mission agency bemoans this. One of the largest denominations over a one-year period received 2,000 offers from candidates anxious to serve in Christ's foreign legion. Only thirty-two were commissioned. Insufficient funds was given as the main reason for the low percentage.

A moment's evaluation of this small portion of pertinent evidence should convince the open-minded Christian of the world's dire need for a greatly increased number of "hearty send-offs." And there can be no argument that Christians are derelict when they fail to respond to the all-time precept, "See that they want for nothing." Prosaic as a supporting role may seem when compared with work abroad, it is nonetheless crucial. Since it would seem that the only effectual preventive to world-wide communization is world-wide evangelization, the question arises, "How shall men preach except they be sent?" *Senders* perform a vital office in the strategy for winning the world.

". . . prepare me . . . a lodging . . ."
Philemon 22

18

LOGISTICALLY SPEAKING

If Christ's Foreign Legion is to win in the world contest, the stay-at-home-missionaries are going to have to supplement their prayers with provisions.

IN THE WORLD struggle one vital factor is being greatly overlooked by the forces of right. It is the matter of *logistics*. Webster defines *logistics:*

"The branch of military art which embraces the details of moving, supplying and quartering troops."

Logistics applied to foreign missions enterprises is most apropos. Transporting workers to distant outposts, housing them and providing their necessary equipment is of great importance. Unfortunately, foreign missionaries find themselves often subsisting on minimal requirements.

Here is an area where the modern Ecclesia is weak. The esthetic is permitted to obscure the practical. A recital of "Thees" and "Thous" is often substituted for down-to-earth duties. To supplicate, "Thy Kingdom come, Thy will be done on earth," then to leave it all up to miracle is obviously to be irreverently presumptuous. Praying cream and practicing skim milk is not the way to win the world. If the Church is going to triumph in her battle for the souls and minds of this generation's masses, she is going to have to supplement her prayers.

99

In his letter to Philemon, Paul writes of both prayer and provision as though they were components of vital worth. Gathering and forwarding material resources is an integral part of a spiritual work. Men should substantiate their supplications with sacrifices.

The provision of food, clothing and weapons for the soldier is the necessary prerequisite for his doing a creditable job of fighting. The same is true for those who do battle for Christ abroad. Failure to help materially is to hinder spiritually. Involuntary and unthinking though our omissions be, the end result may be as calamitous as if they were deliberate. An unknown author emphasizes this point:

> Last month I voted to close all mission stations. Not intentionally or maliciously but carelessly and indifferently I voted. I voted to close all orphanages, schools and hospitals which faithful missionaries labored to build. I voted to recall all the men and women who are giving their lives to carry the Gospel light to those in darkness. I voted for every native worker to stop preaching. I voted for the darkness of superstition, the blight of ignorance and for the curse of greed to settle down on the shoulders of a burdened world. I voted for all this not because I am opposed to what missionaries are doing. Why, *I believe in Missions* . . . but I did nothing to further the cause last month; thus I cast my vote against all that missions stand for.

To care for the logistical requirements of the ambassadors of Christ is a thing divinely owned and appreciated. Jesus taught that to provide for a good man is to receive a good man's reward. To sustain a prophet for his office's sake is to gain the reward of a prophet. A mere cup of cold water bestowed in the name of a disciple is a meritorious deed. Providence invariably sees that such mindfulness is richly compensated.

> "The food I share with others is the food that nourishes me;
> The freedom I seek for others makes me forever free.
> The load I lift for others makes my load disappear,
> The good I seek for others comes back my life to cheer.
> The thing I ask for others when God doth bid me pray
> Doth in that same act, commence to come my way." [1]
> — *Author unknown*

The principle is universal. Elijah in his day was directed to accept help during the time of famine from the widow of Zarephath. "The word of the Lord came unto him, saying, I have commanded a widow to sustain thee." Unaware of the unusual recompense which

[1] "Others," *Log of the Good Ship Grace*, Vol. 6, # 23, 1930.

26961

was to be hers, the nearly destitute widow became anxious at the prospect of sharing her meager store. She was down to her last handful of meal. Nevertheless her faith triumphed. She fed the prophet and a miracle supply lasted throughout the remaining lean years. Never again did she see the bottom of the barrel, nor did the cruse of oil fail (I Kings 17:10-16). It was a case of providing for a prophet and receiving a prophet's reward.

A second blessing was given the woman — then a third. Elijah saved her house from calamity by raising her dead son to life. And he supplied their spiritual needs. All this was consequential to feeding and housing one itinerant prophet.

Similar rewards came to the home of the Shunammite woman at the hands of Elisha. One of the best investments of their lives was made that day when she and her husband decided to build a "prophet's chamber" in the wall of their oriental home. During one of the periodic visits of Elisha, their only child suffered a fatal sunstroke. Elisha restored life to the lad (II Kings 4:8-37). Their hospitality was thus abundantly rewarded.

It was more than a coincidence that Peter's boat so overflowed with a great catch of fish that it almost sank *after* he had made it available to Christ for a pulpit from which He ministered to the throngs on the shore (Luke 5:1-11). It was *after* the Philippians had supplied Paul's needs many times that he assured them: "But [*in consequence*] my God shall supply all your need according to his riches in glory by Christ Jesus" (Philippians 4:19). Obviously, these analogies apply to the present foreign missions picture.

Today, Christ's envoys too frequently have to make do with cast-offs from the proverbial "missionary barrel." They are obliged to walk where they should ride. They are forced to paddle a canoe when they might better travel by plane. In many areas they are still trying to carry out their twentieth-century mission with nineteenth- or even eighteenth-century methods and material.

Were we to visit the mission fields it would be incriminatingly obvious that certain working conditions approximate those of Hudson Taylor's era (1832-1905). He wrote of China's wintry blasts:

> It's pretty cold to be living in a house without any windows and with very few walls and ceilings. There is a deficiency in the wall of my own bedroom, six feet by nine, closed in with a sheet so that ventilation is decidedly free. But we heed these

things very little. Around us are . . . large cities without any
missionary; populous towns with no witnesses and villages without number, all destitute of the means of grace.[2]

Men of Taylor's generation were of pioneer stock and had no
choice but to endure severe hardships and labor under adverse conditions. There was no way to circumvent their difficulties in their
slow-paced world. But the sailing ship period gave way to the steamship era, and the steamship era to the jet age. Ours is a new day,
one of technology, invention and prefabrication. In it we can find
no excuse for a lag of logistics, no justifiable reason for the lack
of a strong support program. Missionaries can be, should be, must
be supplied with every needed comfort, implement, and facility for
their global efforts. Instrumentation and resources should be mobilized and kept in instant readiness to assist their execution of the
Great Commission.

In God's economy, the Church must now rise to every logistical
exigency. Nothing is to be kept back which should be sent to the
forefront of the battle. This may involve our equivalent of a fishing
skiff, a prophet's *chamber,* a *meal barrel* or an *oil cruse.* Whatever
is needed should be kept ready. The owners of the tethered ass
conscripted by Christ for His triumphal Palm Sunday ride into the
Holy City made no remonstrance when the disciples explained, "The
Lord hath need of him." Apparently that was reason enough.

The renowned missioner of the nineteenth century, David Liv-
ingstone, very early in life formed a resolve which not only shaped
his own illustrious career but helped mold his generation.

> I will place no value on anything I have, or may possess, except
> in relation to the Kingdom of Christ. If anything will advance
> the interests of that Kingdom, it shall be given away, or kept,
> just as by the giving or keeping it shall most promote the glory
> of Him to whom I owe all my hopes for time and for eternity.
> May grace and strength sufficient to enable me to adhere faith-
> fully to this resolution, be given me, so that not in name only,
> all my interests may be identified with His cause.

Updating this concept, Dr. A. T. Pierson arouses us to the challenge:

> There is enough jewelry, gold and silver plate buried in Chris-
> tian homes, to build a fleet of 50,000 vessels; ballast them with
> Bibles; crowd them with missionaries; build a church in every
> destitute hamlet in the world; and supply every living soul with

[2] Dr. and Mrs. Howard Taylor, *Hudson Taylor's Spiritual Secret* (Philadelphia:
China Inland Mission), p. 94.

the Gospel in a score of years. Only let God take possession (of our possessions), and the Gospel will wing its way across the earth like the beams of the morning.

When at last we give an account of our stewardship, won't our disappointment and sense of loss be enormous should it be disclosed we did less than we might have done for our men who "hazarded their lives for Christ"? Especially will this be true if it be found that they suffered needlessly, that their useful lives were shortened, or their successes were few because they lacked the help we could have furnished. Suppose Timothy had failed to bring Paul the cloak he had left with Carpus at Troas (II Timothy 4:13)! Suppose for the want of that garment to warm him in the cold, dank Roman dungeon the apostle's earthly ministry had been shortened.

Knowing that things logistical can be turned to spiritual account, that what is done for missionaries in the temporal realm enables them to serve others in matters eternal — does not this provide a great incentive for faithful Christian stewardship? Harnessing the practical for the sake of the spiritual — this is the argument supreme in favor of keeping the supply lines open all the way from the home bases to the strategic posts on the front lines.

Pray for the bearers of the cross we shall, while never forgetting to provide for them logistically, lest the end result be irrecoverable spiritual loss to mankind.

". . . Jesus also suffered *outside
the gate . . ."*

Hebrews 13:12
(Moffatt's Translation)

19

BEYOND THE WALL

*The Cross puts Bethlehem, Pennsylvania,
as near God as Bethlehem, Judea; Nazareth, Texas, as Nazareth, Israel; Jerusalem, Ohio, as Jerusalem, Jordan.*

THE WAY the world is being segmented geographically, politically
and ideologically is unprecedented.

Today there is new talk of partitions. *Iron* and *bamboo* curtains separate Russians and Chinese from the rest of the world.
Barbed wire barricades and stone walls divide East and West Ber-
liners. Political and religious barriers plague the world.

But Christianity knows no walls and builds no barriers. It top-
ples them! Jesus Christ by His atoning death "broke down the
middle wall of partition" which for centuries had divided the human
race into two distinct, hostile camps (Jewish and Gentile), bringing
the hostility to an end (Ephesians 2:14-16).

It is fascinating to note that Jesus Christ was crucified *beyond
the wall* of old Jerusalem. That the exact area where He died should
engage the pen of the inspired writer is of great consequence.

The author of the epistle to the Hebrews (whoever he was —
Paul, Barnabas, Luke, or Apollos — no one seems certain) reminded
Christians with Judaizing tendencies that Christ died beyond Jeru-
salem's wall, thus locating Golgotha outside the legal religious polity

105

of Judaism. He called on them to break with the old parochial order and "go forth . . . unto Him without the camp, bearing His reproach." This proved to be sound advice. Soon all that had been "within the wall" was demolished by Titus when he sacked Jerusalem in A.D. 70.

By established custom, criminals were executed *outside* the Holy City. That the One hailed "King of the Jews" should also leave the Jewish capital to die and thus be divorced from insularism is one of the most significant facts recorded in Holy Writ. It proclaims His universality, obliterating all lines of demarcation which have separated people — Jews from Greeks, bond from free, male from female — in their approach to God (Galatians 3:28). The very moment He died, the Temple Curtain separating the common people from the Holy of Holies was torn from top to bottom — a divine act!

Not one drop of provincial blood stained the old rugged cross. It was not even pure Jewish blood. Interestingly, a glance at Jesus' genealogy reveals the entire human family represented. Moreover it includes some who were not "holy" as we commonly use the term.

Matthew's genealogy of Christ introduces four women besides Mary, two of them Gentiles by birth. Ruth, the Moabitess (not of Israel at all) was destined to be David's ancestor, and hence Christ's. Rahab, the harlot of Jericho, became a woman of faith (subsequently the wife of Salmon), and through her offspring a forebear of the Messiah. The other two women mentioned in Christ's family tree, Tamar and Bathsheba, have questionable moral records according to Old Testament evidence. Christ came *for* sinners and representatively *of* them and *by* them.

The Saviour identified with all men, Jewish and Gentile, even a race of people somewhere in between . . . Samaritans. The fourth gospel lends an exquisite touch here. The Saviour is shown deliberately taking a route of travel usually avoided by Jews. Agelong prejudices and hatreds had worn a different path, one which skirted Samaria. A wall had been erected between the two cultures which had to come down.

Jesus justified His break with tradition by saying to the wondering disciples, that he must go through Samaria (John 4:4). The reason, it proved, was a woman of sordid background and many lovers whom He would meet at the well of Sychar . . . and convert. Her first reaction was astonishment. " 'What? You are a Jew, and you ask me for a drink — me, a Samaritan!' (Jews do not associate with Samaritans.)" (John 4:9, Moffatt). But He was more than a

Jew, and the "living water" He came to give was offered her too. Immediately she raised a controversy over sacred places, whether His temple area inside the walls of Jerusalem, or her own Mount Gerazim beyond the walls was the proper spot to worship. He rejected both.

The hour was near when no one place would be *holier* than another. Christ's death "outside the gate" would put Bethlehem, Pennsylvania, as near the throne of mercy as Bethlehem, Judea; Nazareth, Texas, as near as Nazareth, Israel; Jerusalem, Ohio, as near as Jerusalem, Jordan. (It may be of more than political significance that when modern Palestine was divided, the Holy City fell into the hands of both Jews and Arabs.)

There are other facts which must be regarded as more than simple coincidences. Christ was stripped of the clothing that would have localized Him or given identification with a certain people. Both Jews and Gentiles were present, and accomplices in His execution. The former instigated it and the latter consummated it. Even the inscription on the cross is suggestive. It proclaimed His kingship in the languages of all three major civilizations: Hebrew (actually Aramaic), representing Jerusalem; Latin, representing Rome; and Greek, representing Athens (John 19:19-22). The placard in the chief languages of the earth made sure that all spectators would be able to read the title of the crucified One.

It was not by human whim or caprice that Christ's kingship should be thus universally noted. The conflicting passions of barrier-conscious men would have had it otherwise, had the matter been left to their devices. The Jews angrily demanded that the Romans take down the sign and the Romans peremptorily refused — with the result that the sovereignty of Christ was declared simultaneously in the chief tongues of mankind as an indication of His catholicity. (So at His birth His kingship was acknowledged by the Magi who came from Asia to worship "the King of the Jews" — and angels proclaimed from heaven news of great joy that is meant for all people.)

As at His birth and His death, persons of heterogeneous origin were present throughout His life. A woman of Canaan turned her alien status to advantage, receiving what she sought from Him, when she pled with Christ, ". . . the dogs eat of the crumbs which fall from their masters' table" (Matthew 15:27). Greeks came asking to see Him (John 12:20-22). An African carried the cross down the *Via Dolorosa* (Mark 15:21). A Roman, witnessing the crucifixion testified, "Truly this man was the Son of God" (Mark 15:39).

The conclusion may be drawn that since Christ came *of, by* and *for* sinners, the Gospel must be for all sinners. Iron and bamboo curtains must be rent, walls sundered and barriers breached for its entrance into every bustling city, every plague-stricken hamlet and every native kraal. In the accomplishment of this objective, the Christian cannot be less than a cosmopolitan to fulfill all that is required of him. Wherever the blood-stained banner of the cross needs to be carried, he will carry it. Wherever it needs to be lifted high, he will lift it. He is of the same spirit as the wealthy, dedicated Count Zinzendorf who, when observing the Moravians' missionary devotion, professed: "Henceforth, that shall be my country which most needs my Gospel."

That kind of Christianity is suspect which does not go *beyond the wall* bearing His reproach. "Going forth" is a fundamental plank in the Gospel platform. Christianity knows no walls and will recognize none.

> "If ye fulfill the royal law . . .
> *Thou shalt love thy neighbour*
> . . . ye do well."
>
> James 2:8

20

SECRET FORMULA

*Love alone wins, survives and conquers,
and of this penetrating force, the Christian world may be said to have a near
monopoly.*

AN INCREASING NUMBER of discerning statesmen today are realizing that if the West does not soon discover something besides free enterprise to sell the world, the world will be lost to the Reds. A rediscovery and an application of the old prescript, "Love thy neighbor," is what the war-convulsed earth needs most. The best commodity we have for export is good will. Dispense it openhandedly and efforts to gain the favor of people of other lands will take on a less frantic aspect. Today's battle for men's minds will be won by whoever is successful in the conquest of their hearts. He who loves most, wins most.

There are perhaps not two men in a million on either side of the iron curtain (perhaps not even a thousand in our world of billions) whose hearts are totally hardened against simple, honest-to-goodness love. If anything can move the world in the right direction, love can. It is the *never-failing* force (I Corinthians 13:8). It is so potent that God has reserved it to Himself as the only weapon to conquer rebel man. Love is the beginning, the middle, and the end of everything.

We call *love* the secret weapon in the world struggle because communists profess to know nothing about its strength. Some do not know it exists. Their credo is "To win we must hate," little realizing that hatred is an enervating madness in all who spawn it or spread it; it is weakness itself, able only to destroy. Love alone wins, survives, and conquers (and of this penetrating force, the Christian community may be said to have a near monopoly).

The Good Neighbor Policy predated the Roosevelt administration by centuries. Jesus Christ enunciated its importance when He reiterated the Old Testament command, "Thou shalt love thy neighbour" (Luke 10:25-37). In direct reply to a wily lawyer's query, "Who is my neighbour?" Christ identified him as a certain Samaritan who had compassion on a wounded, half-dead Jew. Here, one's neighbor is not the person next door from whom one may borrow a cup of sugar, or an egg or two, or the lawn mower. He is an alien, a person of another race, culture, or creed whose benefactions would not even be welcomed in ordinary circumstances. Christ named him as one who inconvenienced himself to lift up a fallen foreigner, who went the "second mile" by assuaging a stranger's wounds with his own oil and wine, who walked so the wounded could ride, who contributed of his means so the distressed traveler might be healed of his hurts, who filled the cup of love to overflowing by becoming a surety for the period of convalescence.

Jesus was illustrating a principle that had always been in force, though not always practiced. The earliest books (the Pentateuch) carried God's reminder to Israel warning them of the direst consequences of "tampering with the rights of an alien." The penalty, which all the people were obliged to endorse by answering, "So be it," was on a par with God's judgments upon offenders guilty of removing a neighbor's landmark, misleading a blind man on the road, or committing sexual irregularities (Deuteronomy 27:14-26, Moffatt). To have no love for a foreigner, or merely to disregard his rights, was as heinous a crime in the divine view. Israel was admonished:

> "Devote your heart to Him. . . . For the Eternal your
> God is the supreme God, . . . never partial, . . . and He
> loves an alien, giving him food and clothing. Love the
> alien, then [*if you would be like God*]: for once you
> were aliens yourselves in the land of Egypt" (Deuter-
> onomy 10:16-19, Moffatt).

Not only were maltreatment and oppression of the foreigner viewed as transgressions against God, but failure to love him was a sin also.

"If an alien settles . . . in your land, you must not injure him; the alien who settles beside you shall be treated like a native [one of you], and you must love him as you love yourself . . . I am the Eternal your God" (Leviticus 19:33, 34, Moffatt).

This was an order!

God's feeling for strangers is an ever-recurring theme in the Old Testament. He set up an agrarian program to cover their needs. The Jews were instructed to not discriminate against them simply because they were not of their own clan. The farmers of Israel were forbidden to pick every grape in their vineyards for their own use, or to glean every grain of wheat or barley from the field. The scriptural injunction on the subject was clear:

"When ye reap the harvest of your land, thou shalt not wholly reap the corners of thy field . . . ; thou shalt leave them for the poor and stranger" (Leviticus 19:9, 10).

Palestine's "cities of refuge," sanctuaries of immunity for the one who accidentally slew another, were always to remain open to resident aliens and foreigners (Numbers 35:15).

Charity can begin away from home. The narrow provincialism which disagrees knows nothing of the latitude and longitude of this love. The Apostle Paul wrote to aliens: ". . . you are in my very heart, and you will be there in death and life alike" (II Corinthians 7:3, Moffatt). To others he said in substance:

"I am a Jew . . . you are Gentiles, but Christ brought us together by destroying the racial barrier that kept us apart. You are strangers and foreigners no longer" (Ephesians 2:12, 13).

It is a sobering thought that one day all men will be judged according to their hearts' response toward the needy of other lands. Jesus' own words on this subject leave no room for quibbling. He identified Himself with the hungry foreigner when He said:

"I was an hungred, and ye gave me meat: I was thirsty, and ye gave me drink: I was a *stranger*, and ye took me in" (Matthew 25:35).

Stranger here is the Greek word *xenos* which literally means foreigner and alien. It is even more sobering to discover that to neglect *them* is to neglect *Him*. He who does not espouse their cause will one day hear the Saviour say, "Inasmuch as ye did it not to one of the *least* of these, ye did it not to *me*" (Matthew 25:45).

The story is told of a well-to-do rancher who championed the "Help thy neighbor policy," but within certain geographical limits. He was noisily opposed to foreign missions. Charitable duty began and ended with his near neighbor, and he was quick to make it plain that his neighbors included only those whose land joined his.

When asked to contribute to foreign missions, by the late Dr. William Skinner, his reply was: "I don't believe in foreign missions. I won't give to anything except home missions. I want what I give to benefit my neighbors."

Not easily squelched, Dr. Skinner questioned him further:

"Whom do you regard as your neighbors?"

"Why, those around me."

"Do you mean those whose land joins yours?"

"Yes."

"Well, how much land do you own?"

"About 500 acres."

"How far *down* do you own it?"

"Why, I never thought of that before, but I suppose I own half way."

"Exactly," said Dr. Skinner, "and I want this money for the Chinese . . . the men whose land joins yours at the bottom." [1]

If I am a human being, no one is really *foreign* to me. All men are my neighbors. My surplus food belongs to the hungry wherever they may be; my excess clothing, reserves, or hoarded wealth exist to help the poor of every degree north and south. No distance can weaken love's relationship. No ocean is broad enough to alter true affection. Said a native African child to a foreign missionary: "God sent you from America to Africa. You built a bridge of love from your heart to mine and Jesus walked across." Only let this kind of heart-to-heart affection enlarge in ever-widening circles over the world and down will come communism's colossus. Its doom is sure. Love in action will pull the pedestal from under its feet of clay.

[1] "Our Neighbors," *Prairie Overcomer*, March, 1961.

". . . to the . . . scattered . . . grace
unto you, and peace . . ."
I Peter 1:1, 2

21

PEACE CORPSMEN

*For the sake of Kingdom growth, we
ought to be willing and eager to be uprooted from accustomed environment
and transplanted in alien soil.*

IT IS REPORTED that within twenty-four hours after Sargent Shriver
Jr. put out his call, the Peace Corps Director was besieged with
nearly 5,000 applications. Persons representing a wide variety of
skills, talents and ages were offering their services. Willingly, col-
legians interrupted their educations, business and professional people
left their vocations and senior citizens postponed their retirement
claims, in order that they might fill niches in newly developing
countries.

These men and women (in ratio of sixty-two men to thirty-
eight women, with the eldest nearly seventy) were willing to be uprooted, to give up their accustomed way of life and comforts, and
to be transplanted in strange places, places sometimes inhospitable.
They were willing to live on a monthly stipend of seventy-five dollars, to exchange inner spring mattresses for bamboo mats. Luxury
items such as bath tubs, electric razors, and faucets yielding safe
drinking water would soon be only memories. Amoebic dysentery
could be the penalty for just one sip of water from the village well.

Patriotic Peace Corpsmen have become, unwittingly, the pace-
makers for today's Christian community in all lands. Their freewill

113

enlistment for humanitarian service overseas in the name of Uncle
Sam provides a standing challenge to the Church's rank and file,
to match their strength in numbers and in dedication in the Name
of Jesus Christ.

We need to search our souls. Perhaps we are too snug and too
comfortable. Possibly we are unaware of the holding power of plush
pews and worshipful sanctuaries. Maybe we are too busily absorbed trying to find the publicized but elusive peace of mind for
ourselves to be bothered about the titanic battle being waged for
other men's minds. A "Do Not Disturb" sign may be hanging outside our door. Perchance we are unwilling to be awakened, removed
and resettled for the sake of the kingdom.

The nearly stationary number of foreign missionary personnel
would seem to indicate this. Major organizations dedicated to world
evangelism find recruitment a prime concern. Only a few are briskly
moving ahead. Some are actually on the decline numerically, others
are nearly static. A spokesman for one of the larger inter-denomi-
national foreign missionary societies recently lamented, "Three years
ago we had 816 missionaries. Today we have 817. A net gain of
only *one.*"

The Apostle Peter's appeal was addressed to Christian Jews
scattered far from Zion's templed area. They were exiles of the
dispersion living in such strange-sounding places as Pontus, Cap-
padocia, Bithynia, and Asia. The Apostle here dealt with salient
truths relating to the ministry of those displaced persons.

It should be noted that some of these Jews might have been
in Peter's audience on the Day of Pentecost. Acts chapter 2 indicates that dwellers from these very regions were present in Jerusalem on that occasion. Perhaps some of these "scattered saints" were
among the several thousand converts made on Pentecost morning.

These were not, for the most part, professional missionaries.
The epistle is addressed principally to the laity — ordinary Jewish
believers now subject to the Parthians whose capital was Babylon.
Probably some had resided for a long time in these areas as slaves
(I Peter 2:18). Many others had doubtless found their way to these
distant parts of the pagan world as a direct result of harassments and
persecutions in Jerusalem. "They that were scattered abroad went
every where preaching the word" (Acts 8:4).

Unfortunately for the world at large, the tendency of Christians
has nearly always been to cluster instead of scatter, to stay instead
of to go, to congregate instead of to disperse. The very words "con-

gregation" and "assembly" should be given some serious study in the light of Christ's implied command to separate and increase, to divide and by so doing to multiply. The Church is not monastic, but missionary.

Someone has imagined the scene when the Saviour arrived back in heaven after His thirty-three-year sojourn on earth. Gabriel met Him and the conversation went something like this:

"Master, what plan did you leave for carrying on your work on earth?"

"I have asked Peter, John, James and others to go into all the world and preach the Gospel to every creature."

"But, what if they fail? What alternate plan do you have?"

"I have no other plan!"

If the redeemed lapse in their task through preoccupation or lassitude, and fail to engage in world evangelization voluntarily, then the Lord creates situations and circumstances to cause them to do so involuntarily. The scattering-of-the-saints method has been standard procedure in the past. He may well use it again that the "seed of the Kingdom" may be strewn over the broad, fertile, virgin acres of the earth. The Gospel must be disseminated "unto the uttermost," and He will see to it at whatever cost to His disciples.

Christians ought to be willing, even eager, to be uprooted and then transplanted in alien soil. There should be no reluctance to break with accustomed environment and go to strange realms for the sake of the Gospel advance. This in fact is their commission.

The scattered church is the ideal church, ideal to itself and to the world. Concentrated Christianity is the bane of any generation. The comer-to-Christ becomes a goer-for-Christ. No cloister is to be built on the Mount of Transfiguration as long as there are people in the plain who need the healing touch (Matthew 17:1-21). Enslaved man can only suffer more if the *Go* is taken out of the *Go*spel.

Practical lessons may be drawn from Peter's instructions to the *scattered saints* of his time. Their first concern was to minister "the manifold grace of God" (I Peter 4:10) to foreigners among whom they resided (2:4-25; 3:8-17). As Christian slaves they were to be subject to their pagan masters for Jesus' sake. Nothing was to be done which would nullify their testimony before heathen lords. Possessing only the status of serfs, still, their main purpose was missions in the land of their adoption.

Today, nothing could be more beneficial than a widespread dispersal of Christians over the whole planet, for they are the "light of the world . . . . the salt of the earth" (Matthew 5:13, 14). As the farmer sows grain evenly over the field, so the seed of the Kingdom demands similar even distribution over the world.

It was this reasoning which impelled a former GI who had served overseas to offer his specialty to foreign missions. He heard that the presses in Madagascar were standing idle for lack of repairs, and that the printing of Bible literature, so badly needed, was being held up. He testified:

> "It seemed that God was speaking: 'You are the man. Your hands are trained to do these things.' That is why I am going to Madagascar to set up lithographic equipment."

The present need for Peace-Corps-like volunteers from among the Church's rank and file is monumental. Mission societies are appealing for recruits who are willing to be reset in promising fields of productivity overseas. Bulletins are constantly issued calling for teachers, doctors, nurses, engineers, pilots, lab technicians, builders, and translators. Strategic niches where they can serve are crying for occupancy. Critical vacuums are begging to be filled.

One of the leading spokesmen of the Sudan Interior Mission has issued to Christians in his homeland the following appeal:

> "Doctors, leave your offices; pastors, your pulpits; teachers, your classrooms. Come, help us gather in this harvest of souls. We will give you a dozen for each one you now have, whether patients, parishioners, or pupils."

Representatives of the Wycliffe Bible Translators are calling for 8,500 more linguists over the next fifteen-year period. With these added reinforcements they promise to translate Scriptures into all of the remaining 2,000 Bible-less languages and dialects. While Wycliffe has enjoyed better than average growth (compared to other mission organizations), it still does not have enough missionaries to meet expanding opportunities and requirements abroad.

Perhaps it is the element of personal sacrifice which attracts Peace Corps volunteers in such numbers . . . a factor that the Church may be underestimating in its appeal. Jesus spoke of denying self, of taking up the cross, of cutting off right hands, and the like. He did not gloss the hardships and inconveniences facing His followers. Far from deterring them, this frankness provided an incentive.

In mustering missionary recruits for Africa, C. T. Studd set forth the following stipulation:

> "If any man counts his life of any account, dear unto himself or desires to live many years, he had better seek a softer job. But if he feels that for him, the world holds no greater honor or pleasure than to fight for Christ in the front line, except it be to die for Him in the hottest part of the field, then by all means let him come to the mission field." [1]

They came! And his era came to be known as the era of "wooden ships and iron men."

[1] Quoted by permission of Norman P. Grubb.

"The Lord is . . . not willing
that any should perish . . ."
II Peter 3:9

22

DIVINE INTENTION

The white missionary answered the troubled
Negro boy, "I think the color of His skin
must have been somewhere between yours
and mine."

WHEN IT COMES to assessing the value of an individual human being and his highest role, the Christian and the communistic philosophies are poles apart. By the communists' own admission, a person is of no intrinsic worth whatsoever. He is but a physical animal to be destroyed when he ceases to serve or be of further value to the state. Nikolai Lenin was doubtlessly speaking for all his kind when he asserted that it does not matter one whit whether three-quarters of the people of the world perish in communism's struggle for conquest. "What matters," he said, "is that the remaining quarter are communists."

Judged by such tenets, communists' pretended proletarian concern for the colored races and the oppressed peoples of the earth becomes a ruse. What care they about even the temporal welfare of one Hottentot, one Italian, one Cambodian?

Christianity, on the other hand, says that man is not a clod. He is eternal beyond the stars. The loincloth savage is kin to the sophisticated New Yorker. He, too, is a creature of dignity and worth, with a capacity for eternity. "God . . . will have all men to be saved, and to come unto the knowledge of the truth" (I Timothy 2:3, 4). It can be stated unequivocally that the Lord desires the temporal and eternal good of the whole human race from the most cultured to the most backward, downtrodden peoples.

This is illustrated in the salutation of Peter's second epistle. He invokes "grace and peace" on all who have obtained "faith of equal privilege . . . by the equity of our God" (II Peter 1:1, 2, Moffatt). Reemphasizing this toward the end of his letter, Peter cites certain corrupters who were attempting to pervert the Truth by scoffing at the concept of Christ's existence and His promised return to the world. Even the scorners, contended Peter, were the objects of divine forbearance since God was "not willing that *any* should perish, but that *all* should come to repentance" (II Peter 3:9). There must be no question that the Father's beneficent plan for man is an unbiased one.

Surprising as it may at first appear, the Redeemed are sometimes the most prejudiced in this matter. On occasion the "pure minds" of the first Christians needed to be stirred up "by way of remembrance" (II Peter 3:1) to the end that proper construction be put upon God's patience with pagans. Such a reminder seems superfluous. How can anything so important to the Father be forgotten by His sons?

When God's view of the equal worth of all men became a major issue in the parochially-minded early Church, the leaders at Jerusalem assembled to listen to whatever lame excuses Peter might offer for his fraternization with outcasts. He threw the whole matter over on the Lord by saying, "I could not withstand God." Then he submitted to the pillars of the Church irrefutable evidence of God's paternal solicitude. Only then did they accede.

"When they heard these things they held their peace,
and glorified God, saying, Then hath God also to the
Gentiles granted repentance unto life" (Acts 11:18).

And why shouldn't He have done so? His saving designs could extend to no fewer than *all* His creatures. All places are equidistant from heaven. When "God so loved the world" He loved it all.

Again in the first century a similar situation arose which disturbed the Church fathers. This time Peter stood up to explain why converts from heathenism should be considered on a par with converts from Judaism. His answer was substantially the same as at the first. He contended:

"God, which knoweth the hearts, bare them witness
giving them the Holy Ghost, even as He did unto us;

and *put no difference* between us and them, purifying
their hearts by faith" (Acts 15:8, 9).
This was admissable evidence. In the divine Lapidary's lexicon
there were no *semiprecious* stones. The same Lord over all was rich
unto all that called upon Him. Forgiveness was available for anyone. Jesus Christ was in the "public domain."

A missionary recounts a dialogue between herself and an African child who was greatly distressed with the notion that Jesus
might be the Saviour of white people only. "What was the color
of Jesus' skin?" he asked, hoping the answer would be "Black." The
white missionary, knowing how the Eastern sunshine must have
darkened the Saviour's features, gave this classic reply: "I think the
color of His skin must have been somewhere between yours and
mine." Delightedly the child exclaimed, "Then He belongs to *both*
of us!"

It may be reverently said that when the Heavenly Father looked
down upon the sacrifice of His only begotten Son, He was color
blind. There could not be the slightest trace of partiality. Divine
love embraced the whole erring race. Paul wrote of all men:
"... there is no discrimination: for all have sinned and are
short of the glory of God: for they are freely bestowed
righteousness by the grace of God through salvation
which is in Christ Jesus" (Romans 3:22-24, Aramaic).
Translating Luke 3:6 from the Aramaic brings to light a fine
shade of meaning. The King James version reads, "All flesh shall
see the salvation of God," but the Aramaic says, *"Let* every flesh
see the salvation of God." This agrees with Moffatt's translation of
Titus 2:11 clarifying the King James' "The grace of God that
bringeth salvation *hath appeared to all* men . . ." Moffatt puts it
more understandably: "The grace of God has appeared *to save all
men."* It must be admitted that all men have not seen the salvation
of the Lord. But grace has appeared in order that all men *might* see
it. To help achieve universal application, believers are admonished:
"Prepare ye the way of the Lord, make his paths straight.
Every valley shall be filled, and every mountain and
hill shall be brought low; the crooked shall be made
straight, and the rough ways shall be made smooth; . . .
[so that] *all flesh* shall see the salvation of God" (Luke
3:4-6).
The text conveys the idea of vacuums and empty spaces being
filled, of obstructions being removed to reveal salvation to the whole

world. The inference is that whatever stands between the sinful world and the sinless Saviour must be removed. Mountains of partiality must be leveled and valleys of prejudice filled if "the Eternal's glory shall be revealed before the eyes of *all:* such are the orders of the Eternal" (Isaiah 40:5, Moffatt). Some of the *valleys* to be filled are the minds and hearts which are void of the necessary information and inspiration to motivate disciples into immediate action "preparing the way of the Lord."

Spade work remains to be done if God's will for the world is to be implemented. This can be profusely illustrated. A wrinkled old Eskimo said to the Bishop of Selkirk: "You have been many moons in this land. Did you know the Good News then? Since you were a boy? Did your father know? Then why did you not come sooner?"

This indictment was echoed by a Peruvian living in the snowy heights of the Andes: "How is it that all the years of my life I have never heard that Jesus spoke those precious words?"

A Moor challenged a Bible-seller on the streets of Casablanca: "Why have you not run everywhere with this Book? Why do so many of my people not know the Jesus whom it proclaims? Shame on you! Why have you so hoarded it to yourself?" [1]

Near a little town in India where outdoor billboards advertise Singer sewing machines, Coca-Cola and Standard Oil, an itinerating missioner inquired of certain peasants if they "knew Jesus." One answered flatly, "I never heard of Him." Another replied, "About two miles down the road, you will find a police station. They ought to be able to tell you." From a farmer and his son, who were busily irrigating their field by dipping water by hand from one level to another, the first inquiry got a simple "No." The man of God decided to ask again in another way. Without stopping the rhythm of their movements, the father, manifesting some degree of impatience, said, "I don't know him!" Once more, the missionary ventured the question in a different form. The man straightened up, as though to end the conversation. He answered sharply: "I don't know what he wears. I don't know what he eats. I don't know what his work is. I don't know where he lives. He never came to this village."

How irreconcilable this seems to the Father's determination that Christ be known and worshiped in every hemisphere and from pole to pole. How needless this widespread unawareness of His Saviour-Son.

[1] All three illustrations are from L. E. Maxwell, *Crowded to Christ* (Grand Rapids, Michigan, Eerdmans, 1950), p. 142.

There is no problem in maintaining the Father's willingness to extend every grace and redemption to His erring race. Heaven's last recorded message to earth's inhabitants was this invitation: "Whosoever will, let him take the water of life freely" (Revelation 22:17). The crux of the matter is to be found elsewhere. As we have already said (in Chapter 5), the two greatest obstacles standing in the way of world evangelization are prejudice and indifference, and ignorance is the mother of them both.

If missions languish, if the race exists half-slave, it cannot be charged to divine patronage or disinclination, but to ignorance, prejudice and indifference among Christians. These are the deterrents which must be removed. All that benighted humanity requires is for the Church to launch and sustain a twentieth-century missionary thrust to "cover the earth with the knowledge of the Lord as the waters cover the sea." This God has decreed for His world.

> "Jesus Christ . . . the propitiation for
> our sins, though *not for ours alone*
> but also for the whole world."
>
> I John 2:2
> (Moffatt's Translation)

23

NO FAVORED SONS

How much longer will it take for us to com-
prehend that the Heavenly Father has no
favorite sons and no rejected Cinderellas.

THE MOST FELONIOUS CRIME of this generation was not committed
at Pearl Harbor, not on the streets of Budapest, nor in the burning
ovens of Dachau. History probably will record it as a crime of
omission with Christendom charged as the transgressor. The offense — apathetic neglect of millions of human beings permitted to
perish from spiritual thirst, while the Church slakes its own from
inexhaustible fountains of "living water."

It is said that early in the automobile era a wealthy couple was
being driven across the desert. On the infrequently traveled road
the limousine broke down and the chauffeur was unable to repair it.
Hours lengthened into days. Now and again the driver checked
under the hood. The passengers weakened and died. When authorities found the disabled car, the driver, who had periodically drunk
from the radiator, was in good condition. It was discovered there
was enough water still remaining to have sustained the lives of the
other two until the rescue party came. The chauffeur was tried for
murder.

An eminent religious critic acknowledges the "difficult and embarrassing" situation of his well-to-do denomination in relation to its unmet moral obligation to the thirsty world at large. He points out his church's claim to the Truth and its accountability in spreading it over the wide earth. Yet he draws a frank, incriminating picture.

> We will not agree to a geographical division of territory on the basis that the work be limited to stipulated areas with agreements not to enter others. We assert we have a responsibility to the whole world, yet we devote ninety-seven percent of our total evangelistic and missionary effort to an area which represents but three percent of mankind.[1]

Disparities of this magnitude are not confined to one group. Probably every church body finds far too much self-identity stamped on its activities.

Simultaneously with caring for our own comes the duty of sharing the "living water" with the *have-little* and *have-not* peoples of the earth. If their participation meant the impoverishment of ourselves, there might be some excuse for restricting the supply to a limited group. But the opposite is true. Dividing with others only tends to increase our own supply. It is a time-tested Bible truth.

"One gives away, and still he grows the richer:
another keeps what he should give, and is the poorer."
(Proverbs 11:24, Moffatt)

The chief characteristic of Christianity is its unselfishness.

In the first Christian era certain Jewish disciples felt they had a monopoly on Christ. The Lord had to teach them that His love for "every creature" included more than merely *Jewish creatures.* Nor were the chosen people the only exclusionists of the time. That some of the Gentile believers were afflicted with egocentricity is evident from the Apostle John's "not for ours only" reminder.

The writers of the New Testament used a fair amount of parchment and ink convincing their readers that propitiation for sin was intended not for a few—even quite a few—but for all. The Heavenly Father has no favorite sons, no rejected Cinderellas. In one grand sweep His provision for pardon takes in "every creature . . . of all nations . . . for all time." Whoever was, or is, or will yet be a part of this planet, for him Christ bled and died.

The pinnacle verses of all Scripture draw no restrictive lines:

"God so loved the *world,* that he gave his only begotten

[1] M. Theron Rankin, *What Will You Say?* (Richmond, Va.: Baptist Foreign Mission Board).

Son, that *whosoever* believeth in him should not perish, but have everlasting life. For God sent not his Son into the world to condemn the world; but that the *world* through him might be saved" (John 3:16, 17).

Equitable distribution of the benefits of grace among the nations was something not even the cosmopolitan Paul had considered prior to his call to bypass Bythinia and proceed to Macedonia (Acts 16:6-40). Europe had no Gospel at all and he was contemplating another preaching circuit on a continent where the Light was already shining. True, not every dark nook and cranny of Asia had been brightly illuminated but not a single ray had yet penetrated Macedonia's night. So Paul went abroad. There must be fair play. No longer must there be a premium upon souls in Asia. Gone the day of a discount on souls in Europe.

We may be practically unaware of it and still degenerate into a religious clique. We can present to the world much the same image as did a wind-ripped convention motto hanging outside a sanctuary. In its original state the banner proclaimed to passers-by, *Jesus Only*. The tattered sign, minus the torn-away portion, simply read ——*us Only*.

In far too many cases that bisected sign represents what the Church displays, if unintentionally, before the gaze of a bewildered, longing world. We are a minority engrossed in singing "Oh, How I Love Jesus," hugging Him to our bosoms, while the majority in our world community remain without this consolation. The few feast while the many famish.

If, with full knowledge of his plight, a man through sheer neglect permits his neighbor to starve, he stands condemned before the bar of social justice. The parent who fails to provide for a hungry child is guilty before the law. Remissness is as deserving of punishment as any sin of commission.

> "When Jesus came to Birmingham
> They simply passed Him by.
> They never hurt a hair of Him,
> They only let Him die."
> — *Geoffrey Studdert-Kennedy*

Is it fair to stuff ourselves while others starve? Shall we surfeit while bony hands reach out for their fair share of the Bread of Life? Do we actually require another deeper life conference? Would additional sermons on the atoning death of Christ, or another study on His deity or virgin birth be news? Delightful as discoursing on the Second Coming of Christ might be, it would lose something if, during the exposition, we couldn't get off our consciences the millions who still wait to hear about the *first coming of Christ*.

The favored minority have far more than their prorated share. They need not more for themselves but longer arms and swifter feet to expedite distribution of what is already a great surplus. Too many fit the picture of the oversized, overfed parishioner who met the new pastor in the vestry following his maiden sermon and offered a bit of advice. "All we ask of the pastor is that he feed the flock. Just feed us well and feed us plenty." The new clergyman, eying the enormous proportions of his parishioner, humorously replied: "Brother, what you need is not more food but more exercise." Apocryphal though the story may be, it forcefully illustrates the concept we need to understand.

Only hours away in our shrunken world, millions of people know the torment of inner hunger. At the same time segments of the Church may be found at home busily majoring on feeding the already fed and teaching the already taught, while minoring on quieting the hunger rumblings from abroad. A cry is heard from afar: "Be a saving church, not a satiated one."

Every congregation must inquire of itself whether it is guilty of usurping for its own use what is intended by God for all. Horatius Bonar declared: "We must begin at the inner circle but woe to us if we stop there. Woe to us if we do not take the Gospel to every creature."

If the religion one professes does not meet his own need, he should *give it up*. If it does meet his need he should *give it away*. Failing to do so, he will awaken one day to find himself an unwitting accomplice in crime against humanity — the crime of omission — as conveyed clearly in Christ's own words: "Inasmuch as ye did it not to one of the least of these, ye did it not to me" (Matthew 25:45).

A good rule for immediate adoption and vigorous implementation has been articulated for all in the personal life-motto of Charles Wesley: "I must have the whole Christ for my salvation, the whole Church for my fellowship and the whole world for my parish."

> *". . . this is love, that we walk*
> after his commandments."
>   II John 6

24

IRONS IN THE FIRE

> *True love wears the dust of the road*
> *. . . it is feet on the ground . . . running*
> *God's errands of saving mercy among*
> *men.*

Don't just sit there; do something!

The Christianity that is going to put a soul under the ribs of today's humanistic civilization, and defeat communism's effort to enslave mankind, will not be the sedentary sort. It will not be confined to a cathedral, cloistered in an abbey, or secluded in a monastery. Nor will it substitute sanctimony for service, or apathy for action.

Those who suppose God cares for no other pursuits than reverie and worship are mistaken. Serenading the Saviour from under the church balcony on Sunday (if that is all one does), cannot compare with serving Him in the byways the remaining six days of the week. The pew-ridden are to be pitied.

Christ stressed the point that the Kingdom belonged not to the *hearers,* or to the *sayers,* but to the *doers.* They delude themselves who congregate, saying, "Come and let us hear what is the word from the Eternal today!" and having heard, ". . . will not obey" because "their minds are set upon their selfish ends" (Ezekiel 33: 30, 31, Moffatt). Jesus challenged, "Why call ye me, Lord, Lord, and do not the things which I say?" (Luke 6:46). We could

129

argue effectively that this warped affection is not love in its true dimensions. To call our attitudes and emotions *love,* does not make them so. Testing, not claiming, will prove the genuine quality of anything.

Devotion is always dedication to *duty.* True love is peripatetic. It wears the dust of the road, the consequence of going about doing good. It is not an ethereal something floating around in the air; it is feet on the ground, going God's way and running His errands of mercy among men. Affection may be said to be ambulatory; it *walks* after His commandments.

Love constrains to action where other motives fail. The account of an Army nurse in Korea, reported by Charles S. Ryckman, is an example.

> An American journalist, covering a particularly savage area of fighting, came upon an advanced medical post where a nurse was preparing a wounded man for surgery. He was bloody and filthy, but the nurse went about her errand of mercy swiftly and expertly.
>
> The newspaperman, fascinated by the gruesome evidence of man's inhumanity, and at the same time marveling at the wonderful proof of human tenderness and skill, said softly, "Sister, I wouldn't do that for a million dollars."
>
> The nurse, without staying the flying movements of her fingers, said in even a softer reply: "Brother, neither would I." [1]

It is axiomatic that one can *do* without *loving,* but he cannot *love* without *doing.*

John, the fisherman turned disciple, wrote his tiny second epistle (thirteen verses), to emphasize the fact that truth and love are joined together in pure Christianity, and are outwardly demonstrable. He championed the view that the only admissable evidence of a man's inner charity is his outer conduct. Anything less would be "loving in word and tongue," he said in his first epistle, "not in deed and truth."

> "Hereby we do know that we know him, *if we keep* his commandments. . . . But whoso *keepeth* his word, in him verily is the love of God perfected . . ." (I John 2:3-5).

Christianity is comprised not merely of professions of love for Christ, but of deeds.

[1] Quoted in a sermon by C. Julian Bartlett, published in *Guideposts,* November, 1960.

The Apostle John was building on the Saviour's own words which he had recorded:

"Ye are my friends, *if ye do* whatsoever I command you" (John 15:14).

"He that hath my commandments, and *keepeth* them, he it is that loveth me . . ." (John 14:21).

One may sing ever so piously, "Oh, how I love Jesus," and yet provide no actual proof of the sentiment. Between a gratitude which sings hymns and a thankfulness which does something to lift up a fellowman in Christ's stead, there can be no question which is the better choice.

In his gospel, John records an illuminating dialogue he overheard between his colleague, Simon Peter, and the Saviour. (It took place only a few days after Peter had denied Christ on the eve of His crucifixion.) The highlight of the colloquy is that each of Peter's three reaffirmations of love for Christ was answered by a commission. To the first profession, "Thou knowest that I love Thee," came the reply, "Feed my male lambs"; to the second, "Feed my sheep"; to the third, "Feed my female lambs" (John 21:15-17, Aramaic). The lesson is easily understood.

Love has not one dimension, but two — vertical and horizontal. "Thou shalt love the Lord," is complemented by "Thou shalt love men." Avowals of love for Christ without deeds of love for His creatures is mere pretense. The first calls for putting mind and muscle to the second. Loving the Shepherd involves one spontaneously in the role of an undershepherd. Tending His sheep is the responsibility of every disciple. He cannot be devoted to Christ who is derelict toward men.

> "Love has a hem to its garment
> That touches the very dust.
> It can reach the stains of the streets and lanes
> And because it can, it must.
> It dares not rest on the mountain,
> 'Tis bound to come to the vale,
> For it cannot find its fullness of mind
> Till it falls on them who fail."
> — *Source unknown*

Love for the Lord can be accurately measured by love for the lost. Little love for Him means little love for confused, straying, harassed humanity. Much love for the Master, means much love for mankind.

"The closer we get to Christ," wrote Mrs. J. C. Mason, "the more intensely missionary we become." It is not surprising that those who have no love for God should have no love for His world-redeeming mission. A heart beating in rhythm with Christ's above, cannot be out of step with His work below.

Love has irons in the fire. Going places and doing things is its forte. Paul dazzled the world with his missionary feats and accounted for them on the basis that he was *controlled* by the love of Christ. Heart response made it impossible for him to do otherwise than help to liberate his generation from enslaving, devilish forces. God's will never fails to strike sympathetic vibrations from the devoted soul. When two hearts beat as one, fulfillment becomes spontaneous.

Love for their recently ascended Lord played a large part in the disciples' ready obedience to His last words delegating them to bring "other lost sheep" into the fold. Peter was soon found tending the flock. Love's persuasion overcame racial prejudices, causing him to walk all the way from Joppa to Caesarea where he opened the doors of the Kingdom to believing Romans. Philip left Jerusalem, traveling thirty miles to Samaria, to bring *others* into the fold. Paul's travels covered sizeable portions of Asia Minor and Europe. Thomas, according to legend, traversed Africa and India in search of souls. Loving Christ, as these men did, they could do no less than carry out His wishes. Can we?

The fate of humanity trembles on the brink. Hope hangs by a tenuous thread. One thing alone frightens the godless forces bent on enslaving the earth. It is the prospect that Christians might wake up and start acting their beliefs. Love in action would soon rivet the attention of the world upon Christ, and bring every eye to rest in adoration upon Him.

". . . we are bound to support
such men, *to prove ourselves
allies* of the Truth."
III John 8
(Moffatt's Translation)

25

LOYALTY TEST

*Christendom is widely populated with
professors who have yet to demonstrate
allegiance to Christ by a practical sharing with those who serve Him abroad.*

A FRENCH NEWSPAPER has quoted a communist who conceded the
Gospel to be a superior weapon to communism, psychologically, but
then asked: "How can anyone believe in the supreme value of your
Gospel if you do not practice it, and if you sacrifice neither time
nor money to spread it?"

The editor of *Missions,* a Catholic publication, lends credence
to the accusation when he asks:

> Why do the enemies have so much fire, and we are but flicker-
> ing candles? They sizzle, we stew; they burn, we smolder; they
> are forest fires, we are bonfires. There is more of the devil in
> Communists than there is of Christ in Christians. This is the
> answer to the world crises . . . for the last years we have written,
> begged, pleaded with the Catholic people to make sacrifices for
> the Holy Father, so that he could send missionaries to Africa
> and Asia . . . and how much do we receive . . . from each Catho-
> lic in a year? *Twenty-seven cents!* [1]

[1] *Missions,* November-December, 1964.

Perhaps Protestantism can boast better than this, but its missionary investments are nothing in which to take great pride, nor evidence which could be used to refute innuendoes implying disloyalty to the Cause.

That communists should be justified in their charge ought to be a major concern, and we should be grateful for the nudge, even if given by a communist. A reminder from any quarter is good if it helps us to see more clearly that the momentous issues abroad can be resolved, with greatest blessing to mankind, when Christians in superior numbers get behind Foreign Missions with their time and money. Admittedly, between what is professed and what is practiced in this area lies a chasm greater than the Grand Canyon.

Half of John's minuscule letter is devoted to the subject of missionary partnership. It is addressed to one, Gaius, a man beloved by the writer as a person who demonstrated his loyalty to the Truth by rendering material assistance to those who were propagating it in a more itinerant fashion.

Certain traveling missionary-evangelists who had been entertained by Gaius had afterward mentioned to others the aid he had given them (verses 5-7). News of this generosity reached the Apostle, and he wrote Gaius assuring him of his prayers:

"That thou mayest prosper [temporally] and be in
health [physically], even as thy soul prospereth [spiritually]" (verse 2).

John urged him to continue forwarding others on their journeys by giving them provisions for the way "after a godly sort" (verse 6). His request, "Pray speed them on their journey worthily of God" (Moffatt), infers that to honor God's missionary personnel in this manner is to honor God.

"We are bound to support such men," he wrote (verse 8, Moffatt), clearly defining whom he meant by "such men" as the ones who had gone abroad to witness, "taking nothing of the Gentiles" (verse 7). It was the apostolic expectation that local Christians would put themselves and their substance at the disposal of those who were doing the leg work. The services of both were equally acceptable and necessary in carrying out the provisions of the Great Commission: "Go ye . . ." (Mark 16:15).

It is a source of substantial satisfaction to the earnest-hearted who long to serve as foreign missionaries, and would if they could, to know that effective work can be theirs simply by joining hands across the seas with those who are so occupied.

The story is told of a young man who applied as a candidate for the foreign mission field. Illness in the family prevented the fulfillment of that wish, so his brother went in his place, supported by the business operation of the one who made the first attempt. When circumstances prevent the giving of literal interpretation to the command, "Go," many happily discover they may still "go" by proxy in underwriting others.

Corinthian believers received a gentle reminder of this principle from Paul. He wrote of his intentions to visit them that he might be sent on his way by them to Judea with an offering for the Christians in Jerusalem (I Corinthians 16:1-6; II Corinthians 1:16). The Macedonians he held up as their examples. They "first gave their own selves to the Lord, and [then] *unto us* by the will of God" (II Corinthians 8:1-5). Obviously, the illustration was given lest the wealthy Corinthians should allow themselves to be outdone by the poor Macedonians who had already made themselves partners with Paul's missionizing exploits.

The world would be markedly different if today's Christians would imitate their noble predecessors and make themselves available as aides to intrepid soldiers of the cross. This is "acting loyally." Such support backs up the Christian's claim to discipleship, proving him an ally of the Truth (III John 5, 8, Moffatt).

> "How much do you work for the Lord?" he was asked,
> "How many hours in a day?"
> "From sun to sun," was the strange reply,
> "Unceasingly, I work and pray."
>
> "Why, friend, you are mad," the other said,
> "We humans must rest now and then!"
> "Ah, then, I will haste to explain my good plan
> That makes me the happiest of men.
>
> "My labor begins with the new morning dawn,
> And then when day is done,
> My substitute brave, in faraway land
> Has only his work just begun.
>
> "The money I earn, though not very much
> Is divided between him and me.
> So I work for the Lord twelve hours at home,
> And twelve hours over the sea!" [1]
>
> — *Opal P. Gibbs*

[1] From *Cable,* Overseas Crusades, February, 1963.

A young man and his wife accepted for African missionary service reported in New York City for embarkation. Further medical examination revealed that she would not be able to pass the physical requirements. Heartbroken they returned home, determined to make all the money they could to extend the kingdom of God over the world.

The young man's father, a dentist, pursued the interesting avocation of making unfermented wine for the communion service. The dedicated couple fulfilled their world-missions dream in a unique way, by taking over and developing the business until it assumed vast proportions. Under their stewardship the industry has since contributed hundreds of thousands of dollars to missions. The grape juice still carries the family name, "Welch."

Following this principle, every labor can be a missionary work, as has been dramatically illustrated in every age. Barnabas, a first-century disciple, cared so much that he sold his farm to finance the Church's advance. Paul professed to have "suffered the loss of all things." An illustrious example in more modern times is the young British athlete-intellectual, C. T. Studd. Upon inheriting a large sum of money, he gave it all away to missions, impelled by the logic that "if Jesus Christ be God, and died for me, then no sacrifice is too great for me to make for Him." [2]

The record reveals how on January 13, 1887, Studd issued nine checks. One in the amount of $25,000 went to D. L. Moody, the American evangelist through whom he and his father had been converted. Moody used this money to found Chicago's Moody Bible Institute, the cradle of much worthwhile modern missionary enterprise. The second check provided $25,000 for George Mueller's missionary work; another $25,000 went to the Salvation Army for missions in India; and $45,000 was distributed to others.[3]

Not all contributions are so large, nor need they be. Partnership in missions, equally sacrificial, but on a more moderate level, is the lot of the majority.

Too much cannot be said to emphasize the extreme need of more workmen abroad, but their mission depends upon the quality and quantity of the resources at home. William Carey rallied the faithful to their supporting role with this call: "Yonder in India is

[2] Norman P. Grubb, *C. T. Studd* (London: Lutterworth Press; Ft. Washington, Pa.: Christian Literature Crusade), p. 65.
[3] *Ibid.*, p. 141.

a gold mine. I will descend and dig, but you at home must hold the ropes." His analogy provided the inspiration for these lines:

> "Those at home must hold the ropes;
> The rope of faith, the rope of prayer,
> The rope of gifts we give,
> The rope of brotherhood we hold
> To bid the nations live."

If we are to be frank, we must admit that the communist quoted in our opening remarks was partially right. Christendom is widely populated with professors who have yet to demonstrate allegiance to Christ by practical sharing with those who serve Him abroad. These have yet to prove themselves by scriptural measurements "allies of the Truth."

"I gave all diligence to write unto
you of *the common salvation . . ."*
Jude 3

26

SUPPLY AND DEMAND

*As admitted by its chief exponent, there is
no such thing as a congenital communist
. . . man is without the natural proclivities.
He must first be tampered with.*

ONE OF THE MOST revealing statements ever made by a communist
luminary was Nikita Khrushchev's offhand admission "Men are not
born communists." The world can be grateful for what may have
been an unintentional confession of incompatibility. Apart from
some such explanation, the fact that there are so few unadulterated
communists in the world would be the enigma of this century.

The reason so few people are truly communistic is that the
godless ideology does not meet the requirements of man's innate
structure and capacity. It is not indigenous to his being. Man was
not made for communism, and as it now turns out communism was
not made for man.

Marxism is an inhuman, bloody, ferocious system, hostile to
every inbred, virtuous affection, leaving nothing above us to excite
awe, nor around us to awaken tenderness. The godless system wages
war with both heaven and earth. Its first object is to dethrone the
Almighty, its next is to destroy man. Yet it is propagated with as
much fierceness and contention, wrath and indignation, as if the
safety of the world depended upon it.

Not only are there not many communists now, there cannot

be many ever. Too few people qualify. Reason is out of its element. To have the inner fitness one must first be an atheist, and real atheists are rare.

But then, there need not be many. It is not even the Party's expectation that everyone in the world will be converted to communism, only that they will be controlled by an elite, hard-core minority. No illusions are harbored that the common man has an affinity for the doctrine. As admitted by its chief exponent there is no such person as a congenital communist. Man is born without the natural proclivities for it. He must first be tampered with.

Communism is not for the common man. But how different is Christianity. It is suitable to every being within the classification *homo sapiens*. Paraphrasing Chateaubriand we may say:

> "Christianity assures men that afflictions can have an
> end. It dries our tears and promises us another life.
> On the contrary, in the abominable worship of com-
> munism, human woes are the incense, death is the
> priest, the altar, and the annihilation of deity."

Anthropological proofs abound to support the affirmation that the "common salvation" is in agreement with, and answers to, the inner requirements of the rich and poor, the ignorant and the intellectual, the pygmy Gabonese and the hairy Ainu. The Gospel is not restricted in its application but is appropriate for world-wide acceptance by the totality of men — oriental or occidental, black-skinned or white, cultivated or savage.

Often it is from other than Christian sources that the best evidences are put forth, proving the inadequacy of other systems and religions to satisfy inborn longings and capacities. A missionary mother once said she did her best teaching when she dressed the body of her baby, just taken from her in death, putting on its prettiest frock, brushing back its hair, laying a rosebud in its waxen fingers, and then calling the heathen women to come and view her child. They sobbed out in their astonishment, "You've fixed up your baby to go to a lovely place, and you expect to see her again. When our babies die, we throw their bodies out for the dogs to eat. They have gone into darkness and we have no hope of ever seeing them again. We want to know about your Jesus." [1]

A medical missionary to China was asked by an eager woman, "Give me some of your medicine for cleansing mouths." She told

[1] *Whitened Harvest*, West Indies Mission, April-June, 1955.

of her neighbor who had lately been in the mission hospital for a month. "Before she went there she would answer with the foulest language if she were crossed in any way. Now never a coarse word comes from her lips. I want my mouth to be clean like hers." Medicine for cleansing mouths! Artlessly but movingly she witnessed to an inner need, scripturally defined as, "the washing of regeneration." Here her own pagan religion failed her.

Christianity is as suited to every human being as the air he breathes. Station, social stratum, intelligence quotient make no difference. The Gospel's comprehensiveness distinguishes it from every competitor. It elevates each and all as the incoming tide lifts both yacht and garbage scow, luxury liner and flotsam. Obviously, if divine grace be not suitable *for all,* it is not suitable *at all.*

Jude (not an apostle, and one about whom little is known except that he was probably a younger brother of Jesus) wrote his short letter of exhortation to urge his readers to contend for the "common salvation." Here was something not to be compromised. Salvation was designed for all men, and all men require and are capable of receiving it.

God's inclusive designs are spoken of by almost every Bible author. Simon Peter amplified Jude's statement of *common salvation* by pointing it up as one of *equal privilege* manward and *equal provision* from God (II Peter 1:1, Moffatt). He spoke of Jesus as the "Lord of all" (Acts 10:36). John interpreted Christ's coming into the world as light for "every man" (John 1:9), and recorded the Saviour's promise to quench the thirst of all who would come to Him (John 7:37).

The Apostle Paul championed redemption as a free gift of life *upon all men* (Romans 5:15-18). He set forth Christ's atoning death as "a ransom *for all*" (I Timothy 2:6), and declared Him without reservation to be "the Saviour *of all*" (I Timothy 4:10). He reasoned that the grace of God, bringing salvation, had appeared to save every man (Titus 2:11) from sovereign to subject, and called for prayers to be offered toward this end (I Timothy 2:1-4).

As God's goal is man, so man's goal is God, and anything that leaves him short of this goal leaves him short of his destiny. He is more than a materialistic animal. He, of all creatures, "does not live by bread alone" His needs are deeper and his longings higher than can be met on the horizontal plane. God made him with upright posture and open countenance to survey the heavens and look toward the stars. His vital relations are to God and eternity.

Thomas Carlyle said:

> "The older I grow — and now I stand upon the brink
> of eternity — the more comes back to me that sen-
> tence in the Catechism which I learned when a child,
> and the fuller and deeper its meaning becomes: 'What
> is the chief end of man? To glorify God and enjoy
> Him forever.' "

This explains why disciples of Christ sever their cherished home ties
and migrate to bush veldt, arctic snow, humid jungle and arid desert.

Leaving their native America for a third term of missionary
service in India, the Elmer Berthelsen family bade kindred and
friends farewell.

> "We go back because Christ is the answer to India's
> need. The endless cycles of lives which a man must
> endure to atone for his sins (according to Hindu be-
> lief), becomes a burden too great for him to bear." [2]

They felt morally obligated to cause the Indians to hear the voice
of One, saying:

> "Come unto me, all ye that labour and are heavy laden,
> and I will give you rest. Take my yoke upon you, and
> learn of me; for I am meek and lowly in heart: and ye
> shall find rest unto your souls. For my yoke is easy,
> and my burden is light" (Matthew 11:28-30).

Our "common salvation" is incomparable on the face of the earth.
It meets the highest demands and the deepest needs of collective
mankind. Where Christianity has sown its seed the results have in
every case been the same, says J. H. Seelye:

> "Virtue, social order, prosperity, blessedness; the ele-
> vation and improvement in all respects of human life,
> are the uniform and exclusive inheritance of those who
> receive the Gospel."

Bringing supply and demand together, then, is the high duty
of all Christians. When one experiences in Christ the complete
fulfillment of the soul's requisites, it becomes his sacred trust to do
all in his power to see that "every creature" shall find his place in
the Son. What Christ can mean to one, He can mean to everyone.

[2] *The Missionary Broadcaster*, The Evangelical Alliance Mission, January-
February, 1961.

"Let us not be storehouses, but channels,
Let us not be cisterns, but springs,
Passing our benefits onward,
Fitting our blessings with wings;
Letting the water flow onward
To spread o'er the desert forlorn;
Sharing our bread with our brothers,
Our comfort with those who mourn."

            — *Author unknown*

"And *they sung a new song,* saying,
Thou . . . hast redeemed us to God
. . . out of every . . . people and
nation; . . . and we shall reign on
the earth."

Revelation 5:9, 10

27

TO US THE VICTORY

*The movement which began in a Bethlehem
grotto 2,000 years ago, sweeps inexorably
outward and upward toward its apogee, and
nothing can stop it!*

HANDEL'S MESSIAH reaches a climax with the rapturous "Hallelujah
Chorus," a paean of praise to the Redeemer who stands victorious
at last over the allied forces of evil. Here is graphically portrayed
the scriptural truth that Jesus Christ will never become ancient history
(all communist prophecies to the contrary notwithstanding).

Russia's leaders expect that "all religions will die out within this
generation." They boast:

> "We are pushing religion back. The chemical labora-
> tory is militantly atheistic. So is the astronomical lab-
> oratory . . . it will banish God from the heavens. Be-
> cause we have the ideological weapon we are as sure
> of victory as we are sure the sun will rise tomorrow
> morning."

Their Chinese counterparts confidently predict the Christian religion
will "soon be only a memory in China."

Forecasts of a Red victory would be more realistic if the major

145

premises were true. Communists hold that Christ is the creature of the Christian imagination. The Gospel is a fairy tale about a non-existent Jesus. The Christian missionary society is a tool for aggression and the repression of the colored races. Missionaries are secret agents and saboteurs. Building on such hypotheses, the framers of communism's scheme for world conquest wrote this anti-Christian plank in their platform: "The struggle against the Christian legend must be conducted ruthlessly and with all means at our disposal." [1] There is no room for religious weeds in the socialistic garden.

The Russian textbook *Psychopolitics,* equates Christianity with dementia.

"You must work until religion is synonymous with insanity. You must work until officials of city, county and state governments will not think twice before they pounce upon religious groups as public enemies."

The Red line, voiced by American Communist Langston Hughes is reflected in his infamous writing, "Good-bye Christ." It is so ribald and offensive we prefer not to stain the pages of this last chapter with even an excerpt.

All this is strangely reminiscent of what has been said before by others who labored under similar illusions.

Toward the end of the third century, the Emperor Diocletian, who instituted massive persecutions of Christians, commissioned a monument to be set up in Rome with the inscription "Christianity is dead." It is noteworthy that soon after, at the beginning of the fourth century, the West Roman Empire was proclaimed nominally Christian by Constantine the Great, who later defeated Licinius, King of the East, thereby becoming Emperor of both East and West. He initiated broad reforms, and Christianity flourished throughout the Roman Empire; so was disproved the postulate of his infamous predecessor.

One of Constantine's successors, Julian the Apostate, in his time made a desperate effort to re-paganize the world. He turned violently against Christianity only to later confess the futility of his attempt in his dying moments. Mortally wounded in combat, Julian is said to have caught some of his own blood in his cupped hand, flung it heavenward and cried, "O Galilean, Thou hast conquered."

Scriptures prophesy that the day will come when every knee

[1] Chairman of the Soviet Society for Political and Scientific Research in a broadcast over "Leningrad Radio," quoted in the *European Bible Institute Bulletin.*

will bow . . . and every tongue will confess that Jesus Christ is Lord, to the glory of God the Father (Philippians 2:10, 11). The Apocalypse depicts an era when every creature in heaven, earth, and hell will unite in ascribing *blessing, honor, glory* and *power* to Christ forever (Revelation 5:13).

Bible scholars agree that some of the meanings of the Revelation of St. John are so veiled and obscure that it is presumptuous, from our present and restricted points of view, to give them positive interpretation. This poses no vital problem for us. That which *is* comprehensible, namely the eventual triumph of Christ, is so clearly stated that it should inspire all Christians to work toward the grand finale when Christ shall be "all and in all" (Colossians 3:11). Setting the stage for His universal acclaim (preceded by His second advent) is obviously to be the prime task of the Church.

The last book of the Bible proclaims Christ as Victor in the moral and spiritual conflict of the ages. Since it is the wrap-up of God's revelation to man, it naturally and necessarily sums up His redemptive plan. Genesis foretells the bruising of the serpent's (Satan's) head, the gospels and Acts reveal the plot's development, and the Book of Revelation affirms the final accomplishment. Christ is Victor supreme — "Lord of [all] lords, and King of [all] kings" (Revelation 17:14).

It is not straining the rules of interpretation to regard chapter fourteen of John's Patmos vision as a summary of the ages-long conflict. Two verses in the portion could easily apply to the opening of the missionary campaign which would result eventually in the overthrow of Babylon.

> "I saw another angel fly in the midst of heaven, having the everlasting gospel to preach unto them that dwell on the earth, and to every nation, and kindred, and tongue, and people, saying with a loud voice, Fear God and give glory to him" (verses 6, 7).

John received his apocalyptic vision while exiled to the Mediterranean island of Patmos "for the word of God and for the testimony of Jesus Christ" (1:9, 10). If we were to judge by the adversity of his time, nothing could appear more impossible of fulfillment than that which he was about to foretell. But his eye of faith saw the coming day when the kingdoms of the world would "become the kingdoms of our Lord, and of his Christ; and he shall reign for ever and ever" (11:15). The outward circumstances were delusive, not conclusive.

In our day too the odds still appear in favor of principalities and powers of evil. Obstacles facing the Church loom so large they seem to preclude forever the fulfillment of John's prophecy. Two out of every five persons in our world are controlled to some extent by one monolithic, atheistic system which promises to conquer the other three-fifths and to make the world over according to its own deadly design. Other godless *isms* domineer countless millions. Statistical evidence would seem to belie any hope of imminent, universal acknowledgment of Christ.

Far from breeding apathy and discouragement, the *status quo* only proves why the Church must increasingly give of her sons to bear the Message glorious, and give of her wealth to speed them on their way. The grip of evil only provides the greater incentive for believers to send their intercessions vertically and their ministrations horizontally, linking the beneficent Heavenly Father and the erring world in reconciliation at the foot of the cross.

Nothing should be allowed to interfere with the carrying out of the divine will to sow every acre of the inhabited earth with the seed of the Gospel. The Almighty is determined that His Son shall be known, loved, served and honored from hemisphere to hemisphere and from pole to pole. Whatever hinders this must become intolerable.

If our enemies prophesy twilight, darkness, and oblivion for Christianity; if atheism promises to make the Bible a forgotten Book; if the Russians warn, "Your grandchildren will live in a communist world," there is still no justification for pressing the panic button. We have only to remind ourselves of history's pages, secular and sacred.

> "The kingdom of heaven is like to a grain of mustard seed, which a man took, and sowed in his field: which indeed is the least of all seeds: but when it is grown, it is the greatest among herbs and becometh a tree . . ." (Matthew 13:31, 32).

In parable, Christ pictured kingdom growth in the world by showing a housewife adding a small amount of yeast to a dough mix, ". . . till the *whole* was leavened" (Matthew 13:33). The *transforming element* has been inserted and is even now permeating the earth. Evidence of this can be seen in miniature in the New Hebrides Islands. Armed only with the Gospel, Dr. John Geddie achieved so marvelous a success among the cannibals as to excite the wonder and admiration of Protestant Christianity. Still to be found on the Island of Aneityum is a tablet raised by grateful natives to his memory. Inscribed in the Melanesian language, it reads:

> *When he landed here*
> *in 1848*
> *there were no Christians;*
> *when he left here*
> *in 1872*
> *there were no heathen.*[2]

Because of the "Truth that makes men free," the death knell of all despotism can be heard, if but faintly in the distance. Writes Edward Thompson:

> Christianity is speaking languages more numerous, by tongues more eloquent, in nations more populous than ever before. It is shaking down philosophies that exalt themselves against God; it is making printing presses roll under the demand for Scriptures, giving godlike breadth, freedom and energy to the civilization that bears its name; elevating savage islands into Christian states; leading forth Christian martyrs from the mountains and plains of China; turning the clubs of cannibals into railings for altars before which Fiji savages call upon Jesus; repeating the Pentecost "by many an ancient river and many a palmy plain"; thundering at the seats of ancient paganism; sailing all waters; cabling all oceans; scaling all mountains in its march of might, and ever enlarging the diameter of those circles of light which it has kindled on earth, and which will one day meet in universal illumination, that "the knowledge of the Lord may cover the earth as the waters cover the sea."

The thrilling prospect of Kingdom triumph nerves Christian soldiers for battle. Their knowledge of certain, ultimate conquest is enough. Logically they are admonished:

> "Put on the whole armour of God. . . . Stand . . .
> having your loins girt about with truth, and having
> on the breastplate of righteousness; and your feet
> shod with the preparation of the gospel of peace"
> (Ephesians 6:11-15).

The movement which had its genesis in a Bethlehem grotto, 2,000 years ago sweeps inexorably outward and upward toward its apogee, taking with it the ransomed of all ages. Nothing can stop it. St. John envisioned its climax as though he were already an eyewitness:

[2] Arthur T. Pierson, *God and Missions Today* (Chicago: Moody Press), p. 114.

"I heard a great voice of much people in heaven, saying, Alleluia; Salvation, and glory, and honour, and power, unto the Lord our God" (Revelation 19:1).

". . . *they sang new praise* saying, You are worthy . . . for you were slain, and have redeemed us to God by your blood, out of every tribe, and tongue, and people, and nation . . . . and *they shall reign on earth*" (Revelation 5:9, 10, Aramaic).

James Mills Thoburn (1836-1922), trail blazing Methodist missionary to India, sounded a clarion call to his generation which becomes one to ours:

"The signs of the times, the lessons of the past, the indications of the future, the call of providence, the voices which come borne to us on every breeze and from every nation under heaven, all alike bid us lay our plans on a scale worthy of men who expect to *conquer the world*." [3]

---

[3] Quoted by Sherwood Eddy, *Pathfinders of the World Missionary Crusade* (New York-Nashville: Abingdon Press), p. 95.

EPILOGUE

RACE-REDEEMING THOUGHTS now motivating heart and mind, let us be no longer apathetic, but let us move forward and act in consonance with the Great Commission (see Addenda).

While the fate of mankind trembles in the balance, there seems no course left to loyal soldiers of the cross but to seize the initiative from the enemy and unite in mounting a world-wide, evangelical offensive, commensurate with the present challenge and opportunity.

Touching foreign missions with only the tips of our fingers will not overcome the menaces abroad. We must reach our arms around the world.

> "Soldiers of Christ, Arise!
> And put your armour on,
> Strong in the strength which God supplies
> Through His eternal Son;
>
> . . . .
> From strength to strength go on,
> Wrestle and fight and pray;
> Tread all the powers of darkness down,
> And win the well-fought day."
> — *Charles Wesley*

ADDENDA

I

Interdenominationally constituted organizations comprise a vital segment of the Church's total foreign commitment. These represent strategic endeavors and key countries often beyond any one denominational sphere. Their reservoir of skilled and dedicated personnel eagerly respond to the local congregation's call for help to supplement its own program.

Two associations, serving 80 cooperating societies with a total complement of 14,000 missionaries in 110 nations, can supply you with further information. They are:

Interdenominational Foreign Mission Association
54 Bergen Avenue   Ridgefield Park, N. J.

Evangelical Foreign Missions Association
1405 G Street, N.W.   Washington, D.C.

II

Your Home Church and Its Foreign Mission (Moody Press Compact Book #40), by the author, offers practical guidance in Sunday school application; the church's annual conference, faith promise system, prayer program, mission covenant, *et cetera.* Available in book stores or by writing to Clay Cooper, P. O. Box 1, Spokane, Washington.